Choosing Futures

Choosing Futures offers a wide-ranging perspective on how young people and their parents make choices as they travel through a lifetime of education and training. The authors challenge traditional views of how choices are made of primary school, secondary school, college, university and career, which assume that choices are rational and objective. Instead, this book reveals how choices depend upon a range of factors

- young people's personal experiences;
- individual and family histories;
- their perceptions of education and careers.

The book compares choice for 5 to 11 year olds, and for 16 and 18 year olds, drawing out models of the decision-making process, and at the same time the consequences on schools, colleges and individuals of 'enhanced choice'.

This topical book will be of great interest to professionals in careers guidance, head teachers and principals, who will find it offers important insights into how the choice dimensions of the markets they compete in actually work. Researchers of educational policy and policy-makers will find *Choosing Futures* an up-to-date, challenging analysis of key processes in educational and training markets.

Nicholas Foskett is Professor of Education. **Jane Hemsley-Brown** is Senior Research Fellow. Both authors are based at the University of Southampton.

Education/Educational Management

Choosing Futures

Young People's Decision-Making
in Education, Training and
Careers Markets

Nicholas Foskett and
Jane Hemsley-Brown

London and New York

First published 2001 by RoutledgeFalmer
11 New Fetter Lane,
London EC4P 4EE

Simultaneously published in the USA and Canada
by RoutledgeFalmer
29 West 35th Street, New York, NY 10001

RoutledgeFalmer is an imprint of the Taylor & Francis Group

© 2001 Nicholas Foskett and Jane Hemsley-Brown

Typeset in New Baskerville by Wearset, Boldon, Tyne and Wear
Printed and bound in Great Britain by TJ International Ltd,
Padstow, Cornwall

British Library Cataloguing in Publication Data
A catalogue record for this book is available from the British Library

Library of Congress Cataloging in Publication Data

Foskett, Nicholas, 1955–
    Choosing futures : young people's decision-making in education,
training, and careers markets / Nicholas Foskett and Jane
Hemsley-Brown.
        p. cm.
Includes bibliographical references (p.) and index.
ISBN 0-415-23238-4 – ISBN 0-415-23239-2 (pbk.)
    1. School choice – Great Britain. 2. Decision making in
adolescence – Great Britain. 3. Education – Parent participation –
Great Britain. I. Hemsley-Brown, Jane, 1950– II. Title.

LE1027.9 .F66 2001
373.18–dc21
                                                            00-045704

ISBN 0-415-23239-2 (pbk)

ISBN 0-415-23238-4 (hbk)

Contents

Acknowledgements

We would like to express our thanks to many individuals and organisations who have supported our research at the Centre for Research in Education Marketing. In particular, we are grateful for the time given willingly by so many anonymous pupils, students, teachers, parents, careers advisers and headteachers/principals, without whom our understanding of young people's choice processes could not have even begun. We would also like to thank those organisations who have funded our work. In particular the substantial initial support from HEIST, and of David Roberts, has been invaluable, but we would also like to acknowledge the support and funding from Hampshire TEC, Wiltshire and Swindon TEC, FOCUS TEC in London, and the headteachers of the anonymous schools who supported our work on independent schools.

Of particular importance, though, has been the forebearance of our families, both during the research process and also during the writing of this book. Without their support and the space they have created when needed, this book would still simply be an idea in our minds.

Nick Foskett
Jane Hemsley-Brown

Introduction

This book is about young people's lives and their experiences in moving from the dependency of childhood to the independence of being a young adult. Much of the first two decades of life are focused on preparation for entering the adult world, with an emphasis on acquiring the skills, knowledge, attitudes and values that will enable each individual to enhance their chances of personal success. For many it is not an easy pathway to follow, as the challenges of developing a sense of personal identity and self-esteem, and of finding a place in the adult world, can be strongly dissonant experiences. One of our purposes in writing this book is to try and make sense of the decisions and choices young people and their parents must make, for in better understanding these processes we hope to be able to lay the foundations of improved support and guidance.

The book draws on two major sources of ideas. First, it tries to synthesise the evidence from the research of many individuals and groups to draw out key principles relating to choice and decision-making. The literature on choice, particularly school choice, has grown rapidly during the 1990s, and there is now a sound theoretical and evidence-based foundation for our understanding of many choice processes. Second, we draw strongly on our own research, developed through a number of local, regional and national research projects that we have undertaken through the Centre for Research in Education Marketing (CREM), based in the Research and Graduate School of Education at the University of Southampton. This has enabled us to develop a range of new perspectives in fields where there is already a significant array of research – and also to undertake some important ground-breaking work in specific aspects of choice. We believe that the synergy between our own research and that of others has enabled us to move forward some key conceptualisations and understanding in young people's choice arenas. A list of our own research projects is provided in Appendix A.

The book is structured around the key choice points in an individual's education and/or training pathway. Chapter 1 sets the scene for the analysis by looking at the growth of 'enhanced choice' in relation to education and training arenas, and considers some of the philosophical arguments for and against the development of choice systems in education. Chapter 2 examines the economic and psychological basis of theories of choice, and challenges the notion of rationality and vigilant information search. We then address some of the important methodological and ethical issues in researching choice in education and training markets.

Chapters 3 and 4 focus on school choice. The generic components of school choice processes are considered initially, before we move on to consider choice in two arenas as yet explored very little in the literature – parental choice of primary school (Chapter 3) and choice in relation to the independent school sector (Chapter 4).

Chapters 5 and 6 consider choice at 16+, as young people leave compulsory education and can for the first time choose whether or not to participate in education or training. The psychological challenge of choice at 16 emerges very strongly from this analysis, together with the intimate interplay between education and training choices and the development of self-image and lifestyle by young people as they begin to develop independence from their family environment. Chapter 5 explores, in particular, the nature of programme and institutional choice for those staying on in full-time education. Chapter 6 concentrates on choice in relation to training pathways, drawing significantly on our own recent research in relation to choices of modern apprenticeships.

Chapter 7 considers choice in relation to higher education entry. The importance of early commitment to academic pathways in the school system is clear from this analysis, for a theme that emerges from earlier chapters is the dominant role of the 'holy grail' of university entrance in shaping choices throughout the education/training system.

Chapter 8 looks at the wider issue of career choice, which overlaps into choice at all other points along the pathway. The importance of perceptual models of particular careers in shaping decisions is identified, and the chapter examines some of the influences on how those images and perceptions are formed. The central role of teachers in image development, and the necessity of influencing how those images are developed in the primary school are important findings from the chapter.

Although the book is structured around key decision points in education/training pathways, we emphasise throughout that the process of choice is not neatly compartmentalised. The relationship between images and choices at all stages of the pathways is clear, and supports our thesis that to understand young people's choice we must understand it in its entirety across the 0 to 18 age range. Chapter 9 concludes the book by drawing out some of the key generalisations and developing a conceptual model of young people's choice processes.

We hope that the understanding that emerges from this book will have important implications for policy makers, for politicians, for teachers, and for the Careers Education and Guidance (CEG) services, and will help them to reflect on the nature of choice, its limitations, its complexity, and the implications of enhanced choice. More importantly, though, we hope it will be of value ultimately to young people and their parents by enabling the wide range of formal and informal agencies engaged in education and training markets to better understand what is going on in this process we casually call 'choice'. In this way we hope that more young people will be the beneficiaries rather than the victims of enhanced choice.

Nick Foskett
Jane Hemsley-Brown

Southampton, June 2000

1 Choice, decision-making and the education market place

Choice, society and education

Society is shaped by the process of choice. Choice is a fundamental process of human existence, for in daily life and in the course of our lifetimes the way in which we exist as people is founded on the choices we make for ourselves and also on those made by others. Choice is an expression of human individuality, for through the choices we make we express our beliefs, values and personal priorities. Choice, though, is an interactive process. Our every choice impacts on other people, and their choices impact upon us. The choices an individual, a group or an organisation make result in changes to the world they occupy, and in so doing change the environment of choice for every other individual, group or organisation. The social, economic and cultural environment within which we all operate is the product of choices throughout human history and they constrain and shape the choices open to individuals at any particular moment. Although we are the product of our own choices, many of those choices will be highly constrained by these external environmental structures that define the way in which we live in society.

The domain of choice is a social and political battleground. The history of local, national and global politics is one of tensions between the rights of individuals to make choices and define their own existence, the rights of individuals or groups to be protected from the negative impacts of choice by others in society, and adjusting the balance between the rights and obligations of individuals and the rights and obligations of the communities and societies within which they live. The rise of democracy and the rise of capitalism are expressions of political perspectives on choice as an inherent human right. At the end of the second millennium we may perceive that 'choice' is a 'meta concept' that underpins much of global society and economy, promoted by most political regimes and championed by the corporate capitalism that increasingly shapes the globalisation of human existence. We live in the era of the 'consumer-citizen'.

This book is about choice and young people. By the age of 20 young people find themselves in life circumstances which are, in large measure, the product of a choice system. Some of these choices will be those they have made for themselves, either as positive choices to take particular courses of action or negative choices not to take particular actions. Many of the choices, however, will be decisions in which they played little or no part but which have fundamentally impacted on their pathway through childhood and adolescence into the stage of being young adults. These decisions will have been made in the family, in the community, in the formal systems they participate in (health and education, for example), and in political and economic arenas at local, national and international level. We are all, as individuals, both the masters and victims of choice.

The explosion of the debate on choice in education in the last quarter of the twentieth century has implied that consumer educational choice is a new concept. In reality education has historically always been an arena of choice. In many countries, for example, choice has long existed in the dichotomy between state (public) and private (independent) schools, and has always existed in the decisions to continue education, take up training or move into employment made by young people after they leave the compulsory phase of education. Choice has only been constrained by centralised moves to provide universal compulsory education in an environment of limited economic resource and the belief in the role of the state to provide and fund the main social systems including education. We may regard the 1980s and 1990s, therefore, not as a period of the introduction of choice but as a time during which opportunities for choice were increased.

'Choice' is not a singular idea which is either present or not. Rather, it occurs across a wide range of circumstances. At one extreme we may as individuals find ourselves in circumstances where we have no choice or almost no choice. In education, for example, traditional ideas of fixed school catchments have meant that for most parents there was no choice – attendance at school for their children was a legal requirement, and the only school available (other than for those who could choose private education) was the local catchment school. At the other extreme we may be faced with circumstances where there is a bewildering range of choices. At age 18 we may choose to participate in higher education or to pursue a job with or without training. The choice of jobs and careers is potentially very large, and the choice of higher education courses is enormous, with over 15,000 courses available at over 300 institutions in the UK alone. Choice is, therefore, a highly contingent concept, and to understand its operation we must move away from generalisations about the presence or absence of choice to an understanding of the precise circumstances under which choice is operating. It is common, for example, to speak of 'compulsory education' and 'post-compulsory education' (PCE) to distinguish those phases of education and training where participation is statutorily required by government and those where participation is voluntary. In PCE compulsion, by definition, does not exist, but choice will still not be 'free' for it will be strongly influenced by government policy and social expectations. In compulsory education, on the other hand, while there is no choice about whether to participate, there may or may not be considerable choice about which school and which curriculum a child might experience.

The notion of choice in education has generated a strong debate about the rights and wrongs of its expansion and its relative role, concealed in a debate about the rights and wrongs of its existence. The argument is not about whether choice does or should exist, but about how far this choice should be constrained or unconstrained by external intervention. Should the shape and nature of education and training systems be driven by the choices of individual 'consumers' or should choice be strongly limited to provide more direct control by government on the outcomes of the system? There are strong moral, economic, ideological and political arguments within this question which will be explored later within this chapter. Irrespective of the views that emerge from that debate though, there is an imperative to understand the nature of choice in relation to education, training and careers. We need to know how choice occurs, what the outcomes of choice processes are likely to be, and what factors influence and shape choice. Only then can we fully understand the interaction of individual choice and the socio-economic structures, systems and decisions within which choice is made.

Enhanced choice and social policy

The expansion of enhanced choice in education has occurred in response to two parallel processes. Increasing social and economic expectations have resulted in the expansion of participation in post-compulsory education, which has led to an increase in provision and hence an increase in the options for choice. More important, though, has been the ascendancy of choice in the context of the application of market theory by governments around the world in the sphere of public service provision. This process of marketisation has its origins in the economic ideas of Adam Smith (Copley and Sutherland, 1995) in the eighteenth century, but modern market theory is attributed to the work of Friedrich von Hayek (1976), and is strongly associated with the thinking of Milton Friedman (Friedman and Friedman, 1980). The contention of market theory is that competition and consumer choice stimulate 'providers' of goods and services to strive to satisfy consumer 'wants' as closely as possible, and to compete by minimising their costs through better and more efficient ways of producing those goods or services. Entrepreneurship amongst producers and freedom of choice for consumers are central elements of market theory, and external intervention in the market, for example by government through policy or statutory constraint, is regarded as reducing the efficiency of such a market system.

The application of market theory to public sector services, including education, has been a feature of many 'western' economies during the 1980s and 1990s, based on a fundamental ideological and philosophical thrust that has captured the high ground of policy-making internationally. Although often initiated by conservative administrations, continuity with limited change has been the policy stance of successor governments across a range of political persuasions. The argument for marketisation, and hence enhanced choice, is based on a number of assertions and aspirations.

Most pressing on politicians has been the pursuit of the efficient use of resources. This is in part a reflection of an ideological and economic commitment to limiting public expenditure to sustain economic competitiveness in a global economy. It is not without significance that the most rapid growth of public sector marketisation is associated with periods of economic downturn in national economies. More important, though, is the desire to expand education for social and economic objectives without proportional increases in expenditure. Markets are perceived as driving down unit costs, as providers seek to compete for resources, and customers, which feeds through to efficiency gains in the overall education and training budget.

Tightly linked to the short-term economic benefits of marketisation is the pursuit of higher levels of individual skills and competency within the economy to optimise long-term competitiveness. Such a view sees individuals as 'human capital', a resource which can be invested in to produce increased economic gains. The generation of a trained, flexible future workforce is one of the principal aims of the education and training 'business', an objective emphasised by the Department for Education and Employment's (DfEE) explicit target of 'supporting economic growth by promoting a competitive, efficient and flexible labour market' (Rajan *et al.*, 1997, p. 2). Indeed, the economic future of the UK in the next century is frequently described as being dependent on our ability to create an internationally competitive economy and raise standards of education and training (FEFC, 1997; Fryer, 1997; DfEE, 1998b). The aim is to raise standards and attainment levels in education and training to match those in other developed countries, for there is a marked economic advantage for societies with skilled, adaptable and learning work forces in an increasingly global economy (Tuckett, 1997, p. 1). This has been an important driver for government in England and Wales in seeking to raise the levels of skills and education within the labour force (Petherbridge, 1997), and led to the establishment in 1991 of the National Advisory Council for Education and Training Targets (NACETT, 1995). Most of the key reorganisations of the education and training system in the last two decades have been predicated on such economic priorities – the push towards enhancing vocational pathways post-16 through the development of GNVQ, the proposals of the National Committee of Inquiry into Higher Education (Dearing, 1997), and the establishment of Curriculum 2000 (DfEE, 1999) are but exemplars of this trend. In particular, the equipping of entrants into the labour market with 'pre-installed' intellectual and practical skills and the skills necessary for lifelong learning, career re-orientation and adaptation to the technological and work practice needs of a post-industrial, post-modern society has become a priority in government education and training policy.

But what is the evidence of such objectives being achieved? The answer lies in the pursuit of increased output performance indicators – 'standards' has become the watchword of education and training policy across the globe. By establishing markets in which the principal criterion of success is deemed to be output standards in terms of student performance, governments have sought to raise overall levels of economic competency through the choices of individual young people and their parents in the education and training market place. The 'standards' debate finds its expression in the institutional (school) effectiveness and improvement movements (e.g. Reynolds and Cuttance, 1992) which have had a high profile in the evolution of professional practice in schools and colleges in many countries. The simple logic from policy-makers goes something like this:

1   We need to raise standards of achievement of young people in education and training to ensure global competitiveness for our economy.

2   Schools and colleges make the difference. It is how they operate the technical processes of education and training that determines whether each young person optimises their achievement. We can identify what processes enhance achievement, and schools and colleges can be charged and directed to follow these principles.

3   To drive schools and colleges to ensure that they manage resources and processes most effectively, an education market is created in which they must compete for resources. Key elements in such a market will be individual choice of school, college or training programme, and to both facilitate choice and demonstrate public accountability of each institution key performance indicators will be identified.

4   Schools and colleges will then be left to make it all work. Furthermore, if it doesn't work, then because of the empowerment and autonomy of the institutions, policy-makers can blame them for the failure. If it does work, though, then the policy-makers can take the credit.

Social market development has also been founded on an ideological/ moral commitment to the empowerment of the consumer in society, though, and issues of personal liberty and autonomy. In the context of education such a perspective is enshrined in the UN 'Universal Declaration of Human Rights', which indicates that 'parents have a prior right to choose the kind of education that shall be given to their children' (Almond, in Halstead, 1994, p. 14). Such a libertarian perspective stresses the rights (and responsibilities) of the individual within society, and enshrines these rights in the freedom of 'consumer choice' and in the operation of market forces to make 'producers' accountable. In this way power within society is 'wrested from professional protectionism and producer capture' (O'Hear, 1991, p. 56) and returned to the individual, whose choices and decisions then shape the form of society and economy in which they live. Two tensions exist within such a perspective. The first is that liberty as a concept may be in conflict with issues of equity, and the ability of choice-based systems to protect individuals from the inequities of the consequences of choice may be limited. This requires intervention in the market and the choice process by government. The second is the contradiction between libertarian objectives and conservative objectives. Libertarianism emphasises the freedom of the individual to exercise choice in pursuit of self-determination, without external intervention by government. Conservatism focuses in contrast on centralised statutory control and constraint, processes which may be necessary to protect individuals in society from the negative consequences of choice and to ensure that overall government ideological objectives can be met. Herein lies a significant tension for the right-of-centre administrations which have promoted markets. Markets are essentially about libertarianism, yet to ensure that the markets produce the outcomes that policy requires there must be strong intervention in the making of those markets, to create surrogate markets in public sector arenas. It is from these libertarian-conservative tensions that many of the issues in relation to choice and markets emerge.

Enhanced choice in education and training – counting the costs?

The arguments for 'enhanced choice' sound compelling, and have certainly been warmly received in a range of political regimes. The global policy shift towards the development of 'enhanced choice' in education at all levels, however, has not been without strong resistance in the debates about its moral basis and its social and economic consequences. Set fair against the strong 'push' factors of economic and libertarian gain range a number of substantial arguments which see the possible benefits of enhancing choice being outweighed by the negative effects. In broad terms these arguments may be grouped into four themes – the social engineering debate; the humanitarian education debate; the education as partnership debate; and the win–lose debate.

The social engineering debate

One of the arguments mustered to promote marketisation and the enhancement of choice in education and training is the need for education to reflect individual student–parent wants and to move away from social engineering. Friedman and Friedman (1980, p. 32) believe that 'social engineering is not the purpose of education, and it is unfortunate that schools are now regarded as a means of promoting social mobility, racial integration and other objectives only distantly related to their fundamental task'. State provision of education and training, however, is built on the notion that the purposes of education go far beyond simply satisfying what individual consumers want but are about meeting a range of wider economic and social needs. At a political level education and training is one of the main mechanisms of shaping the future development of society in pursuit of specific ideological intentions. At the level of individuals, education and training is one of the ways of reducing the consequences of socio-economic polarisation within society, and of pursuing the moral imperatives of 'equity'. The establishment of markets in education may itself constitute social engineering, of course, in that it reflects the pursuit of a specific social organisation and morality (market accountability) by the imposition of market forms created by legislative constraint. The promotion of enhanced choice and marketisation is simply a different form of social engineering than centralised, command-based public service provision.

The humanitarian education debate

Extending from the idea of education and training systems as social engineering is the view that education has a range of aims that go beyond the classical-vocational purpose of producing young people prepared to play a role within the economy. Two other substantive ideological views of education may be described as a 'critical-reflective' perspective, which sees education as seeking to produce reflective and socially-critical young people able to participate actively in shaping and re-forming the society in which they live; and a 'humanitarian' perspective which sees education as about self-growth and the development of the individual in personal, social and intellectual terms. The balance between the three perspectives is an issue of political belief, and the shift in the last two decades globally has been to emphasise the 'vocational' view of education and training. The humanitarian view would argue not against choice in education and training but in favour of constrained choice to protect all young people to enable them to be nurtured in relation to their own needs. As Wilson (1991, p. 228) suggests, 'we should neither over-protect our children from the hard (and inevitable) fact of human differences in talent, ability and motivation, nor make the children's lives wholly into a competitive game which gives them no other identity', reflecting, in turn, Jensen's view that 'human variation should be dealt with constructively by bringing to bear on it as much knowledge, humaneness, generosity, reason, wisdom and farsightedness as society can possibly muster' (Jensen, 1991, p. 169).

The 'education as partnership' debate

The engagement of parents and young people in education and training is in part a utilitarian process in the pursuit of educational achievement, qualifications and other personal gains that will enable them to compete in the labour market after leaving school or college. However, this is not the only perspective on education and training, for such stakeholders are not simply 'customers' in an educational market, but may see themselves to varying degrees as partners seeking to develop a much wider relationship with the school or college. The ability to satisfy these wider relationship needs may be a factor in the choice of institution that parents and young people make. However, many parents have wider societal interests that go beyond self-interest and may wish schools and colleges to pursue strategies that are in the interests of young people in general. Indeed, parents may be willing to subsume personal advantage for wider social benefit, preferring constrained choice with wider equity than enhanced choice with increasing social polarisation. The libertarian view that choice is 'a good thing' *per se* may not always be the perception of parents and young people forced to make education and training pathway choices. We shall return to this issue of parental views of themselves as consumers in a later chapter.

The 'win–lose' debate

Amongst the arguments against enhanced choice in education and training perhaps the most strongly contested have related to the belief that the outcome of the operation of markets in all spheres is the production of winners and losers. Markets are perceived as a mechanism which leads inexorably to the redistribution of resources – as Ranson (1993, p. 338) suggests 'markets institutionalise an unequal game of winning and losing'. Those succeeding in the market will, over time, make significant resource gains at the expense of those unable to compete successfully. While this may be regarded as an inevitable consequence of commercial and business markets, in education and training the reinforcement or exaggeration of differentials in society may be seen as fundamentally opposed to the equity principles of education in most societies.

Polarisation may occur at the level of both individuals and institutions. At an individual level parents and young people are not all equally equipped to play a role as active choosers in education and training markets. Some will possess much higher levels of 'cultural capital' (Bourdieu, 1997) than others, enabling them to choose more effectively than others. One of the key concerns about the impact of marketisation is the domination of active choice by choosers who are 'privileged/skilled' (Gewirtz *et al.*, 1995) and the polarisation effect it may have both on young people and on institutions. Such polarisation may in turn structure the market within which choice is made and condemn some schools and colleges to a cycle of decline in recruitment and in their performance in relation to measures of effectiveness and others to a cycle of increasing primacy in the market and 'effective performance' as a result of positive feedback processes. Where there is competition for places in 'popular' schools, colleges or universities, some choosers will have the skills, knowledge and 'market value' to ensure their acceptance in those institutions at the expense of others. In the context of schools Whitty, Power and Halpin (1998) identify the idea of the 'commodification of parents'. This represents the consequences of choice in markets where demand for places in popular schools exceed supply, and where schools perceive parents as valued commodities within a market where the schools make choices. Parents with high levels of cultural capital, usually expressed in terms of middle-class attitudes and a positive orientation to the benefits of academically focused education, are seen as having significant market value for the school. Those without such attributes will, through such mechanisms, have their choice restricted. We may perceive, therefore, that the aggregate of individual choice is enhanced choice for some and less choice for many.

It might be expected that the same outcomes at the level of institutions. Just as we may recognise the idea of 'cultural capital' in relation to individuals, so schools and colleges will vary in their 'institutional cultural capital' (Foskett, 1996). Some will have inherent advantages because of their history, location and reputation. This may be enhanced by their skills at competing in the educational market place through effective marketing and promotional expertise. Others, less well endowed with such cultural resources, may find that with or without the use of strong promotional strategies, they cannot compete effectively in the competition to attract the choices of young people. As a result some schools, colleges or universities gain in the market place – and others lose. The consequence of winning or losing is self-reinforcing through a process of positive feedback. Schools or colleges that 'win' will attract more resources, more potential for success in relation to output indicators, an enhanced reputation and so increased institutional cultural capital. Their ability to compete effectively will be greater. For the losers, their ability to compete will be diminished. The predicted outcome of enhanced choice, therefore, is increased polarisation at both individual and institutional levels in society.

The prediction of increased polarisation resulting from enhanced choice in education and training markets has generated two responses in educational debate. First, it has been seen as inevitable, and indeed an intended outcome of the introduction of marketisation by conservative political groups. Ranson (1993, p. 334) has suggested that 'markets are designed to justify, perpetuate and rationalise the existing social status quo', while Ball (1993, p. 16) sees the market as a mechanism for social differentiation and for 'the reinvention and legitimation of hierarchy and differentiation via the ideology of diversity, competition and choice'. It may be perceived, indeed, as an outcome which results at the end of a cost-benefit analysis in overall net gain for the economic well-being of a particular society, with the losers simply representing the unfortunate but recognised 'downside' of a process which is in the wider social interest.

Second, the existence of enhanced polarisation has been questioned, or where it emerges, it may be explained as the consequence of ineffective school/college management rather than an inevitable result of enhanced choice systems. With the relatively recent introduction of 'enhanced choice' in education in many countries the evidence base for drawing conclusions about polarisation effects has simply not been available. Linking changes in institutional performance to specific policy and market changes is extremely difficult. In part this is because of the complexity of educational systems and the lack of simple links between inputs and outputs. It is also related to the time component in change, for changes may take several years to produce recognisable effects, and overall changes may be masked by short-term 'noise' in the system. Gorard (1997) has stressed the importance of recognising that markets evolve through time, and their form and processes are dynamic. Examining new and immature markets may not necessarily indicate what will be found in an 'established' market. Thus increasing polarisation of institutions in the first year or two after marketisation and 'enhanced choice' are introduced, may be a function of the early uptake of choice by active choosers, a common characteristic observed in most diffusion of innovation (Rogers, 1983). As others begin to participate in choice, though, some of the polarisations may become less emphasised. Alternatively, polarisation may be an accelerating process.

The search for evidence of whether 'choice' and the marketisation of education actually increases or decreases segregation has become a priority as the markets/choice experiment enters its second decade in many countries. Most of the research on polarisation resulting from 'enhanced choice' has focused on secondary schools. This provides some useful insights into the processes resulting from enhanced choice, but clearly extrapolation of the outcomes to other sectors of education and training will need to be undertaken with some caution. Nevertheless, we shall use the example of schools to explore the issues of institutional polarisation in markets.

The evidence on polarisation is contradictory at times and may suggest that the precise circumstances under which marketisation is operating at any particular moment will influence whether segregation increases or decreases. Woods, Bagley and Glatter (1998), for example, found little conclusive evidence of increasing segregation in their study of 12 micro-markets in central England, with the pre-existing contrasts in socio-economic mix between the schools simply being reinforced by the market and choice processes. Whitty, Power and Halpin (1998) have reviewed the evolution of secondary school choice in England and Wales, the USA, Australia, New Zealand and Sweden. They conclude that there is evidence that in societies which are already strongly stratified by socio-economic status the introduction of choice may increase the inequalities that exist, but that the identification of exactly how those inequalities will emerge, in what form and with what intensity is hard to model. This reflects the importance of local and national contextual factors in filtering and catalysing the market processes that choice sets in motion, and the huge number of factors that are influential in shaping outcomes.

Thrupp (1999), working with schools in New Zealand, has examined the issue of how far schools may themselves be responsible for any identified increase in polarisation. His work focuses in particular on the constraints to school improvement that derive from the social context within which the school operates, and which have such a major influence on school choice. Examining the thinking underpinning the school effectiveness and improvement (E & I) movements (e.g. Barber, 1996), Thrupp shows how they are based on the notion that changing pupil performance is a technical process, most of which is driven by variables that the school can manage and control. Failure of achievement or progress in such a model is portrayed as failure of the individual school, its managers and its teachers. The 'politics of blame' is based on the premise that in educational markets:

> Schools which 'lose' (...) are seen as those whose teachers and principals have not been able to improve enough to boost their reputation and hence the size of their student intakes.
>
> (Thrupp, 1999, p. 7)

Thrupp's empirical evidence suggests, however, that the polarisation of schools in terms of social mix that results from parental choice processes makes this analysis untenable. Parental choice favours affluent, professional, middle-class parents from the dominant ethnic groups (usually white), and the schools they choose are benefited at the expense of others. Since the cultural values underpinning school improvement and effectiveness strategies are more congruent with middle-class values, then the inevitable result is that advantaged schools will show, overall, much more improvement than disadvantaged schools. Central to this analysis are what Thrupp terms 'school mix effects', which are interlinked but distinct characteristics of schools that are fundamentally tied to the social mix of the school intake. He identifies three components of school mix effects:

1 *'reference group effects'*, i.e. the reinforcing effect of the sharing of cultural values between pupils where a school has an increasingly concentrated proportion of its pupils from a particular social background. These have a positive feedback impact on the two other aspects of social mix effects, which are:
2 *'organisational and management effects'*, i.e. the relatively straightforward challenge of managing a 'middle-class school' as opposed to a 'working-class school' because of the congruence of management approaches, educational aims and middle-class attitudes; and
3 *'instructional effects'*, i.e. student engagement (or not!) with the established curriculum that meets the needs of middle-class rather than working-class children more directly.

The interaction of these three groups of effects tends to enhance polarisation between the successful and the least successful schools as school choice begins to impact. As a result, Thrupp is clear that these school mix effects are crucially important in influencing the likely success or failure of school improvement strategies, for:

> While schools make some difference to student achievement this is likely to be smaller than typically assumed by E & I literature because of the way school mix affects school processes.
>
> (Thrupp, 1999, p. 182)

Thrupp's key conclusion is that policy-makers and educationalists must 're-emphasize the social limits of school reform' (op. cit., p. 182), and recognise that it is in the differences between schools and their pupil intake that the main handicaps to enhancing school effectiveness, as defined by the rhetoric of the market, actually resides. Hence the promotion of enhanced choice in relation to schools will inevitably result in polarisation effects, which may reduce the likelihood of 'raising standards' across the whole school population. Choice may, therefore, be impeding rather than promoting the achievement of one of the fundamental aims underpinning its introduction.

Lauder and Hughes (1999) have pursued a similar line of reasoning. Their analysis of the schools within the Smithfield Project, in two cities in New Zealand, shows the marked polarisation of schools as a result of the operation of parental choice and market forces. The impact on school performance through feedback processes that re-emphasise school contrasts is also strongly demonstrated through their data – and once the polarities are firmed up, then 'circuits of schooling' (Gewirtz, Ball and Bowe, 1997) are established. For schools at the bottom of the league, operating in the market becomes impossible, for as Lauder and Hughes show for one such school, 'all the marketing in the world has not helped Kea College' (op. cit., p. 109) where, despite large investment in promotion, the children who can do so are still being sent to other schools. Lauder and Hughes conclude that 'the school mix or composition of the student body is such a key factor in school performance, it is important that schools have student intakes which are as well balanced on variables such as prior achievement and social class as is possible' (op. cit., p. 136). The domination of choice by those with high levels of cultural capital makes this difficult to achieve.

Gorard and Fitz (2000) occupy the middle ground. Using data from schools in England and Wales they have developed an Index of

Segregation. This suggests that schools became more socially mixed during the period from 1993 to 1997, a period covering the first few years of the operation of more intense parental choice. From 1997, however, their data suggests that segregation has increased almost back to the level of 1993. The causes of this fluctuation are not clear but appear to coincide with economic cycles – a key indicator used by Gorard and Fitz is the level of free school meals in each school, and this reflects, to some extent, the state of the economy outside the school. Gibson and Asthana (2000) challenge the validity of Gorard and Fitz's conclusions on the basis, *inter alia*, of their concern about the validity of the Index of Segregation. They contend that social polarisation is in fact much more marked than Gorard and Fitz suggest. On the basis of an analysis of GCSE results from over 1500 schools they conclude that schools which are particularly attractive within their local markets are improving their GCSE results at a rate that is three times as great as those which are least popular. Their contention is that this demonstrates a polarisation of school performance on the basis of a polarisation of socio-economic profile in schools. While the jury is still out on the depth and significance of the negative effects of choice on social segregation, it appears that the evidence of its existence is now fairly well established. What is still missing, though, is any attempt to measure the aggregate gains and losses of choice and marketisation, for without such an analysis it is not easy to make judgements about the benefits and disbenefits of marketisation which are based on anything other than a concern for issues of social equity.

The nature of education markets

For choice to occur there must be in existence some form of market place within which that choice process can operate. Understanding the nature of markets in general, and of public sector markets and education/training markets in particular, is important to understand both the context of choice, and the impact of market processes on choice outcomes. Much of the literature on education markets during the late 1980s and early 1990s (e.g. Hatcher, 1994) focused on such analysis, but pursued a rather sterile line of argument by seeking to damn the introduction of education markets by showing that they did not compare to the classical notion of the 'free market' or by caricaturing them in the light of common critical perceptions of the idea of 'selling'. Brighouse (1992), for example, complains of school markets as 'bewildering bazaars', while Hargreaves (1991) has characterised marketisation as the introduction of 'Kentucky Fried Schooling'.

Bowe, Ball and Gold (1992) identify the characteristics of markets as the existence of:

1   Competition between more than one 'provider' of a product or service.
2   Choice for consumers.
3   Free and full information for consumers on which to base their choice.
4   Rational choice processes by consumers. This is based on the idea of Individualistic Rational Calculus (IRC), which assumes that consumers make objective, rational, fully-informed choices on the basis of comprehensive, vigilant decision-making.
5   Some form of 'exchange mechanism', e.g. money.
6   Diversity, and active differentiation between 'providers', demonstrating differences between products or services that enable choice to be made by the consumer.
7   Some form of 'marketing' organisation and activity by the providers.

This summary reflects a view of 'free markets' and 'perfect competition' in classical economic terms (Beardshaw *et al.*, 1998). In reality, such perfect competition rarely if ever exists, and the characteristics of real markets will differ from the model presented by Bowe *et al.* (1992). Some markets, for example, may have a supply side with many providers, while others will have few. Some will have a direct 'cash' transfer between customer and provider as the exchange mechanism, while others may be based on different forms of exchange. On the 'demand' side of the market some customers will make more vigilant or rational choices than others. Hence the term 'market' is a highly generic one, which is operationalised in the real world by an almost infinite variety of forms. In the context of the public sector, Le Grand (1990) coined the phrase 'quasi markets' to emphasise their distinctiveness from 'free markets'. Public sector markets are quasi markets because, *inter alia*:

•   Producers, or suppliers are mostly 'not-for-profit' organisations.
•   The state, through national government, tightly defines and constrains the 'product', and hence choice, for example, by defining curricula (e.g. the National Curriculum) or by imposing quality assurance systems and quality standards.

- Exchange mechanisms are not direct between consumer and provider. The exchange takes place via a third party (central funding organisations).
- Public sector organisations are statutorily constrained from acting as 'true' commercial organisations – for example, most cannot raise independent finance from private financial institutions.

Despite this concern over precise definition, though, it is clear that a market exists wherever customers can make choices between different services or products, whether the differences are small or large, and whether the choice is 'free' or highly constrained. In educational and training environments, for example, choice occurs at a variety of scales, ranging from choices between state and independent school pathways, or between academic or vocational post-compulsory educational pathways, to choices of individual subjects for study at points in the pathways where option choices can be made. Each choice, though, is made in a specific context of a market existing at a particular point in space and time.

In examining choice in education markets, therefore, it is important to recognise the central idea of the micro-market. The unique nature of the operating environment of each education or training institution means both that there are challenges to macro scale conceptualisations of markets and that transposing any such macro models to a specific market environment must occur with caution and a recognition of the importance of locally-defined factors. Gewirtz *et al.* (1995, p. 3) indicate that:

> It is our basic contention that there is no one general education market in operation in England. Education markets are localised and need to be analysed and understood in terms of a set of complex dynamics which mediate and contextualise the impact and effects of the Government's policy.

Markets are dynamic and individual, defined as much by local geography and history as by any overriding principles of the economics of supply and demand. They are also strongly shaped by the socio-economic characteristics of the clientele that they serve, whose decisions and choices are the key 'driver' in generating market outcomes. These socio-economic characteristics are, themselves, the result of the history of the local community, and are the sum product of the individual personal biographies and histories of members of that community. These 'micro-markets, or 'competitive arenas' (Woods, Bagley and Glatter, 1998) each generate, therefore, their own patterns of outcome, according to the relative influence of a whole range of factors. Strong and aggressive competition, for example, may push young people and their parents more strongly towards a highly consumerist response, while institutions that collaborate, cooperate or collude (Hall, 1999) will shape an entirely different market place. The importance of institutional culture both within individual schools and colleges and within markets is important, and strong in shaping this will be the attitudes and personalities of individual headteachers and principals (Foskett, 1998). Woods, Bagley and Glatter's large-scale study of a range of such competitive arenas demonstrates the multiplicity of outcomes that can emerge and how the interaction of choice and institutional response in itself shapes and influences both future choice and future institutional response.

Two brief examples illustrate this notion of micro-markets. Firstly, Foskett and Hesketh (1997) have distinguished between contiguous and parallel markets in choice at 16 for young people. Contiguous markets exist where a number of institutions overlap in terms of the catchments or market areas that they serve, so that there is strong competition between them to attract in students. Parallel markets occur where an institution serves a self-contained catchment so that there is only competition at the margins of its operating arena. The processes at work are very different in a parallel market than in a contiguous market, for example in the role of promotional activities in influencing institutional choice – promotional activities (such as open days or advertising) are much more important, for example, in a contiguous market. Even within these two groups of markets, though, there are contrasts over time and between different market scenarios. Contiguous markets in one city may be quite different in the detailed way they operate than in another city. Similarly, the dynamic nature of markets and the continuous feedback of outcomes into shaping and reworking the form of the market means that any market place will be different from year to year, and possibly from month to month or week to week. As choice decisions occur over a long period of time this means that the market in which those choices are being made will in practice be a moving backdrop against which there is a constant need to reassess choice as the market conditions and choice influences shift.

A second example is found in the markets for independent school choice (Foskett and Hemsley-Brown, 2000). Two dominant market forms exist within the independent school choice arena – 'competitive supremacy markets' and 'rivalistic markets'. Competitive supremacy markets have some strong similarities with the parallel markets of the post-16 market place, for they occur where a school has no significant competitor within the niches of the independent school market in which it operates. Here choice for parents is essentially between the independent and state sectors, not between different independent schools. Both the decision-making frame for parents and the marketing frame for the schools are quite different in these circumstances than in the 'rivalistic markets', where a number of similar schools provide virtually the same service. While the response of schools in such circumstances may be strong 'cut-throat competition', most frequently it results in very careful collaboration between the schools, which may make choice for parents much more difficult. The precise outcome in a rivalistic market will depend on the precise local circumstances, emphasising the importance of understanding the full nature of the local micro-market as a prelude to understanding the choices parents and young people are making.

Throughout this book we stress the importance of 'knowing the local market' to an understanding of choice. However, the evidence we present also demonstrates that local processes and outcomes are simply variable patterns painted on a backdrop of common principles of choice and decision-making. Such principles are transferable ideas which can provide the important point of departure for analysing local circumstances. Knowing how and why such local patterns differ from the patterns that might be predicted from the generic principles provides empowerment to institutions, individuals and policy-makers in educational and training markets. Although each market place has its own local internal dynamics, therefore, we believe that the generalisations that emerge from an attempt to identify the generic characteristics of choice in education markets are important for 'both levels of macro and micro research are complimentary and essential as they represent two sides of the same education market coin' (Foskett and Hesketh, 1997, p. 302).

The growth of enhanced choice in education/training markets

The development of enhanced choice in education and training arenas for parents and young people is an international phenomenon. Just as there is an infinite variety of market forms within one national setting and one market segment (e.g. primary education), so there are significant differences between the arenas of choice in different states. The development of enhanced choice internationally has been described by the OECD (1997). This emphasises strongly the different starting points, political processes and precise socio-economic aims that have driven the expansion of choice. In some national settings (e.g. Spain, France), for example, educational choice has been enhanced but to a lesser extent than in other states such as New Zealand and Australia, where, as in the UK, consumer choice has been at the heart of fundamental educational reform processes (Waslander and Thrupp, 1995). Both as an exemplar of such change and as a background to the detailed analysis of choice within this book we shall consider briefly the time line of enhanced choice in England and Wales in each of the three main sectors of education/training – schools, further education and higher education.

Choosing schools

Choice in the compulsory phase of education in England and Wales has always existed in the dichotomy between state and independent school sectors. Even within the state sector, though, some elements of choice existed where local authorities maintained different forms of school (for example, single-sex and mixed secondary schools), where parents had the choice of faith-based schools (usually Catholic or Church of England schools), or where local authority boundaries made access to schools in more than one authority a practical possibility. In the period following the election of a Conservative administration under the leadership of Margaret Thatcher in 1979, though, the foundations of enhanced school choice were constructed through the enshrinement in statute of parental rights to information about their children's schools. The 1981 Education Act, for example, required schools to produce a prospectus for parents with tightly defined types of information, while the 1986 Education Act required school governing bodies to produce an annual report for parents. Such developments, though, were simply a prelude to the substantial reform embodied in the 1988 Education Reform Act (ERA).

The 1988 ERA was designed to 'carry the concept of parental choice to the heart of our educational system' (Baker, 1988, p. 1), built around three key features. First, 'open enrolment' removed the limitations from schools to take pupils only from a local clearly defined catchment area, and enabled them to recruit pupils in numbers up to the physical capacity of the school. Parents, in theory, therefore, could choose any accessible school for their children rather than simply their local 'catchment' school. Second, the introduction of 'local management of schools' (LMS) delegated financial responsibility from LEAs to schools, with the level of funding for each school determined by a formula in which the key element was pupil numbers. Hence schools were not only made responsible for their own financial management but were *de facto* encouraged to recruit more pupils to increase their income. Third, diversification in the nature of state educational provision was encouraged by the establishment of two new types of school – Grant Maintained (GM) schools, which received their funding direct from government and were thus independent of the local authority, and City Technology Colleges (CTCs), also independent of the LEA and with a strong focus on specialist provision (e.g. in music, the arts, modern languages or information technology). Such schools were enabled to provide distinctive provision to create competition with LEA schools and so enhance choice.

The statutory establishment of the broad structures of a market for parental choice of primary and secondary schools in 1988 was the prelude to a number of strategies to enhance parental choice during the first five years of the new market place. The promotion of choice as both a right and obligation for parents was enshrined in the Parents Charter (DfEE, 1994) which passed the responsibility for monitoring and raising standards in schools to the attentiveness of parents in exercising choice. To ensure a sound basis for choice, government also introduced a number of measures to provide parents with a range of information about school performance. The publication of the reports of school inspections by the government's OFSTED agency, and of 'league tables' of school performance in public examinations, attendance and school exclusion became a statutory requirement, and the nature and detail of information to be contained in school prospectuses was further enhanced by legislation. Diversification of schools was also strongly promoted by government through the encouragement of schools to 'opt out' of LEA control into GM status, with strong financial incentives to do so, and the continuing promotion of CTC schools. Parents were strongly driven to become active 'consumers' of education, making choices on the basis of readily accessible public domain information that enabled them to compare schools before choosing.

By the mid-1990s parental choice was an important feature of the management and operation of schools. Its impact on the culture of schools, their objectives and their operation was widely observed by research. Gewirtz, Ball and Bowe (1995), for example, record changes to professional and management culture as schools became more competitive and focused on output performance indicators. Levacic (1995) has noted the effects on financial management processes of operating within choice-driven markets, while Woods, Bagley and Glatter (1998) have identified the changing relationship between schools and parents. The embeddedness of choice was reflected in its continuance under the Labour government elected in 1997.

School choice in England and Wales operates in a government defined market place, whose precise form continues to be modified. Parental choice as such has been replaced by the notion of 'parental preference' which has moved the ultimate decision-making in relation to the allocation of school places more firmly back into the hands of individual schools. Free choice has been replaced, for those parents who wish to express choice, into a calculated risk game in which they gamble their assured place in their local school for a place in another school of their preference. Governors' appeals committees now spend significant time dealing with the appeals of parents unsuccessful in their application for entry to popular schools. Just as the choice system has changed so the range of choices has been modified by the transfer of GM schools back to LEA control and the creation of the new category of 'foundation schools', to include ex-GM schools and Catholic/Church of England schools. Choice is still, though, a strong component of the educational scene as parents and their children pass through the compulsory phase of education.

Choosing further education and training

Choice has always been a feature of the education/training scene encompassed by the Further Education (FE) sector, since young people, by definition, could choose whether to participate or not. However, under the guiding hand of LEAs planned provision meant that little inter-institutional competition existed and young people chose between the (frequently) monopolistic single provider of vocational training within their locality and the providers of academic programmes in a single sixth-form college or in the sixth forms of schools. Independence from the LEA for FE institutions was established by their incorporation as self-managing corporate bodies under the 1992 Further and Higher Education Act, and the transfer of much of their funding to the newly-established Further Education Funding Council (FEFC). There followed a period of strong marketisation in which 'choice' by potential customers became a paramount element of institutional development and survival. The funding models applied by the FEFC sought to both increase efficiency by driving down unit costs in colleges, and to expand 16–19 participation rates for young people. The result was a highly competitive market (Hemsley-Brown, 1999b). The maintenance of funding levels from year to year was dependent on expansion as an 'efficiency gain' was imposed each year, and colleges were set expansionist recruitment targets to raise overall participation rates by 30% over the period from 1990 to 1996. In such an environment the persuasion of young people's choice by colleges and other providers became all important, and the individual potential student was strongly empowered within the market place. Just as consumer choice has been supported in relation to schools by enhanced information flow based on strong quality assurance (QA) systems, so in FE inspection and the publication of league tables have been established to underpin consumer choice as well as public accountability. Each institution has striven to persuade more of the existing FE demand in its locality into its compass, and to increase overall demand by seeking new markets, locally, regionally, and in some cases nationally and internationally (Davies, 1999; Hemsley-Brown, 1999b). The impact of the development of enhanced choice in the sector has been substantial in both cultural and operational terms for, as Hemsley-Brown (1999b, p. 82) suggests, there has been ...

> a shift from a 'collectivist' (...) operational environment, dominated by a culture of collegiality and a humanistic philosophy with colleges working in partnership with LEAs, to a culture of managerialism within a rational-economic philosophy, operating in a competitive market environment managed by the FEFC.

Choosing higher education

Choice in higher education until the late 1980s was characterised by a strong selection system. Demand exceeded supply of places in an academically elitist system, and choice was, in practice, limited to those individuals of high academic achievement seen as desirable by all universities. Expansion of HE participation rates from 14% in the late 1980s to 33% in the mid-1990s though, accompanied by the use of funding models by the Higher Education Funding Councils (HEFC) which required very substantial reductions in the unit of resource for HE institutions, resulted in strong competition and increased empowerment of young people as choosers in the HE market place. Expansion of the system, by increasing numbers and incorporating the former polytechnics into university HE, provided individual students with greater choice, and institutions were moved to establish strong marketing systems to support and influence that choice (Smith, Scott and Lynch, 1995). In addition, as with schools and FE, the emphasis on accountability by government established strong quality inspection systems and the publication of perform- ance data to enable comparison between institutions by potential customers. League tables and inspection (now by bodies such as the Quality Assurance Agency (QAA)) are as much a part of the HE scene as they are in the schools and FE scene.

Choice and widening participation

Both FE and HE in the UK in the 1990s have seen substantial expan- sion in participation. An important element of this expansion has been the policy drive to widen participation amongst socio-economic and community groups hitherto under-represented in the sectors – for example, those from socio-economic groups 3, 4 and 5, those who had 'missed out' on FE/HE as young people, and those from under-represented ethnic groups. The drive to widening participa- tion is strongly linked to a commitment to the idea of lifelong learn- ing, in which learning, education and training are not seen simply as something to be undertaken by young people. It is based in the par- allel political aims of raising attainment levels to increase economic competitiveness in the global economy, and also in the humanitar- ian view of the need to facilitate individual achievement (Kennedy, 1997; Fryer, 1997). In this way it brings together wider economic needs with the empowerment of individuals through the enhance- ment of choice. Widening participation is fundamentally about widening choice for individuals.

Widening participation has two quite different components. The first involves *facilitating choice*, enabling an engagement with learning for those who consider this as a choice option but reject it because of the circumstances in which they find themselves. Economic, social, cultural and community barriers, or the structural characteristics of admissions or teaching and learning systems (for example the very limited availability of child care facilities or the traditional emphasis on long courses taught during the daytime) mean that individuals who might wish to participate are prevented from doing so. The second involves *increasing demand* for education and training by persuading those groups who have either not considered engaging in learning or have actively rejected it to consider participation.

Facilitating choice is the easier of the two to achieve, but is not without a requirement for very significant systemic change. In the UK, increasing the availability of places in FE and HE, providing alternative entry pathways, for example through Access programmes, and incentivising the recruitment of non-standard entry students (or at least removing some of the major disincentives for institutions) have enabled groups previously unable to enter FE/HE to do so. However, while increasing numbers of individuals from ethnic minority groups, or mature applicants, or those from socio-economic groups with no strong tradition of FE/HE participation has occurred, lowering such barriers also enables more young people from traditional participating groups to enter. Expansion of FE and HE in the UK in the 1990s has largely been the result of increased participation rates amongst white, middle-class young people (Trow, 1998).

Increasing demand is much more problematical. We shall demonstrate later in this book how the choice of education and training pathways is rooted in early experiences of education and training. Decisions made by and for primary and secondary phase children, and the influence of parents, teachers and the media during compulsory education years are fundamental in shaping what choices are made later along those pathways. Those choosing not to participate in learning as adults or in their late 'teens' are making those decisions on the basis of earlier experiences. Those experiences, in such cases, will often be about failure, rejection, or exclusion in relation to particular choices, making participation in learning as older individuals much less likely – as Fryer (2000) suggests, 'people do not volunteer to be humiliated a second time'. We would argue, though, that widening participation as an objective requires a full understanding of how choices are shaped as young people progress through their lives in compulsory education and on into post-compulsory arenas. Furthermore, breaking through the challenge of increasing demand in post-compulsory education requires a fundamental re-appraisal of how the perceptions, attitudes and beliefs of young people and their parents can be modified by changing the types of experiences they have and the messages they receive both from within the education/training system and from society as a whole. We have to find ways of enhancing the value of education and training as choices for young people once they have left compulsory education.

In summary

The expansion of enhanced choice underpins government aims in many countries both in relation to their objectives for school sector outcomes, in relation to improved benefits from further and higher education and in the pursuit of goals relating to lifelong learning and widening participation. Understanding choice processes, their development as young people move through the education/training system, and the influence of individual and external factors on those processes is essential in such a context. The chapters that follow explore these ideas, and seek to draw out the important elements and common themes in the choices of young people in education and training markets.

2 Motivation, rationality and the reality of choice

Rationality and the roots of choice

At the heart of the pursuit of enhanced choice in education and training markets in the 1980s and 1990s has been a belief in the economic and libertarian benefits of choice. The commitment to facilitating market forces as the key determinant of social and economic outcomes has, in turn, been based in a belief in the decision-making models of classical economics – what we may term 'economically rational models' of choice, based on the notion that choices and decisions in the market place are the result of rational and conscious economic calculations (e.g. Becker, 1975; Friedman and Friedman, 1980; Schotter, 1990; Johnes, 1993). But how far do young people's decision-making strategies follow the economically rational decision-making models which underpin government rhetoric and legislation (CBI, 1989; CBI, 1993a; CBI, 1993b; Dearing, 1996; and Dearing, 1997)? As background to the discussion of choice processes through the rest of this book this chapter examines such models of decision-making behaviour, drawing on a range of research from the traditional fields of economics and psychology. To provide a critique of rational decision-making, motivation theory and the realities of choice the chapter examines the key features of these models, and considers both the inherent problems of rational models of choice, and the challenges of applying them to the arenas of education and training where their application is comparatively recent. This analysis demonstrates the imperative of research within such decision-making arenas, and the chapter concludes by exploring some of the methodological and ethical issues that emerge when we seek to research choice and decision-making in public sector, and particularly education/training, markets.

Choice, motivation and rational decision-making

Traditional theories of 'choice' draw strongly on the models of classical economics. McLean (1987, p. 3) defines economics as 'the study of rational decisions, whether in the market, in politics, or anywhere else', and emphasises that within economic theory there are a number of important standard assumptions, *viz*:

> that there is no accounting for tastes, but that whatever an individual wants, he prefers more of it to less; that the more he already has of any good, the less he will want more of that good in preference to some other good; not, that he is procedurally rational in making consistent and transitive choices; that goods or options can be placed in order, but not normally compared cardinally.
>
> (McLean, 1987, p. 182)

For the individual, the choice process is central to this view of the world, requiring him or her to engage in decision-making processes involving 'the formulation of alternatives and the subsequent choice between them' (Radford, 1977, p. 1). Radford goes on to define decision-making as

> a procedure to select a course of action from those available that will transform what is judged to be a less desirable situation into a more desirable one that can be attained at some time in the future.
>
> (Radford, 1977, p. 2)

This process of decision-making is recognised as being neither instantaneous nor constant and predictable, and Edwards (1961) refers to the process of choice as dynamic decision-making. This suggests that important life decisions, such as career choices, are incremental in nature, the final outcome of a series of small decisions that progressively commit the person to a particular course of action (Janis and Mann, 1977). Although we may perceive each small decision in isolation, in real life, decisions occur in sequences, and information available for later decisions is likely to be based on the nature and consequences of earlier ones. Preferences may well change over time, too, in response to the influence of others, or through the media and advertising, for in a situation where a decision-maker is not fully informed of all aspects of the choice being made, marketing may have a part to play in providing information which could have a bearing on outcomes.

Within this context of a dynamic environment, though, traditional economic rational models make assumptions about the processes involved in the choice decision. Whether in the arena of business and trade involving goods and services, or in community and public sector fields, or within the bounds of an individual's personal life, this view of choice and decision-making is based on four key tenets:

1   That individuals will seek to maximise the benefits they will gain from the choices they make – so-called, *utility maximisation.*
2   That individuals will make choices that are entirely based on *self-interest.*
3   That choices will be made after a process of *vigilant information collection.*
4   That the process of considering alternatives and making choice will be entirely *rational.*

We shall examine each of these assumptions below.

Utility maximisation

Utility maximisation is the assumption that a decision-maker will seek to optimise utility or benefit from their choice. Choice relies on the notion of utility, which may be defined as 'goods and services that have the power to satisfy the wants of mankind' (Whitehead, 1981, p. 2). This perspective assumes that

> individuals are utility maximisers. This means that they make use of the most appropriate of the available means to pursue their ends, and that they exhibit a well behaved preference structure.
>
> (Downs, 1957, pp. 49–50)

In the choice of goods and some services making judgements about utility maximisation may be relatively straightforward for individuals. Choosing one make of car as opposed to another, for example, may bestow clear additional utility advantages to a potential purchaser. In the arena of education and training choices such utility maximisation is not so easy to determine, however. Education and training are both intangible and, usually, very long term in their delivery of benefit. A young person choosing whether to go to college, for example, may want to know how much additional income is generated throughout his or her life by spending longer in education. Becker (1975) argues that an important factor increasing the difficulty of anticipating this rate of return is that the return is collected over a very long time. While business investments are often said to pay off within five or ten years, the payoff from college takes much longer. Furthermore, the benefit that will accrue to the individual is dependent upon future, perhaps unpredictable, circumstances, and will result from the complex interaction of education and training outcomes with social, economic and political environments and labour markets that, also, cannot be foreseen with any confidence. For the individual, judgements of utility maximisation can only be based, therefore, on assumptions extrapolated from historical evidence of the benefits of education and training, yet the past is not necessarily a good predictor of the future. Where young people are the primary choosers in the decision-making process their own knowledge of the interaction of education and labour markets may be insufficient to facilitate an informed choice – indeed, it is from the education process they are yet to undertake that such knowledge may eventually derive. Where it is their parents leading the choice process it is more likely to be based on historical evidence of utility from those parents' own experiences. Either way, seeing the future return on education and training is likely to be very difficult, if not impossible.

It is perhaps unsurprising, therefore, that such rates of return models appear not to be a significant influence on the choices of further and higher education made by young people. Johnes (1993, p. 51) believes that 'the consumers of education do not receive labour market signals sufficiently clearly to make efficient decisions about how much education to consume', and concludes that

> the importance which potential students attach to the financial returns of study is not, in general, as great as the weight they assign to non-pecuniary aspects, such as academic interest and personal satisfaction. (...) Overall, therefore the available evidence suggests that labour market signals do not feed through into the demand for education. Both the quantity of education demanded and the form of education required vary with labour market events.

> (Johnes, 1993, p. 60)

We may conclude, then, that the pursuit of utility maximisation is an unrealistic expectation in decision-making. As Miller and Starr have suggested,

> the work of the psychologist would certainly tend to confirm the assertion that human beings have a variety of diverse motivations which do not lend themselves to maximisation of utility – at least so long as utility is defined in terms of the satisfactions resulting from marketplace phenomena.
>
> (Miller and Starr, 1967, pp. 254–5)

Self-interested motivation

The motivation for choice within markets has been an important focus of research within economics and the social sciences. The centrality of the importance of economic motivation originates in the writings of Adam Smith (1776), the classical economist who first envisaged the workings of the free market economy and the notion of 'the invisible hand of market forces' (Copley and Sutherland, 1995, p. 62). He argued that buyer behaviour is based on self-interest, and in 'pursuing his self interest man (*sic*) carefully calculates the advantages and disadvantages of any given purchase' (Baker, 1992, p. 165). Such self-interest would operate on both the supply and demand sides of the market. For the customer, self-interest is operationalised in the pursuit of goods and services that meet their precise wants and needs at the lowest possible cost. For the supplier, it operates through the pursuit of increased profits by satisfying customers' needs and wants through meeting those needs more closely than competitors and at a lower price than competitors. In this way, Thompson *et al.* (1991, p. 3) explain, 'the pursuit of self interest by individually motivated (...) individuals leads to the best outcome not just for them, but also for society', even though those individuals are not motivated by collective outcomes and 'will not make a decision which is based on their common interests' (Hindess, 1988, p. 12).

But what drives the 'customer's' self-interest, and how is it expressed implicitly and explicitly within the process of choice? A wide range of motivation theories have been developed (e.g. Schein, 1985), most of which stress not a consistent and predictable pattern of motivations for individuals but the contingent and variable nature of motivation at the micro scale. Maslow (1943), for example, suggests that human 'needs' can be classified into a simple hierarchy, which individuals will seek to satisfy in order of precedence:

1   Physiological needs (food, shelter, etc.);
2   Safety needs;
3   Love needs;
4   Esteem needs;
5   Self-actualisation needs.

The importance of each need will clearly vary from time to time and from individual to individual. In education and training markets, for example, both young people and their parents may vary considerably in the stages in the hierarchy they have reached at the time when they are making important decisions about their future. Those who have reached the stage of self-actualisation, for example (i.e. those who have achieved a measure of satisfaction in terms of the first four essential needs), may be 'immune to marketing techniques and have a very clear view of what it is they want, and want to do' (Baker, 1992, p. 173). Young people who are struggling, however, to fulfil basic physiological, safety and love needs, may approach their decisions in a way which satisfies their self-esteem, for example, rather than their need for 'self-actualisation' – or a need to fulfil their best potential in the future. Furthermore, the choices that young people make in education and training markets are not detached from those they are making about all the other components of their lives, and the need to make other choices that relate to more basic needs in Maslow's hierarchy may militate against 'high order' motivations for choices about education pathways.

Maslow's model strongly emphasises the importance of both economic and social motivators in decision-making. One of the earliest models of choice behaviour was developed by the social psychologist Veblen (1899), and emphasises the importance of social class characteristics and social relationships in shaping the needs, wants and hence choices of individuals. Veblen argued that many choices, including 'purchases', were not motivated by need as much as by a concern for social status and prestige. In the context of education, this is an important idea, for it recognises that education may, in economic terms, be a 'positional good', whose value lies in the enhanced status and prestige that accompanies its possession. While it is now generally acknowledged that there is considerable mobility between social groups and social class may no longer be a reliable predictor of consumer behaviour (Baker, 1992), this suggests that we must look beyond economic motivation for an understanding of choice in education and training markets. In such a consideration of social motivations towards (or against) choice as a concept, we must also recognise that parents in particular may eschew the notion of themselves as consumers in relation to education and training for their children and make decisions that they believe are in the interests of society as a whole.

Vigilance and decision-making

Vigilance refers to the pursuit of evidence-based decision-making which brings together all relevant information to support the choice process. It refers to the intensity of the search process, and is a requirement of rational decision-making – without vigilance in the information search, how can any choice be fully rational? The vigilant decision-making process was described by Janis and Mann (1977), as comprising seven stages:

1 Canvassing a wide range of alternative courses of action.
2 Reviewing the full range of objectives to be fulfilled and personal values to be considered in the choice.
3 Weighing up the costs and risks of both negative and positive consequences of each alternative.
4 Searching intensively for further new information relevant to the choice.
5 Assimilating and taking account of any new information or expert judgement, even when the information does not support the initial choice of course of action.
6 Re-examining the positive and negative consequences of all known alternatives, including those originally regarded as unacceptable, prior to making a choice.
7 Making detailed provision for implementing the chosen action, including attention to contingency plans that may be required if known risks materialise.

(adapted from Janis and Mann, 1977, p. 11)

In order for a decision to be considered rational, Janis and Mann suggest that each stage must be completed. They observe, however, that people will rarely, if ever, work through all stages of vigilant decision-making or retain the precise sequence. Indeed, they believe that there may be disadvantages to the decision-making process of keeping rigidly to the choice model, for a high degree of selectivity may often save the decision-maker from unproductive confusion, unnecessary delays and waste of his resources in a fruitless quest for an elusive, faultless alternative.

(Janis and Mann, 1977, p. 13)

In practice, therefore, we must presume that vigilant decision-making is impracticable or undesirable and that most if not all choices are based on a process that, rather than being non-vigilant, is sub-vigilant in its approach. Indeed, the development of effective decision-making skills may involve the honing of skills which enable individuals to estimate implicitly when the additional returns from increased vigilance become very small.

Rationality

The principal requirement of economically rational decision-making behaviour is, of course, rationality. The term rationality is used to describe decision-making behaviour which 'maximises the satisfaction of preferences' (Hindess, 1988, p. 24), and it has been argued that

the crucial fact about economic man (*sic*) is that he is rational. This means two things: he can weakly order the states into which he can get, and he makes his choices so as to maximise something.

(Edwards, 1954, p. 15)

There is little support for the belief that the decision-maker usually reaches the most rational or optimum solution for his/her own benefit, however. If a rational decision is one which has been made through a process of vigilant information processing, and a process which attempts to reach an optimal solution, then research by many writers including Simon (1957), Downs (1957), and Janis and Mann (1977), does not support the view that decision-makers are consistently behaving 'rationally'. From this research we can identify three reasons to question the reality of optimally rational behaviour:

a   It is not possible to identify what the most rational choice in a particular set of circumstances may be, and some observers may perceive decisions as being more or less rational than others might.

b   The information, and the search paths necessary to acquire it, to ensure rationality may not be available to individuals because of practical and, particularly, economic constraints. Chisnall (1985), for example, argues that choice behaviour in markets is complex and influenced by a wide range of factors, some of which may conflict with so-called rational decision-making models. One of the features of complex decision-making is that the information available to people is often incomplete and this prevents decision-makers from working in a totally rational way.

c   Individuals may not be motivated by the pursuit of the perfectly rational choice, but may be seeking a choice that is 'good enough'.

This view that decision-makers do not necessarily act rationally is supported by Hindess who claims that 'human behaviour frequently departs from the canons of rationality, so that rational choice models are not realistic' (Hindess, 1988, p. 10). Decision-makers may like to think they have made a rational choice, or one that will be judged to have been rational in the light of future events, but 'those dealing with complex problems consciously or unconsciously abandon approaches involving comprehensive models and the goal of a uniquely optimum solution' (Radford, 1977, p. 16). Janis and Mann (1977) see each individual making choice

> not as a rational calculator always ready to work out the best solution, but as a reluctant decision-maker – beset by conflict, doubts, and worry, struggling with incongruous longings, antipathies and loyalties, and seeking relief by procrastinating, rationalising or denying responsibility for (their) own choice.
>
> (Janis and Mann, 1977, p. 1)

This concern that fully rational decision-making is unlikely is the basis of an important concept in decision-making, that of 'bounded rationality'. The notion of 'bounded rationality' (Simon, 1957) reflects the limited cognitive capacity of decision-makers and implies that decisions are often less than fully rational. Bounded rationality is a type of decision-making behaviour 'under conditions of uncertainty in which a satisfactory rather than optimum alternative is selected' (Radford, 1977, p. 199). In such circumstances the decision-maker 'satisfices' rather than 'maximises' – that is, he or she 'looks for a course of action that is "good enough" that meets a minimal set of requirements' (Simon, 1972, p. 170). As a result, decision-makers may confine their search to a more restricted and less thorough investigation, and economise on the collection of information and the evaluation of alternatives 'by searching only for a course of action that achieves a satisfactory result' (Simon, 1972, p. 170).

In such a model, 'the first step that participants take towards resolution is to review existing knowledge of the problem and to gather as much additional information as available time and resources allow' (Radford, 1977, p. 37). The next step, though, might be to search fairly superficially for information, based perhaps only on the information provided by others, or information easily available to the individual, such as from friends, teachers or family. A young person applying a 'satisficing strategy' would then only consider each course of action in order, until one that 'will do' is discovered. Simon (1957) argues convincingly that decision-makers generally censor their intake of messages in a biased way to protect their current beliefs and decisions from being attacked, and people tend to seek out information which will support the beliefs, opinions and attitudes they already hold, especially when negative information is provided which might affect confidence. The decisions people make are dependent, then, upon views, attitudes and opinions already held and choice involves an interplay among three broad sets of variables: predispositions, influences, and product attributes (Cox, 1968). This suggests that final decisions will be influenced by an individual's conscious, or unconscious prejudices, and that people typically start the decision-making process with preconceived ideas about the subject in hand, rather than with an open mind, ripe to sift information in an objective way. Decision-makers, of course, vary in terms of how vigilant they are, from hyper-vigilance to random choice. In all cases, though, it is clear that individuals do not 'maximise' by behaving in a rational way throughout, but 'satisfice' by working in conditions of partial ignorance and uncertainty to reach a conclusion that is satisfactory to their needs.

Full vigilance and a concern for optimisation are not common features of choice, therefore, but how far can decisions which have not been made through a 'vigilant' and 'optimising' decision-making strategy be considered to be 'technically rational'? A decision which has been reached through a process of 'satisficing' rather than 'optimising' might be described strictly as 'non-rational', although in practice an individual may reach a conclusion that is rational within the constraints of sub-optimal information and without having gone through all the stages of 'vigilant' decision-making. It may be more accurate, therefore, to describe such choices as 'sub-rational' or 'sub-optimal'.

Factors influencing rationality

Many factors, of course, may be influential in the reasons why choosers operate in a sub-rational way and which operate to constrain rationality. Janis and Mann (1977) recognise that important in understanding such sub-rational behaviour is the effect of the interaction of an individual's explicit perspectives based on ideas of utility, and implicit factors which reflect the individual's concerns about their position within the world and their own community. The decision-maker does not necessarily rely on a criterion which an observer considers to be high priority, therefore, but

> also takes account of a multiplicity of intangible considerations bearing on the probable effects of the chosen and unchosen courses of action on relatives and friends. Anticipated feelings of high or low self-esteem with regard to living up to his own personal standards of conduct also affect his preferences for one alternative rather than another.
>
> (Janis and Mann, 1977, pp. 24–5)

Five associated factors may be considered to affect the rationality of decisions: 'self esteem' (Maslow, 1954); the permanence and importance of the decision; 'conceptual blocks' (Janis and Mann, 1977); inertia; and 'dissonance' (Festinger, 1964).

Self-esteem refers to the individual's feelings about themselves in relation to the choices they make and the situations they find themselves in. Important within all choices is the issue of how a decision will be perceived by those observing from outside. How far will the choice be valued by others? How much will the individual's social and personal position be raised or lowered by the choice? How far will the reaction of others to this change influence the individual's feelings about themselves? The need to conform in behaviour, lifestyle and decisions is often seen as important to facilitate acceptance in peer or other social groupings. Self-esteem might be very important when a decision-maker is choosing between alternative careers, or colleges or schools, where social class perceptions, and personal standards are being judged by onlookers, parents and friends. These factors might not always be openly expressed by decision-makers, but may be a vital, but unstated, consideration in the process of sifting information about the alternatives available. Baker argues that such peer group pressure affects choice, and claims that

> many consumer products are promoted as having attributes which will enhance one's acceptance with the group, or occasionally are sold on the basis that the lack of a possession could lead to ostracism or exclusion from the group.
>
> (Baker, 1992, p. 173)

In anticipation of feedback from peers, the individual may have to provide reasons which were not necessarily crucial in the decision-making process itself, but which would help to convince others that the decision was the right one.

The permanence of the decision which is to be made, according to Janis and Mann (1977), may also have a serious influence on how vigilant a decision-maker needs to be in the information search, before reaching a final conclusion. If the decision is reversible the decision-maker might only undertake a superficial search for information. If the decision is not reversible then this may stimulate a more vigilant search process. In the context of education/training choices, for example, if a young person is able to accept a place at a college (or more than one college) with the knowledge that the place can be turned down later, the search for information might be less thorough than it might have been had no opportunity of reversing the decision been available. Choices of school and college are, of course, ones that may be changed – a child may be moved to a different school or a student may change course or institution. However, the resocialisation that such changes require for the young person involved and the fact that such changes, because of constraints of academic years and cycles, make starting at the beginning in a new setting very difficult, there is strong inertia in the period after a choice has been put into action. The reversibility of such choices is quite constrained, therefore, not so we might expect that such a perception would stimulate behaviours in education/training choice as if the choices were permanent and irreversible. We shall explore in later chapters whether this is in fact the case.

Radford (1977) has identified the importance of 'conceptual blocks' as a limit on the information search decision-makers may carry out. Conceptual blocks are an expression of the pre-existing ideas that individuals bring to the choice process that constrain their perview of choice and their information seeking. Attitudes, values and beliefs, for example, about the nature of education in particular types of institution, or about 'the sort of people' who pursue particular pathways in education or training generate what Radford terms 'information blindness' which will lead to an individual limiting the areas in which s/he is prepared to search and sift information relating to a decision. Attitudes and beliefs about 'Oxbridge' or about universities which had previously been polytechnics may constrain choice of higher education courses and institutions, for example. Beliefs about the nature of grammar schools, or independent schools, may restrict some parents (and their sons/daughters) to only consider, or to not consider at all, these types of institution. Radford identifies four types of conceptual blocks:

> Perceptual blocks may result in stereotyping and labelling of individuals or actions, and the consequent introduction of biased information into the process of problem solving. Cultural or environmental blocks result from exposure to a particular set of cultural patterns or from operation in a particular social or physical environment. Emotional blocks may arise from aversion to uncertainty and risk taking, related possibly to fear of failure or mistake. Intellectual and expressive blocks result in an inability to generate ideas and to communicate them to others.
>
> (Radford, 1977, p. 62)

Inertia is a constraint to vigilant decision-making in that the availability of an easy and readily available 'choice' may deter an individual from seeking other possibilities. Such a perspective suggests that until a person is challenged by some dissonant information or event that calls his/her attention to a potential 'loss' in the immediate future, s/he will continue to be complacent about whatever course of action (or inaction) s/he has been pursuing (Janis and Mann, 1977). This suggests that an individual may remain unconcerned and allow events to take their course, unless something happens to prod them into action. In the context of education and training such inertia may be important at major transitions. Allowing a young child to attend the local primary school may be an easy practical option, and then allowing them to transfer at age 11 to the local community secondary school with their friends may provide a 'good enough' line of action. At 16 many young people who are in a position to remain in the school they have attended since they were eleven may choose to take the easiest option – that is to do nothing about moving to another school or college, unless some significant event occurs to prompt them into action. Only with the arrival of information that demonstrates explicitly that taking the line of least resistance will produce a negative outcome for the child or young person will there be enough momentum to overcome the inertia of such choices.

The idea of dissonance in decision-making has emerged from theories of cognitive dissonance (Festinger, 1964). Dissonance is the existence of contradictory ideas that an individual cannot reconcile. It may occur both in the choice-making process where the individual must deal with ideas and information which challenge existing beliefs or views, and also in the period after a choice has been made when discrepancy between the expected satisfaction and benefits of a choice and the reality of an experience emerge. This is described as post-decision dissonance. Chisnall (1985) suggests that individuals respond to dissonance by pursuing strategies to avoid or minimise its existence, through, for example:

i   actively pursuing a more vigilant search to identify information to reduce the dissonance;
ii actively ignoring information which creates dissonance;
iii seeking information which justifies the decision they have made and which can be used to justify that decision to external audiences. This will be reflected in an increased tendency towards 'selective exposure' (Janis and Mann, 1977), as individuals may select information favourable to their choice, to bolster their confidence (and that of others) in their choice, and at the same time to distort or dismiss unpleasant facts (Baker, 1992). Festinger (1964) recognised that an act of 'purchase' itself may create some uncertainty in the mind of the buyer, who will then seek reassurance that s/he has made the correct decision. Once the individual has made the decision, he/she has to deal with the announcement of the choice to his/her social network, and for this reason it is important for the decision-maker to have clearly identified all the positive advantages of the choice. This may contribute to the effects of bolstering and help commitment to the decision, and to reduce 'dissonance'. The decision-maker, therefore, has to be quite certain that he/she can cope with the challenges he/she meets from any group of people involved in the decision.

These ways of coping with the conflict an individual experiences after reaching a solution form a major part of the process of avoiding regret after the decision is announced. Dissonance is in some ways a form of psychological stress, and produces an impact on the choice process that can be similar to that generated by stress from external sources – for example, pressure to make choices being imposed by other people, such as the pressure from parents on a 17 year old to choose what they will do after A-levels. Janis and Mann's study of the effect of high and low levels of stress on individuals' decision-making processes suggested that when the decision-maker is under no stress only a casual low-level interest is taken in messages and information bearing on what is considered to be an inconsequential issue (Janis and Mann, 1977). Young people who are anxious to make a decision about their post-16 alternatives, however, and who see the importance attached to the decision, and some competition to gain a place of their choice, might experience more stress when making decisions than 16 year olds who are unconcerned about pursuing post-compulsory education.

Janis and Mann have also identified the importance of defensive avoidance as a response to cognitive dissonance. Defensive avoidance involves choosing strategies that deflect the responsibility for a choice on to other individuals or on to factors outside the chooser's control. Defensive avoidance mechanisms serve to enable the decision-maker to deal with any challenges encountered later on when the decision is announced, and to boost the individual's self-confidence about having made the best decision in the circumstances. Three discrete forms of defensive avoidance may operate singly or together:

> One form (of defensive avoidance) consists of procrastinating; a second involves shifting responsibility for making the decision onto someone else. The third form consists of bolstering the least objectionable alternative by exaggerating the positive consequences or minimising the negative consequences.
>
> (Janis and Mann, 1977, p. 87)

These forms of defensive avoidance seem to prevail in cases where the individual feels s/he has not really been able to make an entirely satisfactory decision, through lack of real choice, or where significant dissonance exists after the choice has been made. Janis and Mann (1977, p. 205) claim that 'when conditions making for defensive avoidance are present the individual becomes closed-minded and biased in his information preferences'. This is exemplified in young people's choice of FE institution where research shows that individuals tend to bolster the attractiveness of the organisation they have selected, giving a higher attractiveness rating to the chosen organisation and lower ratings to the unchosen ones, compared with their initial ratings for the same organisations (Vroom, 1966).

An important dimension of defensive avoidance has been demonstrated by Harris and Harvey (1975) who provide evidence of the tendency for individuals to absolve themselves of responsibility for a sloppily made, ill-fated decision by denying freedom of choice. Brehm (1966) has shown that when someone expects to have a free choice, an alternative foisted upon them will become extremely unattractive regardless of its intrinsic merits. In the case of young people making choices about education and training pathways, it is possible that a young person who later feels his/her decision was ill-conceived, might blame others, such as parents, for that decision, saying that he/she did not have free choice. Furthermore, a young person who is not given a choice of post-16 institution by parents, but is impelled to attend a particular establishment, might be unwilling to acknowledge any of the positive attributes of the alternative foisted upon them. The result of being given virtually no choice of action is a cycle of negative feedback about destination and outcomes. This phenomenon was studied by Worchel (1971) who showed that 'restrictions on freedom evoked considerable hostility in college students; the hostility occurred no matter which alternative, the most attractive or the least attractive, was foisted upon the subject' (Worchel, 1971, p. 294). This perspective has been confirmed by the work of Liem (1975), who has shown that whenever a young person is under coercive pressure from an authority figure to choose an unsatisfactory course of action, s/he usually resents the demand even if s/he reluctantly gives in.

Rationality, choice and the research imperative

This chapter has provided a critical review of some of the principal themes in decision-making theory as it relates to the choices made by individuals within markets. Central to the concept of free-market economics is the conviction that individuals should be free to make their own choices in the market place from amongst the competing alternatives available. Furthermore, it assumes that we can predict the outcomes of such markets on the basis of an economically rational model of choice, based on the central concepts of rationality, utility maximisation, self-interest and vigilant information search. These models provide some considerable challenges as a basis for understanding choice in social markets such as those established in education and training arenas, however. Janis and Mann (1977), for example, have provided a critical review of the idea of vigilant decision-making and have suggested modifications to such models that bring them into closer approximation to real world processes. Simon's 'satisficer' model (1957) also helps to clarify some of the processes we may observe at work in choice arenas. However, it is clear from this analysis that, as Baker argues, 'the most important feature of social science explanations of choice behaviour is that none of them individually provides an adequate explanation of the real world' (Baker, 1992, p.168).

The development of 'enhanced choice' in education and training markets in the last two decades, therefore, has imposed a research imperative, for there has been a need to investigate the nature of choice processes in these fields. We need to identify *who* makes choices in such markets (parents, young people, or education/training providers); *when, how and why* those choices are made, and what influences the choice processes; and *what impact* choice has on the choosers, other participants in the education/training system, the outputs of education and training, and the institutions or organisations constituting the supply side of the market place. In particular, we need to test existing theories of choice and decision-making to see how far they can explain the observed outcomes we find in the system, and to develop new perspectives and models that help us more closely to describe, explain and understand choice in education/training markets. Only in this way can we get closer to being able to model and predict the effects of changes that impact on choice, markets and other mechanisms of resource allocation.

Methodological and ethical issues in researching young people's choices

What approaches might we take in researching young people's education and training choice? We can identify two broad methodologies that have been adopted and used. The first, based principally in a quantitative, positivist view of research, has sought to describe and understand choice through identifying the factors which influence parents and young people in the decision-making process. Using both questionnaire and interview processes researchers have sought to identify the relative importance of unitary influences, such as 'proximity of the school to the child's home', or 'the school's public examination results'. The product of such research is typically some form of prioritised list showing that some factors are more influential than others across a broad group of parents or young people. This approach was predominant in the early 1990s during the earliest researches into school choice processes, and is typified by the studies of Coldron and Boulton (1991), Hunter (1991) and West and Vaarlam (1991a; 1991b).

The second approach is based in an ethnographic research tradition, and draws on the key assumption that the choice process is unique, eclectic and unpredictable at the micro-scale level of individual choice. Although broad patterns of choice may emerge from the macro-scale summation of such 'stories', the reality of choice lies in the personal experiences and accounts of choice by individuals. The use of extended, in-depth, qualitative research methodologies is an essential requirement of researching such a view of choice processes. Such an approach has emerged as a response, in part, to a recognition that early factor analysis studies seemed to provide little real insight into the process of choice itself, and has characterised many of the studies in the latter part of the 1990s (Gewirtz, Ball and Bowe, 1995; Maguire, Macrae and Ball, 1999; Hemsley-Brown, 1999a).

Analysis of factors of choice as a route to understanding decision-making about secondary schools has been subjected to significant criticism within the research literature. Gewirtz *et al.* (1995), for example, are strongly critical of an analysis of choice in markets that concentrates on macro-scale summative analysis and ignores the personal responses of individuals at the micro-scale in what they term 'lived markets' (op cit., p 5). While recognising that 'certain general trends, patterns and changes are evident across local markets' (Gewirtz *et al.*, 1995, p. 4), they are critical of the 'abstract and theoretical level' of research conducted about 'who chooses and how' based on a statistical analysis of choice making and 'artificial empiricism through social arithmetic' (op cit., p. 4).

As a research methodology the use of questionnaires or interviews asking parents and pupils to select individual factors has appeal because of its relative simplicity, yet in its simplicity and also in its assumptions it may lead to important distortions in our understanding of the choice process. Critics cite a number of important concerns, some rooted in the validity of the methodological practice, and some in the assumptions underpinning the methodology (e.g. Gorard, 1999). Two issues have emerged.

First, the responses obtained appear to vary according to the timing of the research process within the period leading up to formal choice, suggesting that factors change in importance over time and within the process. Listing important factors must always, therefore, be tempered by an indication of the time within the process, and even then there is little evidence that the length of time over which the process occurs or the stage in the process reached by each parent/child group will have any consistent pattern. Interviewing parents three months before formal choice must be made will certainly include some who are well advanced in a long choice process and some who have not begun a short process, which may itself be very intensive or not. In short, we cannot assume we are comparing like with like when we question a range of parents.

Second, linked to this view is the concern that such factor analysis is a *post hoc* process, in that parents and children are asked to recall what they considered as part of a previous process. The vagaries of memory, the desire to demonstrate a reasoned process, a concern about or an inability to reveal complex emotional and cultural reactions, and the problems associated with *post hoc justification* (Hemsley-Brown, 1999a) conspire to suggest that the ideas that emerge are highly questionable. There may, clearly, be a difference between true motives and rationalised motives, for people are sometimes unaware of the exact nature of drives initiating their behaviour patterns. They may attempt to account for their behaviour through rationalisation by assigning motivations which are acceptable to their personality structures (Cox, 1968).

At a more philosophical level, concerns have been raised that using factor analysis imposes an assumption of logical rationality on choice that may not be valid, and, worse, may suggest that researchers have themselves been captured by the rhetoric and discourse of rational choice. If choice is the outcome of a process that brings together emotion, personal history, values, ideology, and the implicit assumptions and aspirations of an individual's *habitus* (Bourdieu and Passeron, 1992), then indicating or teasing out the role of individual 'objective' factors will be almost impossible. At best such analysis may impose a false simplicity on the interpretations researchers make. At worst it may act to promote and appear to confirm the notion that choice is a straightforward rational process. Gewirtz *et al.* (1995, p. 20) are critical of the approach which 'treats choice as a decontextualised, undifferentiated and neutral mechanism'. Bowe *et al.* (1994), Gewirtz *et al.* (1995), Carroll and Walford (1997a) and Gorard (1997) emphasise that approaches to researching parental choice which focus on parents' prioritisation of lists of choice factors legitimise choice as a rational process and minimise the complexity and social embeddedness of the choice processes at work. Gewirtz *et al.* assert that such methodologies are

> ... sociologically and politically naive ... (since) ... (t)he view that factors and reasons form the basis for human behaviour bears a strong resemblance to the assumptions that underlie economists' abstract accounts of market behaviour (especially the individual rational calculus of classical economics).
>
> (Gewirtz *et al.*, 1995, p. 6)

As Foskett (2000, p. 110) indicates:

> Put simply, the contention is that such a research approach promotes the notion of rational choice, and in its findings supports its existence. It ignores the contentiousness of such a perspective, and in so doing is not ideologically neutral. In effect it promotes the virtues and values of the market as a resource allocation mechanism.

Much of the most recent research into choice, therefore, has developed methodologically from the recognition that choice is dependent on personal histories, experiences, perceptions and interpretations of the influence of implict and explicit socio-economic and cultural pressures. It is more complex and exploratory than 'factor analysis', researching with individual young people over longer periods of time, and observing the choice processes, the emergent choice outcomes and the interaction between them as choices develop from 'the partly unpredictable pattern of turning points and routines that make up the life course' (Hodkinson and Sparkes, 1997, p. 33).

The tension between the two research approaches has generated significant academic and methodological debate (Tooley, 1997; Ball and Gewirtz, 1997), which has been entertaining to observers but may have generated more heat than light. Such debates risk polarising the arguments and dividing the research perspectives, implying that there is a 'right' and a 'wrong' way of researching choice in education markets. Researchers and students new to the field may feel pressure to join one of the gangs, and not to recognise that both approaches have both value and limitations. Developing a full understanding of choice requires both macro-scale and micro-scale analysis, recognising that the broad patterns described by large-scale analysis lose their applicability in understanding choice at the level of individual choosers. Future research into choice must draw on both traditions and seek to integrate the findings of research from each perspective into more sophisticated and complex multi-level models that help us both to analyse how young people (and their parents) really make choices and how policy developments may emerge from that understanding.

Finally, within this chapter we wish to address an important but relatively unexplored methodological issue in educational markets and choice fields, that of the ethical dimension of the research. Researching choice generates a number of significant ethical challenges for educational researchers that emerge from researching real people, real lives and their choice processes within competitive situations. Two particular issues will be explored here – the problem that research on choice may provide distinct market advantage to either individual organisations or particular groups of parents; and the need to consider the personal significance to individuals of the consequences of current or past choices in educational markets.

Research into choice in the public sector is a new phenomenon, yet all adults and many young people are familiar with the idea of 'market research' in their role as consumers in commercial markets. 'Market research', *sensu stricto*, is research into the nature of a market in terms of its size, location, components, etc., and we should more properly use the term 'marketing research' which encompasses studies of 'buyer behaviour', 'customer satisfaction' and even product research to identify the wants and needs of potential customers. Research into choice in education and training markets may be seen as akin to studies of 'buyer behaviour' in commercial settings.

The problem for academic researchers is the confusion for both education/training organisations and for individual young people between commercial marketing research on the one hand and academic research into markets and marketing on the other. The latter is an objective social science process seeking better understanding of a particular socio-economic system, and to be objective in providing a balanced critique to inform public domain understanding. The former is designed to provide one or more supply side organisations with information which will enhance their sales and market performance, and provide them with distinct commercial competitive advantage. Herein lies the ethical issue for researchers, for organisations may see their participation in or facilitation of research as a means of undertaking marketing research for themselves to gain market advantage from the process. A traditional payoff for participation in educational research has been making data available to participating schools and colleges for their own use. Where the gain is enhanced teaching and learning, or more effective management, this provides no ethical conflict for the researcher. Where the gain is a market advantage for one organisation, with a consequent market disadvantage for another, though, there are strong moral issues involved. Research data on choice, buyer behaviour and market activities by consumers has real commercial value in the market place, and the researcher must be aware that he or she is strongly empowered in the market because of access to this data. Even without the data, though, mere participation in the research may advantage an organisation by facilitating reflection on marketing by those working within that organisation. We have discussed these issues at greater length elsewhere (Foskett, 2000), but would high-light a number of specific moral questions for choice researchers here:

1   Should research proceed where there is a clear market gain for one of the participants? Will the distortion of the market by the access to expertise or data of one participant have negative impacts on other individuals or organisations?

2   Who owns the data on choice in relation to particular organisa-tions in a specific market? Does it belong to the organisations that have provided access to young people to discuss their choices, or does it belong to the individuals involved in the research?

3   When should data from research be released? Should it be released to participant organisations before it is made available in the public domain?

4   Should research present data that would be strongly disadvan-taging to a particular organisation? Should evidence on the negative perceptions that young people have of particular organ-isations or programmes be released into the public domain, and so advantage their competitors?

Within these moral and ethical questions there are no simplistic right or wrong responses, and individual researchers must make appropriate decisions according to the precise conditions that prevail.

We have implied above that these are ethical questions relating specifically to engagement of research with organisations, but most must be considered too in relation to engaging with individuals in research into their choice processes. Carroll and Walford (1997b) have demonstrated, for example, how some parents are acutely aware of their rights to exercise choice and their power in the market as consumers. Such parents, or young people, may see an opportunity to engage in research on 'choice' as a means by which they may gain additional information or have their skills and opportunities in the choice market enhanced. There are ethical issues in this in relation to advantaging some people and disadvantaging others through the research process, and the researcher must be vigilant in distinguishing their role as researcher from that of 'unwitting consultant'.

The second broad ethical arena links closely to the question of researching with individuals, particularly in sensitive areas such as personal choice and related issues of 'success' and 'failure' in education and training arenas. Work with individuals clearly imposes 'standard' ethical constraints on the researcher, such as confidentiality of data, the respondent's right to withdraw from the research, and the minimisation of intrusion. Researching choice requires researchers to investigate experiences and choices that may have strong negative emotions attached to them, or strong memories or feelings of stress. Our research on the choices of young people taking up modern apprenticeships, for example, has shown how the research can be personally challenging for respondents, recalling very negative experiences of education, school and training. There is an imperative on researchers, therefore, to identify the ethical boundaries in their intrusion into personal histories. As we have said elsewhere, 'the sensitivities required to explore these issues are akin to the skills of counselling, in which the individual is encouraged to explore their perceptions and ideas themselves' (Foskett, 200, p. 111).

With most ethical issues in research, the most important step is the recognition that there *is* an ethical dimension to the work. Researching choice is not an ethically neutral activity and researchers seeking to make a contribution to developing understanding in this field must consider their stance on the ethical issues their research generates. Without this, researchers may find themselves 'tarred with the brush' of moral derision that is sometimes directed at those working commercially in advertising or marketing and restrained from access to undertake useful research because of their inability 'to demonstrate that they are worthy as researchers and as human beings of being accorded the facilities to carry out their investigations' (Cohen and Manion, 1994, p. 354).

In summary

This chapter has explored some of the traditional views of choice in markets that have derived from economic and psychological research. It has presented the issues that emanate from the disparity between models of rational decision-making and the reality of the choice process, raising important research questions for those investigating choice in education and training markets. The debates about alternative research methodologies in education and training choice have been considered, together with some of the important ethical issues that researchers must address. This has painted the backdrop to the research evidence on choice in specific education and training arenas that the chapters which follow will explore.

3 Choosing schools

Parents and pupils in the market place

School choice – the context

For the majority of parents and their children, choosing schools is one of the most important decisions that they engage in. In the United Kingdom each child spends at least 15% of their life within school between the ages of 5 and 16, and the impact and influence of that experience on both their life as children and adolescents and on their long-term futures and prospects is fundamental. For most parents there are two major points of choice – when their child enters school at about the age of 5, and when they transfer to secondary education at about the age of 11. In some localities, though, different systems of school organisation (for example into first, middle and high schools) increase the number of choice points, and the expansion in participation in pre-school education may provide an additional choice point for some parents as they choose a nursery for their child. Mobility within the labour market, and the dynamics of family life, however, mean that many parents may also need to make further choices as they move locations over short or long distances. Typically, therefore, a family will make two or three choices of school for each of their children before they leave compulsory education at age 16.

This chapter and the following one examine the process and pattern of school choice. Chapter 3 draws on the extensive body of research evidence to develop an understanding of how and why choices are made. Most of the research has focused on choices at transfer from primary to secondary school, and there is much elsewhere in the literature that provides a rich picture of choice of secondary school. We have chosen, therefore, after an initial examination of generic ideas, to focus on two less well developed areas of school choice research – in the latter part of Chapter 3 we examine choice of primary school, and Chapter 4 is a study of choice as it relates to the independent school sector. This enables some of the broad principles of choice to be considered in a number of discrete contexts, and underlines the differences that are to be found between the broad market segments that are state primary education, state secondary education, and independent primary and secondary education.

Researching school choice

The notion of choice is fundamental to marketisation in public sector services such as education, yet school markets were introduced in many countries during the 1980s and 1990s without any evidence-based objective understanding of the choice process. Gewirtz *et al.* (1995, p. 20) are critical of the 'caricatured versions both of how parents choose and of the effects of their choices' that underpinned the market systems established during the late 1980s. To address the deficiencies of understanding, research into school choice has focused on two principal themes, which, while fundamentally related, have rarely been considered in terms of their interaction. Early research focused on the factors cited as the reasons for school choice by parents and pupils, in an attempt to produce a rational model of decision-making. The second theme has been that of the decision-making process, an examination of the journey of reflection, investigation and consideration that choosers make prior to the decision-taking point. Within this second approach can be built the sub-rational, implicit and often subconscious sociological processes that parents and children engage in as they interact with education and social systems. Both these themes, though, emphasise the demand side of education markets, suggesting that the key influences in shaping the market are the processes associated with choosers. Much less research has been invested into the supply side of the market, examining how schools and colleges react to, and strategise and operate in, their own markets to constrain or shape 'parental' choice. It is clear that markets are an interaction of supply and demand, and understanding the choice process is dependent on understanding this interaction. Only recently has evidence started to emerge of the relationship between parental aspirations, school responses and parental choices of school (see for example Glatter, Woods and Bagley, 1996). The sections that follow discuss the evidence of the influence of a range of factors on school choice, and then consider what we currently understand about the process of school choice.

Factors in school choice

Research into school choice has identified 73 factors (Gorard, 1997) which are cited as important by parents and pupils. Most studies have been undertaken using pre-determined lists of factors from which parents were asked to indicate either which factors they considered when they made a choice of school, or the order of importance of the factors. Comparability between studies has been complicated, however, by the fact that no two investigations used precisely the same lists, and the interpretation by researchers has been built around grouping the factors in different combinations.

Analysis of the large number of factor-based studies suggests, however, that there are five groups of important factors in school choice (Gorard, 1999) – academic criteria, situational criteria, organisational criteria, selective criteria and security criteria. Academic criteria relate to the performance of a school in terms of, for example, examination results and success in enabling pupils to proceed to highly valued destinations (a high status secondary school, university, or a particular career or professional field), as well as a reputation for good quality teaching staff or facilities. Situational criteria are those reflecting school location and related access/travel convenience, and include factors such as travel time to school and proximity of the school to home. Organisational criteria reflect the ways in which the school operates in terms of curriculum and management, and may be explicit or implicit, and directly linked to the educational process or not. The wearing of school uniform, for example, is explicit but not directly linked to 'performance', while the types of ability grouping used by the school (streaming, setting or mixed ability grouping), or class size limits, are explicit and performance linked. Implicit organisational factors include the notions of 'ethos' and 'atmosphere', although these may simply be summative terms relating to other explicit factors. Selective criteria are those linked to the inclusion and exclusion of certain groups of pupils, and range from choices between single-sex or mixed schools, faith-based schools, or selection by the school on the basis of prior or predicted educational attainment. The latter approach provided the traditional distinction in the UK between the academic grammar schools for the top 20% of the ability range as defined by examination (the 11+ test) at age 11, and the secondary modern schools for the remaining 80% who failed to pass the 11+. The history and importance of such selection by ability is deeply ingrained within the value systems of many (particularly middle-class) parents, mostly with very positive connotations, and still plays a large part in the choice process long after the demise of such selection in most parts of the country. Finally, security factors are those reflecting the child's well-being and safety in or on the way to school. Discipline, bullying, vandalism, location of the school, and transport arrangements to school, are important as direct or strongly associated factors within this category.

A consideration of the wide range of studies in the UK and internationally shows that the relative influence of each factor or group of factors on choice is highly contingent, and is strongly linked to the socio-cultural and economic characteristics of the choosers and the nature of the market place within which a particular school is operating. Hammond and Dennison's study (1995) of choice in rural areas of north-east England, for example, shows the relative lack of choice of school in such localities and the low influence of travel issues, while Coldron and Boulton (1991), working with parents in Sheffield, show how proximity to home and the choices made by friends are more important in urban areas where transport is less problematical. These contrasts are confirmed by Foskett's study of rural and urban schools in south-central England (1995). Similarly West and Vaarlam (1991a; 1991b) and Carroll and Walford (1997a; 1997b) have shown how many Asian families prioritise single-sex provision for their daughters. Woods, Bagley and Glatter (1998) have considered the influence of choice factors in selection amongst 12 schools as part of the PASCI project, and group the factors into three major classes of 'academic', 'child-centred' and 'access' factors. The incidence of factors within these groups mentioned by parents in relation to their first choice school is highly variable – for example the incidence of citation ranges from 53% to 4% for academic factors, from 34% to 14% for 'child-centred' factors and from 19% to 0% for access factors, and the ranking of the three groups of factors varies from school to school. The contingent nature of school choice factors has also been emphasised by many studies outside the UK. Lauder and Hughes (1999), for example, examining school choice in New Zealand, show important differences in the relative importance of choice factors between Maori and European parents, while Gaffney's research in the USA (1981) emphasises the importance of a strong, morally based caring ethos in school combined with high academic achievement amongst parents opting for Catholic schools.

What is clear from this analysis is that the priorities of every chooser may be different, both in terms of the order of importance of factors and in the relative weighting between them. Similarly there will be variations from school catchment to school catchment, such that each school must, to clarify key factors, undertake research amongst its own current and potential choosers, and amongst those who have rejected the school in their choice, to identify the dynamics of their market. Despite this recognition of the significance of micro-markets, however, it is possible to identify the factors most frequently identified as the most important in school choice.

Most important, overall, are the security criteria, and particularly those elements that relate to the physical and emotional safety of the child. In choosing primary schools, safety of access is an important underpinning factor in the citing of proximity as a key choice factor. In choosing secondary schools this is a little less significant, but the school's reputation for dealing strongly with bullying and maintaining a purposeful, emotionally secure environment is important. An interesting dimension of the security issue has emerged from some small-scale studies amongst working-class communities (Walters, 1998). Here, choosing the nearest school is important for explicit security reasons, but also to avoid the ostracism that emerges for a child from its peers when parents are seen to have aspirations for their child beyond the socio-cultural norm by seeking a different and 'better' school. Children from low ses (socio-economic status) communities entering selective grammar schools have often been reported as experiencing such social exclusion.

Second most important are the academic group of factors. High attainment aspirations by parents are an important motivation for seeking entry to academically selective schools, including the independent sector. Ball, Bowe and Gewirtz (1995) identify 'circuits of schooling' in which parents make choices within groups of schools regarded as having similar status, but rarely choose outside those groups. Academic reputation is important in placing schools within these implicit groups, with schools achieving high levels of examination success for very high proportions of their pupils occupying the highest circuit, and those with low performance indicators occupying lower circuits of choice. However, academic factors are not only of importance to those parents actively choosing schools with high absolute achievement track records. Even where other factors have been more important, as for example amongst working-class parents, the importance of relative academic success is high, and schools with records of good achievement in any output measure (including, for example, lower levels of under-achievement than a neighbouring school, or fewer permanent exclusions of pupils) will be deemed as academically successful by *some* groups of choosers. Academic achievement is a relative as well as an absolute concept in the choice process.

The third most important group of factors appear to be those relating to selective criteria. Amongst active choosers, most include selection on the basis of gender, attainment or religion as an important choice factor. Important within this is the notion of social groupings, and of gaining access to particular social circuits and networks, and perceptions of social *cachet* may be important in defining which schools are within which specific 'circuits of schooling'. Ball, Bowe and Gewirtz (1995, p. 70) stress that 'part of choosing and not choosing is concerned with who your child will go to school with', and the importance to parents and children of being selected to be an insider within a particular social group cannot be underestimated. The significance of social inclusion is emphasised where, for example, parents choose to pay for private schools with limited academic output records but which bestow evidence of socio-economic and cultural status on both the child and their parents.

An important consideration in the analysis of choice factors is the relative role of those making the choice within the family context, and the balance of influence of each parent and the child within the choice process. As Glatter indicates, 'parents are a highly diverse group, and choice is often a complex and ambiguous process for families' (Glatter *et al.*, 1996, p. 200). Most research studies (e.g. Reay and Ball, 1998) have identified that choice is the product of joint parent and child decision-making, with the balance in their relative influence varying according both to the age of the child and many other factors such as socio-economic class. The relationship between social class (and gender and ethnicity) and the importance of different factors has been drawn out through the range of studies in this field. A broad generalisation would suggest that academic factors are more important amongst middle-class parents than amongst working-class parents, for example, and that security factors are more significant in parental choice of school for daughters than for sons. Such macro-scale trends, however, mask very significant differences within groups at the level of individual choosers. The role of the family in choice is an important component of any model of micro-scale understanding of responses to education markets, for the household domain is the arena in which the processes of choice mostly occur. Sociological theory has frequently drawn out the marked differences in aspirations and choice processes between working-class families and middle-class families (e.g. Reay and Ball, 1997). In the context of school choice Reay and Ball (1998) suggest that the choice process in middle-class families is dominantly one of guiding, shaping and providing limits to choices within which some options will fall and some options will not. Amongst working-class families the decision is often delegated much more to the children themselves. Reay and Ball attribute this in part to a view that the child will know the education system and their own place within it better than they do as parents perhaps because of their own limited engagement with the system as a child/young adult. In addition, it may reflect a working-class perception of powerlessness in the context of a system and curriculum designed more to meet middle-class needs and the needs of the powerful groups within the community.

So, who in the family *does* make the choice of school? In choosing a primary or infant school the impact of child preference will be extremely limited, but by the age of transfer to secondary school the child's part in the process will be much more significant. Notwithstanding choice in single-parent families, the role of each parent in the process may differ. Reay (1998) has indicated that mothers may be more important in the choice process than fathers, although fathers may be important in defining limiting criteria and confirming or vetoing final choices. The balance of the roles will vary from family to family, with key influences at the macro-scale being socio-economic status, child gender and ethnicity.

Several studies (e.g. Stillman and Maychell, 1986; Thomas and Dennison, 1991) have indicated that at age 11 most children indicate that they were the dominant influence on the choice that was made of secondary school. This may be true, or may be the child's expression of their growing independence, for this view is not necessarily confirmed by their parents. In the same studies parents indicate that their child has played an important part in the choice process, but has, in effect, chosen from a short list derived jointly by parents and child. Foskett and Hesketh (1997) have identified the concept of a *framed field of choice* to describe this process. This suggests that parents identify 'boundaries' to their child's choice according to key factors and the outcomes of the choice process. These boundaries may enclose one or more schools, including the parents' preferred choice and others that would be acceptable or, at least, not unacceptable, and the child is then allowed to choose within this frame. Choices within it will be acceptable, although the child may still be steered towards the parents' top preference. Choices outside will, however, be vetoed. These 'frames' may coincide with the 'circuits of schooling' identified by Ball *et al.* (1995), but may be defined dominantly by any combination of factors in the choice process.

The importance of understanding the roles of parent and pupil in choice is indicated by research which shows a difference in the importance of key factors in the choices of children and parents (e.g. West *et al.*, 1998). For children at age 11 academic factors assume much less importance than they do for parents. Of more importance are the choices made by their friends, as they attempt to preserve peer friendship groups, and a school's reputation in relation to security factors, especially relating to issues of bullying. These two may be seen to be linked in relation to a child's concern about transfer from the familiar and small world of primary school, where they are the oldest and dominant group, to the large and unfamiliar world of secondary school where their status is much lower. Beyond security factors, the importance of extra-curricular activities is greater for children, and for boys, particularly, a strong reputation for sport is often a key influence on their choice.

This suggests that the analysis of choice factors in secondary school transfer needs to be considered in relation to two separate but intertwined stages in the choice process – the establishment of the choice frame, where parental influence may be much greater, and the choice of school from within the frame, where the role of children is greater. In this way academic criteria may be essential factors in the framing process because of their importance to parents, but of minor importance in the final selection process. In the selection process friendships, a warm welcome from secondary school teachers, or a reputation for sport may be critical, while in the framing process such factors will have assumed a minor role.

The process of school choice

The highly contingent nature of the prioritisation of school choice factors means that understanding the *process* of school choice is of considerable importance. If we are to understand how factors affect choice we must identify how choice processes operate and how each factor plays a role in each part of that process. Several studies in the 1990s (e.g. Gewirtz *et al.*, 1995; Carroll and Walford, 1997a; 1997b) have explored the process of choice by working with parents over extended periods of time, using qualitative, ethnographic research approaches. Emerging strongly from this research is the recognition that the precise process is unique to every choice that is made as a result of the complex interaction of many personal, social, historical, cultural, economic and contextual influences on the process. Within a family, the choice process for each child will differ, even where those children are similar in age. However, while recognising this idea, a number of important general findings have emerged which can help to frame our understanding of the choice process.

The idea of parents as consumers of education as a service, engaging in active choices in a vigorous market place is an important principle of marketisation in education. Most of the research studies, however, suggest that the majority of parents either do not engage in an active choice process at all or only consider a very small number of schools. Carroll and Walford (1997), for example, distinguish 'active' and 'passive' parents, an echo of Willms and Echol's (1992) distinction between 'alert' and 'inert' parents, although they are clear that the distinction is complicated by the fact that 'families could be "active" and "passive" to different degrees on various elements' (op. cit., p. 11) of the choice process. Some parents, of course, may have no choice at all, in that their location, perhaps in a rural area, means that only one school is realistically available to them. Where realistic choice exists, though, most parents still do not actively engage with the choice process. Smedley (1995), for example, has shown that only 25% of parents consider more than one school, although this is higher in some urban localities and amongst higher ses groups, while Foskett (1995) indicates that as few as 10% of parents may actively choose between more than two schools.

Choosing not to choose may be understandable, though, despite the encouragement to engage in the market place. Choosing is a substantial and complex process, that is stressful, difficult and a potential site of conflict within the family and within the community. It exposes people's values and principles to scrutiny, generating feelings of vulnerability. It passes to parents a moral responsibility for their children's futures that could, without school choice, be firmly attributed to 'authority', distancing them from any notion of blame for any subsequent failure or sub-optimal performance by the child. School choice also challenges parents' confidence in their own skills as parents, for it requires them to show that their own knowledge of their children is good enough to make choosing a school that best matches their needs a possibility. Finally, of course, school choice can be very hard work, which it would be easier not to engage with. Gewirtz *et al.* describe the process and its challenges very graphically:

... from the interplay of unclear or contradictory social principles, of diverse aspirations, desires and concerns related to
their children and their children's futures, and of multiple
sources of impression and perception, choosing a school often
emerges as a confusing and complex process. In some ways, the
more skilled you are, the more difficult it is. The more you know
about schools, the more apparent it is that no one school is
perfect and that all schools have various strengths and weaknesses.

'I found that the more choice we had the more we went
round in circles' (Mrs Morden, 31 December 1991).

(Gewirtz, Ball and Bowe, 1995, pp. 26–7)

In understanding the ways in which individuals operate with and
relate to social systems the concept of 'cultural capital' (Bourdieu
and Passeron, 1990) is important. The concept can be illustrated by
comparing stereotypical groups within society. A professional,
middle-class individual will possess high levels of cultural capital.
Their income, housing and lifestyle will reflect their effectiveness in
operating within the dominant social, cultural and economic
environment, and their values and moral perspectives will be those
of the dominant social groups. In contrast, the unemployed,
working-class, single parent will have low levels of cultural capital,
associated with low socio-economic status and a limited ability to
operate in key socio-cultural systems, and low levels of perceived
status and influence amongst the dominant social groups. The relationship between cultural capital and school choice is not simple, for
both Ball *et al.* (1995) and Carroll and Walford (1997a) show
examples of active school choosing and non-choosing across the
social spectrum. Carroll and Walford (1997b), for example, have
undertaken research with parents in the West Midlands which challenges ethnic and socio-economic stereotypes very strongly, and
shows how very active choosers are found across any presumed socio-
cultural divides. Indeed, low parental ses may be a powerful motivator for either parent or child to seek social or economic
advancement through the school choice process. Nevertheless, active
choosers appear predominantly to be those with high levels of cultural capital, exploiting a number of key advantages they hold in the
market place – knowledge of the choice system; knowledge of the
sources of information to assist choice; the financial ability both to
extend the range of choice (e.g. schools further from home) and to
support the choice process (e.g. travelling to open days, paying for

child care while visiting schools); social contacts to exert influence on the selection process of schools; and value in the market place in that they represent 'desirable parents' to many schools, share their educational aspirations (university entrance, for example), and may have children with higher achievement levels.

The importance of such active choosers in shaping the nature of schools may be a matter of some concern, too. Although they may be the minority of parents, they represent the totality of the group which contributes to the expanding or reducing margin of pupil numbers in each school. Attracting such parents and children will be important to prevent a school entering a cycle of decline. Fail to attract such parents, and the decline in formal performance indicators that ensues may also stimulate the start of a decline in a school's perceived success and status. Providing a school system that meets the desires and ambitions of such parents is a priority for many schools, therefore, and moves towards 'streaming' and an all-consuming focus on examination results may be interpreted as not just about 'raising standards' in the school but about appealing to middle-class values. Middle-class parents and schools may be seen to interact in their responses to market processes to underline the embeddedness of a curriculum and a culture that is strongly academically based. As Woods *et al.* (1998, p. 196) suggest, this mutual reinforcement produces 'not only a school or school system for the elite but ... a heightened prestige attached to tight academic focus and selection which helps generate and reinforce social class division focused on a minority of middle-class parents'. The whole character of schools may be driven, therefore, by the market choices of a minority of parents, and schools are confident enough to know that the inertia that exists once a child is in place in the school means they are likely to retain the child through to the final year of the school. Hirschmann (1970) emphasised this inertia in the phrase 'exit, voice or loyalty'. This suggests that once a child is within a school, parents have three options – to be loyal and accept what the school does without too much response; to express concern about issues through appropriate channels; or to remove the child to another school. In practice, 'exit' is a strategy of last resort for most parents, and is rarely exercised.

Gewirtz, Ball and Bowe (1995) in their study of school choice in London, extended this analysis to identify a simple classification of parents into strongly class-related categories of privileged/skilled choosers, semi-skilled choosers and disconnected choosers. The privileged/skilled parents are those with both a high inclination towards active choice and a high capacity, because of their cultural capital, to exercise that choice. They have not only a good understanding of the bureaucratic systems of school admissions but also the ability to 'decode' (Gewirtz *et al.*, 1995, p. 25) the explicit and implicit information from and about the school. They know and can use both formal and informal networks, and 'know how to approach, present, mount a case, maintain pressure, make an impact and be remembered' amongst those with influence in the school's choice process – it must be recognised that oversubscribed schools choose the children they will admit, and that this restricts significantly the reality of the idea of 'parental choice'. Sensitivity to, and the ability to scan and interpret information about, school culture is regarded by Gewirtz *et al.* (op. cit) as an important component of their choice process, and the matching of an individual child's perceived cultural and academic 'needs' is seen as underpinning the choice process. School culture or ethos, while open to some formal analysis (Prosser, 1999), is highly complex and often subjective in its interpretation, yet it appears that this personal analysis and interpretation of culture and ethos is an important component of choice. This observation emphasises the difficulties of criterion-based studies of school choice, for such cultural sensing is not only difficult to analyse systematically but may be a process that parents, although consciously aware of, cannot express in the rational, objective frameworks that many traditional studies of school choice use.

Gewirtz *et al.* (1995) suggest that semi-skilled choosers are those with a high inclination towards choice, but limited capacity to engage with the choice process. The limited capacity may be economic in that the demands of work or child care prevent them from accessing key elements in the choice process, such as open days or the opportunity to visit schools further away from home. Often, however, it is more socio-cultural in its nature, in that they lack the insider understanding of the process of choice and of the mechanisms for influencing that process overtly or covertly. Such parents may simply lack the strategies to approach schools, headteachers and appeals committees because their personal and family histories have not equipped them with the confidence, insight or experience to be part of the privileged chooser networks. As a result they are 'relatively' disadvantaged in the overall process of school choice, and their ability to access the higher status 'circuits of schooling' (Ball *et al.*, 1995) of 'elite, high profile' maintained schools, local independent day schools, or faith-based schools, may be limited. However, the significance of these parents in the school market place should not be underestimated, for they are still exercising active choice, and, particularly, in urban areas where the number of available school places makes choice a reality, their choices can have an important impact on a school's perceived popularity and status. The lowest level circuit of schooling, the local, community comprehensive schools has, inevitably, a smaller market share of the privileged choosers, and it is amongst the semi-skilled choosers that much of their market influence can be exercised. Such schools are the default choices of the privileged choosers, but they are the principal *actual* choice of most of the semi-skilled choosers. By engaging in such choice their actions and decisions may be very influential in opinion forming within the community, and in shaping the 'word of mouth' processes at work.

Disconnected choosers, who will almost always be the significant majority, have a low inclination to engage with the process of school choice, either by choice, in eschewing a choice process they could engage with if they so desired, or by default. Disconnection is not a function of a lack of concern for their child's well-being, but reflects a view of social expectations and of the nature, value and purpose of schooling that makes a complex choice process largely irrelevant and wasteful of limited personal resources. Gewirtz *et al.* (1995) suggest that such choosers perceive schools as having little to differentiate them from each other. Such parents also have a concern only with short-term goals for their child, such as security from bullying or happiness in the company of friends, and a belief that the school curriculum is of only marginal influence on the child's life prospects. For such parents choice is, at best, a selection between the two nearest schools, and is principally influenced by the confirmatory experiences relating to the community grapevine, and the child's perspective. Official influence on their choice is limited for

> Disconnected parents do not speak the language of secondary educational meanings. Authoritative accounts are sought from within local social networks, or from direct experience – rather than from sources of 'public' information.
>
> (Gewirtz, Ball and Bowe, 1995, p. 48)

Underlying the differences in choosers appears to lie a fundamental difference in perceptions of the role and purpose of schools within the community. The notion of consumer choice is premised on the allocation of value to the choices that are available. There is no suggestion that those who are disconnected choosers in terms of schooling are not active in their choice as consumers in relation to other services or products, but exercising active consumer behaviour depends on a belief that exercising such choice is important and of value to the chooser. Amongst the privileged and semi-skilled choosers the market value of education and of the benefits of success in school are seen as both high *and* attainable, and informal cost-benefit analysis suggests a net gain in taking care over such choice. Amongst the disconnected the informal cost-benefit analysis suggests the costs (social, cultural and economic) outweigh the advantages of choice. This suggests a strong perception that the structure and organisation of schools and their curriculum is little related to the realities of life within their own communities and social networks. Disconnection with school choice is a symptom of disconnection with the underlying values in the education and social system, and raises much more fundamental questions for education policy-makers than simply those relating to the success or failure of school marketisation.

The timing and intensity of the choice process in relation to secondary schools has not been explored in depth through formal research. David *et al.* (1994) and West *et al.* (1995) suggest that many families start the secondary school choice process only in the final year of primary school, for example, a fact confirmed by Foskett (1995), but based on parental *post hoc* recall. Others, however, have based their choice of primary or infant school on a decision about their child's secondary school needs (West *et al.,* 1998; Foskett and Hemsley-Brown, 2000). Some of the timing is driven by the choice systems themselves, for open days and school visits may be an important stimulus in 'kick starting' an active process of choice. In the UK there is some evidence (Foskett, 1995) that competition between schools has caused some to move their initial contacts with pupils in feeder schools to earlier and earlier dates. In relation to the overall choice process, though, the evidence from research on educational and training pathway choice at other key points, suggests the process is much longer than *post-hoc* recollection might suggest, and that the 'forming' of choice and the development of the choice frameworks takes place both consciously and subliminally over long periods of time. We shall explore this in more depth in our examination of independent school choice in Chapter 4.

The policy drive towards parental choice and marketisation has been accompanied by the expansion of choice information systems. In the UK, legislation has provided a strong drive to this process by establishing centralised systems to present comparative data (inspection reports, and 'league tables' of examination performance and truancy, for example) and by requiring schools to provide information to the public domain, even defining the minimum content that such communication must cover through prospectuses and governors' reports to parents. Schools have, themselves, 'bought into' the importance of communication, and the growth of marketing and promotion by schools has been noted by many writers (e.g. Headington and Howson, 1995; Gewirtz, Ball and Bowe, 1995; Foskett, 1998; Hesketh and Knight, 1998; Woods, Bagley and Glatter, 1998). But what has been the impact on the process of parental choice? How far do such communications shape and influence choice? Can the supply side of the school choice market substantially affect the choices made by the demand side through their promotional activities?

While many promotional strategies are used by schools (Devlin and Knight, 1992) the most important sources of direct influence on *parental* choice are visits to schools for open days, and on *pupil* choice are the open days, the use of school facilities such as swimming pools by the community or by feeder schools, and the visits by school representatives to feeder schools. The 'glossification' of prospectuses is not reflected in their significance in influencing choice, in part because of the way they are used to emphasise achievement of the common high expectations demanded by government (high examination results, good behaviour, etc.) rather than to distinguish schools from each other in the market place (Hesketh and Knight, 1998; Woods, Bagley and Glatter, 1998).

Much of the provision of information is beyond the direct control of schools, however, for 'word of mouth' emerges as the single most important influence on choice, through the community grapevine and what Beischer (1994) describes as 'school gate gossip'. Influence on 'word of mouth' is harder for schools to effect, although the management of image presentation issues (e.g. pupil behaviour outside school, school uniform and media coverage) can be important. More significant, though, is the performance of the school in its management of the quality of its educational provision and the way that it manages community links and affairs, for these are the primary source of 'word of mouth'.

We have considered so far the broad principles of school choice, both in terms of the influence of a range of factors on decisions and through an examination of current understandings of the process of choice. In the section that follows we shall examine parental choice in the context of their first important decision – their choice of primary school for their children.

Choosing primary schools

The importance of primary school choice by parents lies only in part in the choice of school *per se* for '... choice of primary school is often the first of several strategic decisions involved in the careful construction of their children's school career' (Gewirtz, Ball and Bowe, 1995, p. 26). Recognition that the ultimate outcomes of a school career (university entrance, good employment, economic security) are the product of the value added at each stage of the pathway is important, and choices will often be based on the presumption of enhancing access to subsequent stages of the education/training route. A concern about achieving admission to a 'good university' to undertake a degree programme leading to a high-status professional career will strongly influence choice of secondary school. The need to access a good secondary school will in turn influence choice for children at age 4/5, especially in the circumstances where primary schools have strong links with particular secondary schools and, more important, with schools in the higher status 'circuits of schooling'. This linkage between choice at different stages is confirmed by Reay (1996, p. 581) who suggests that

> ... understandings of choice that view choice as decontextualised and also posit it as a discrete, once and for all activity are too simplistic. (...) The significance of choice making is most apparent when children start school and transfer at age 11. However, these choices can be viewed as the apex of a hidden pyramid of choices mothers are making on a daily basis.

For high-aspiration parents, therefore, choice at age 4 or 5 may be a key factor in setting their children on a desired pathway through the education/training process. While it must be recognised that *actual choice* in relation to any transition phase in the pathway is confined at any time to the next transition, this is important in including or excluding *potential choice* options at future stages. This process of *future choice enhancement* is indicated by West *et al.*'s (1998) observation that 42% of parents choosing private primary education cite 'preparation for transfer to secondary school' as an important element in their choice. Failing to choose a primary school that places children on to particular pathways may simply close down later opportunities, or at best severely limit them, so for many parents primary school choice is of prime importance in shaping their child's education and training opportunities.

The broad nature of the choice process in relation to primary schools has been examined by West *et al.* (1998) in London, who considered the choice process of the parents of 111 children, of whom 77% attended state primary schools and 23% attended schools in the independent sector. The study demonstrates a range of influencing factors on choice and variety in the nature of the choice process, but emphasises the differences between parents choosing the independent sector and those choosing the state sector.

Some twelve different factors were cited as important in the choice process by more than 20% of the sample, with five factors mentioned by more than 50% of parents:

- a belief that the child will be happy in the school (80%);
- the quality of education in the school (74%);
- the school will suit the child's needs (61%);
- the atmosphere of the school (52%);
- the discipline and behaviour of the children in the school (51%).

This pattern of influencing factors repeats in large measure the importance of the factors identified from research on school choice in general, and suggests that similar influences are 'at work' in primary school choice as in later choices. More detailed analysis, though, shows some important differences between sub-groups of parents within the study. Amongst the parents of children in the independent sector, the quality of education offered was the most important factor, while for parents of children in the state sector the principal factor was the belief that the child would be happy. Other major differences emerged in relation to the importance of small classes, and preparation for transfer to secondary school, which were much more important to 'independent school parents', and the school's reputation for being good with special needs children and having a high proportion of gifted children, which were of much greater importance to 'state school parents'.

The difference in choice factors between the two groups of parents was also exemplified in the parents' views of when they started the choice process. Amongst those choosing state schools the percentage starting the choice process increases from the child's birth to peak at age 3. Amongst those choosing independent schools the peak of choice time is 'at or before birth', with 65% of parents indicating that the choice process started before their son or daughter was born, and a further 19% indicating the choice process started in the child's first year. This contrast in timing is underlined by an examination of the age at which primary school applications were made. Amongst those choosing independent schools 66% had made an application before the child was 1 year old, while amongst those choosing state schools 67% applied when the child was 3 or 4 years old.

West *et al.*'s study provides an important insight into the nature of choice in a metropolitan area where transport links make access to a number of schools possible even within small distances. The importance of proximity within their study is small, with only 17% of 'state school parents' and 4% of 'independent school parents' citing 'nearness to home' as a factor in their choice. We might assume that this reflects the fact that in a metropolitan area there is almost always a primary school in close proximity to a child's home, so this can be excluded from the choice process as a decisive factor.

Other studies provide some contrasts with the choice models suggested by West *et al.*, and demonstrate a consistent pattern of important elements in the primary school choice process, viz:

1   the significance of 'locational factors' in the choice process;
2   the importance of the notion of 'reputation' in shaping choice;
3   the importance of social class in choice.

Hughes *et al.* (1994) examined the primary school choice process through interviewing 138 parents in south-west England. Their research indicates that 'location' and 'reputation' are the two most significant factors in primary school choice, with 'location' cited by 56% of parents as important and 'reputation' cited by 48%. The use of both terms, however, raises a number of analytical issues, for both may be seen to be 'condensation terms' which are used to express an amalgam or network of concepts. The use of these terms is both problematical and helpful.

The problems derive from the variation of meaning attributed to the terms by individual parents, and the complex genesis of the term for each individual. The notion of reputation, for example, is difficult to refine and is ambiguous in its use by parents, frequently being used as a summative term to include ideas of both academic performance and a friendly, caring ethos. Furthermore, these elements will have both historical and contemporary components. Stokes (1999, pp. 2–27) suggests that

> reputations are based on perceptions which often go back a long time and are therefore behind the current 'facts' of the situation, but which are notoriously difficult to shift once embedded in parents' minds.

This confirms the perspective of Hughes *et al.* (1994) that

> for some parents the reputation of the school was a long-lived thing and did not necessarily bear any reference to recent experience.... For other parents the reputation of the school went back even further still and was based on their memories of when they themselves attended school.
> (Hughes *et al.*, 1994, pp. 83–4, quoted in Stokes, 1999, pp. 2–27)

Teasing out the real meaning of the term 'reputation', therefore, requires in-depth qualitative investigation at the level of individual parents. Similarly, the notion of 'location' is complex, as indicated earlier in this chapter, comprising both real and perceptual elements of distance and social and economic space. The underlying complexity of these terms, however, is in part balanced by their value as summative notions which may aid interpretation and classification of how parents choose schools.

Stokes (1999) has synthesised the range of factors in primary school choice to identify the primacy of two elements in the choice process – location and image, the second of which incorporates elements of reputation, academic achievement, atmosphere, discipline and facilities. Using these two dimensions he has developed a matrix model of parental choice (Figure 3.1) with four decision fields within it.

The 'best of both worlds' is the situation which parents who are located close to a school with a good reputation find themselves in, where scanning the choice environment serves merely to confirm the positive characteristics of the local school. In contrast, those parents in a location where, because the school is over-subscribed, some may be rejected according to the preference criteria of the school, or who move into a locality where the schools are already full, may be seen to be in 'the worst of both worlds'. However, 'other parents are faced with a trade-off between choosing a nearby school with a relatively negative image ... or looking further afield to inconveniently located schools with better reputations' (Stokes, 1999,

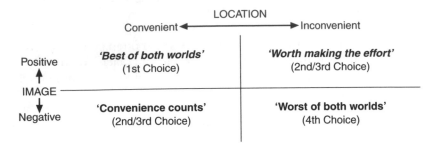

LOCATION

Convenient ◄─────────────► Inconvenient

Positive ↑	**'Best of both worlds'** (1st Choice)	**'Worth making the effort'** (2nd/3rd Choice)
IMAGE ↓ Negative	**'Convenience counts'** (2nd/3rd Choice)	**'Worst of both worlds'** (4th Choice)

Figure 3.1 A matrix model of parental choice of primary school (after Stokes, 1999).

pp. 4–21) and it is these parents where the choice process is most difficult. It is clear from this analysis, therefore, that choice is shaped very strongly by the nature of the local school market place.

The importance of social class in the choice process in relation to primary school emerges strongly from the study by West *et al.* (1998). Similar findings are found in the work of Nice (1997), who has undertaken a small-scale interview-based study of parental choice of primary/infant school in two adjacent localities in southern Hampshire, one of which is a predominantly working-class community and the other of which is a mainly middle-class community. The working-class community is served by three 4–11 primary schools, while the middle-class community has three primary schools and a Catholic primary school. Both are served by a number of private playgroups and nurseries. Little movement across the boundaries between the two areas in terms of school choice occurs.

Nice identifies from the study a number of important observations. First, amongst the parents in the middle-class community the process of choice was more complex and detailed, with parents engaging strongly in the process of 'child matching', and considering both private and state provision within the choice process, even though private education was then rejected by some on grounds of cost. Parents considered schools outside the cluster of primaries within the locality, although all decided ultimately that proximity was an important security and cost constraint on their choice. Important within the choice process was the social mix of the schools, a view summarised by one mother in terms of her concern for 'protection, from language and that sort of thing. I know its snobby but, you know, [we want] a nice class of children'.

Second, amongst the parents in the working-class community there were far fewer strategies used to weigh up the choices available to them, and many appeared to base choice simply on proximity backed up by reputation within the local community. As one mother indicated in explaining her decision about one school, 'I had heard that they was (*sic*) behind with their reading when they went up [i.e. transferred on to secondary school], but they're not any more' and 'they got no bullying down there, at least people don't say they have'. Nevertheless, even in the context of a less vigilant and active choice, parents in the working-class community were still basing their choice on 'child matching' processes.

Third, a range of factors appeared to be shaping the impressions of schools that underpinned the final selection process. Of key importance was confidence in the headteacher providing a focus in the school on progress with children's learning, on dealing strongly with bullying and 'anti-social behaviour', and being both firm and in control on the one hand but approachable and warm to both children and parents on the other. Linked to this was the 'front of house' style of the school, with the warmth of manner from the school receptionist/secretary on the parents' first contact with the school and the nature of the reception area on the first visit leaving strong first impressions.

Nicc's identification of the importance of primary school headteachers in parental choice processes is of some importance, for they emerge as key gatekeepers both in terms of entrance to primary school and exit to secondary school. In the context of a small organisation such as a primary school the role of the headteacher in shaping the school's reputation in terms of processes within the school, representing that reputation in tangible form, and managing and planning the projection of the reputation to parents and the community, cannot be underestimated. In many real senses the headteacher is the embodiment of the school. Foskett (1999) has shown how the marketing of a small village school in Hampshire has been successful because of the headteacher's performance in each of these roles, and how this illustrates the practice of many of the key principles of relationship marketing.

The significance of responsiveness to parents in the 'relationship marketing' environment of primary schools is clear from both Foskett's study and that of Minter (1997), yet there is only limited evidence that schools have yet begun to adjust their ways of working in response to parents. Such changes may be emerging, but as recently as 1997 Hughes has shown the limited responsiveness of schools to parents. Hughes describes the main findings of the PAKSO Project ('Parents and Assessment at Key Stage One') which explored the interaction of parents' views on school performance in statutory assessment for children aged 7 and the school's classroom practice. He concludes that teachers and schools are not significantly aware of parents' views, nor are they likely to modify their classroom practice in response to any knowledge of parental perceptions that they do have. Rather,

> ... the major influences on teachers' views and practice appear to lie in factors ... which might be loosely termed 'producer interests' (and which) ... include teachers' sense of themselves as professional educators and teachers' perception that their primary responsibility is to children, not to parents.
>
> (Hughes, 1997, p. 83)

Despite the limited responsiveness suggested by Hughes, however, Stokes (1999) has conceptualised the operational elements of this relationship management which may be so important in primary school choice. Stokes suggests that relationship marketing in the context of a primary school is based on the establishment of a marketing mix which he terms 'the four 'I's':

- *Information* – the provision of information about the school through parental letters, newsletters, etc.
- *Image-building* – the management of controllable factors such as pupil behaviour and facilities.
- *Involvement* – the encouragement of parental involvement.
- *Influence* – the promotion of informal word-of-mouth recommendation by parents.

Each of these elements is substantially under the control of the headteacher and his/her effectiveness in managing them and projecting the desired image of the school is important in influencing choice of primary school by parents.

As we have suggested earlier, an important element in choice of primary school is the connections between particular schools and subsequent educational choices. Primary school headteachers are important gatekeepers in influencing school choice at the transition to secondary school at 11, and choice of a primary school where the headteacher facilitates the desired choices for parents at age 11 may be an important factor in choice at 5. This role of heads is a reflection of three components:

a   Their own patterns of influence and engagement in professional networks. Their influence (or lack of it) with secondary schools may be important in shaping the image secondary heads or selectors have of pupils from their primary school.

b   Their role in providing references for transfer into selective or non-neighbourhood schools. The ideological perspective of heads to selection or to independent education or to the tenets of comprehensive education may shape implicitly, or even explicitly, the way in which pupils are promoted through references.

c   Their role in providing information about schools to parents seeking to access the information networks. This, too, may be influenced by the Head's own personal perspective, ideology and beliefs, but may also be driven by his/her view of the importance of linkage and continuity between schools. Information on choice options beyond the local secondary school may or may not be promoted to parents, and will, in any case, be interpreted and mediated by the Head's own frames of knowledge and understanding, attitudes and values. Objectivity is unachievable in such circumstances, yet choices by parents may be based on assumptions of the objectivity of the Head's advice and information provision.

It is clear that while primary school choice reflects the broad principles of school choice described earlier in this chapter, the process of choice is especially strongly influenced by the school's image/reputation and by its headteacher. The role of the headteacher in the process in particular is clear, for he or she is the principal gatekeeper to education pathways, a key element in shaping the image and reputation that the school has, and the keystone in developing relationships with the community that both create the image and reputation of the school and diffuse those ideas through the community grapevine. The notion of 'relationship marketing' is clearly paramount to primary schools in influencing parental choice.

In summary

The analysis presented so far has demonstrated the complexity of school choice and its embeddedness in individual circumstances at the level of individuals, families, communities and macro socio-economic environments. While the general influence of the wide range of factors that impact on choice is clear, as is the primacy of security and academic achievement factors, the precise set of circumstances that impinge on a particular choice at a particular time will be unique. Furthermore, the complexity of the process, and its capacity for generating dissonance and stress, is considerable. As a result of these inherent characteristics of choice, and also of the socio-cultural implications of engaging with a process that reproduces many components of a divided society, many parents are reluctant to engage in the choice of schools other than at a minimalist level. There is much still to be understood about this process. As Reay suggests,

> schooling is no unitary, homogeneous product, either in terms of curriculum-offer or relationships with parents. Educational provision appears to be shaped by a combination of the perceived needs of different pupil intakes and the power of demands made by their parents. It is in the cocktail of teachers' expectations of children, parental expectations of school, differential relationships of power between parents, teachers and children, and the intricate layering of discourses informing both parents' and teachers' understandings of the relationship between culture and educational achievement that a more complex picture of parental choice can be built up.
>
> (Reay, 1996, p. 586)

In Chapter 4 we shall demonstrate these issues in relation to choosing independent schools.

4 Choosing independent schools
A parental dilemma?

Education in the independent sector

The existence of a strong, popular and academically successful independent school sector is a distinctive feature of the British educational environment. Some 7% of pupils are educated in the sector, a rising figure and a proportion which represents children primarily from more advantaged socio-economic groups. In some localities (e.g. London) up to 10% of children attend independent schools. While this may appear to be a relatively small proportion of the total school population its significance to choosing in education markets is substantial – if most parents are not active choosers, then the 10% of parents choosing in relation to independent education may be a high proportion of all the active choosers in the market place. Their choice processes will be of particular interest, therefore. This may be only the tip of the iceberg, though, for as many as 55% of parents would prefer to use the independent sector if they could afford to do so (Walford, 1999). The independent sector is itself quite diverse in nature, and the differences between the character and ethos of independent schools is at least as large as the perceived contrasts between state and independent schools at the macro level. An important distinction, though, is between independent boarding schools and independent day schools, within each of which groupings lies a wide range of schools distinguishable by age range served, single-sex or co-educational status, faith-based ethos, pupil ability range, approach to teaching and learning, and other distinctive characteristics. The independent sector, therefore, is in reality an amalgam of distinct market segments in relation to parental choice.

Researching independent school choice

Set against the background of extensive research into school choice in general, however, the process of choice in relation to the independent school sector has not been subjected to extensive public domain research. This is perhaps surprising in view of the fact that independent schools have always operated in a market place where parental choice is essential to the school's survival and well-being. This may reflect in part the small scale of the sector within the total UK educational arena, but is also the result of a number of other characteristics of the market:

a   The competitive nature of the market has meant that collaboration on research has not been acceptable between schools. The desire to keep understandings of the market and research data confidential from competitors has been strong. Indeed, schools may fear that the mere process of undertaking research may be seen by parents and competitor schools as indicative that a 'problem' exists in the school, and for this reason many have not engaged with public domain research. In recent years many schools have undertaken marketing research on their own behalf through the use of consultancy and market research organisations, though, and have changed their promotional strategies and, on occasion, their fundamental character as schools (for example, by becoming co-educational in the sixth-form). In many cases such research has also focused on specific issues (for example, sixth-form entry) rather than seeking to provide a wider picture of the operation of the market place, and so is of less generic value in understanding independent school markets at a macro scale. Such research findings are regarded, in any case, as commercially sensitive and are, therefore, almost always confidential.

b   The *overall* trends in the independent school market in recent years have been towards growth in pupil numbers, and the demand for independent day school places in many localities exceeds supply. Pressure to undertake research has not, therefore, been strong.

c   Research is an expensive process. Without the pressure of specific issues to address, schools may feel that the use of resources to research their markets is not justified, and that the enhancement of facilities for pupil learning or the wider school experience is almost always a higher priority for expenditure.

The few public domain studies that have been undertaken have comprised either relatively small-scale studies undertaken by individual researchers (e.g. Fox, 1985; Johnson, 1987; Edwards *et al.*, 1989; West, 1992; Falconer, 1997), or externally funded projects which have been able to access larger samples of parents or pupils (e.g. MORI, 1989; West *et al.*, 1998). As with all studies of school choice, this research emphasises strongly the significance of micro-markets in defining the detail of the mechanisms and processes of choice. From these studies, however, a number of important generalisations about independent school choice have emerged:

- A significant proportion of parents have such a strong commitment to the idea of independent education that they do not consider state education as an option within their decision-making process. Fox (1985) suggests that in the most high status schools, typically those day and boarding schools within the HMC (Head Masters Conference) and GSA (Girls School Association) groups, up to one third of parents fall into this category. For such parents, their choice process is confined to a consideration of different independent schools.
- The timing and duration of the choice process is different amongst parents eventually choosing the independent sector than amongst those choosing the state sector, for 'the process of choosing a school begins earlier in the private than in the state sector' (West *et al.*, 1998, p. 58). We have shown in Chapter 3 how a high proportion of parents choosing independent primary schools have made that choice before the child is born, and have mapped out a pathway through the independent sector long before the child starts school.
- Parents choosing independent schools place a strong emphasis on the importance of excellent academic achievement at school as a prerequisite for entry into higher education and thence into good jobs, with a strong focus on future employment for their children in 'the professions' such as medicine and law.
- This commitment to the importance of academic achievement as a motivation for choosing an independent school is strongest where no state selective grammar schools exist in the locality. Where state grammar schools exist this becomes a less significant factor in choosing independent schools *per se*, although this is not to suggest it is not an important factor within the choice of school parents are then making.
- A perception of the comparative lack of success of state schools

in achieving high academic results is an important justification for independent school choice amongst many parents, although this is a relative concept for many rather than an absolute dissatisfaction with the state system. MORI (1989), for example, found that while most parents commented favourably on the achievement of independent schools, only 21% expressed dissatisfaction with the state sector schools in their locality.

- The perception of the presence of a well-disciplined environment in such schools in comparison to state schools, and a parental belief in the importance of this both to academic achievement and to the development of young people's attitudes and values is seen as an important justifier of independent school choice.

- 'The child's happiness' is an important factor that is an explicit priority for almost all parents in the choice of both state and independent schools. Qualitative investigation of this idea, however, suggests that the notion of 'happiness' may be differently interpreted by state school and independent school parents. West *et al.* suggest that 'the child's happiness may refer in some families to the child not being upset/being content, whilst in others it may be more linked to the child being able to fulfil parental expectations and ambitions' (West *et al.*, 1998, p. 59). The emphasis on the existence of a disciplined and safe environment as a factor in independent school choice, may, however, have removed the concern for the first of these notions of happiness for parents and enabled them to emphasise the second of the two interpretations. The importance of parental expectations and ambitions on behalf of the child may be the feature which distinguishes parents who are the most active choosers in school markets.

In summary, the existing research has confirmed commonly held perceptions that those parents considering independent education are active choosers, engaging with the process of choice at a very early stage of the child's life, and focusing on the pursuit of high academic achievement as an entry to high-status professional employment. There is clear evidence of the benefits of independent education for those seeking academic achievement and university entrance. At 18, although only 25% of young people are educated in the independent sector, two thirds of the highest grade A-levels (grades A to C) are awarded to candidates from private schools. Beyond 18, some 18% of undergraduates are from an independent school background, a figure much enhanced at the most prestigious universities. At Oxford University, for example, in 1999, 48% of entrants were from private schools, as were 43% of entrants to Cambridge University (*The Guardian*, 26 May 2000). The independent sector appears to be very successful in achieving the aims that parents opting for private education are seeking for their children. We shall explore here some of these ideas in relation to the independent day school market.

The 'Parental Attitudes to Independent Education' research project

Understanding the decision to choose an independent rather than a state school is important both to independent schools and to state schools. The 'Parental Attitudes to Independent Education' Project (Foskett and Hemsley-Brown, 2000), conducted during 1999–2000, was undertaken to examine this choice process. In particular, its aims were to identify the factors which have influenced the choice of parents to invest in independent day school education for their children, and to investigate whether the priorities influencing choice are satisfied by schools, leading to parental satisfaction with the sector or some element of dissonance. In addition the research sought to identify trends in these factors, particularly in relation to the changing environment of family finance in the UK. It is clearly recognised that a *sine qua non* of independent education is parental ability to pay school fees, and trends in family finance may link strongly to changes in the choice process.

The research focused on a small sample of single-sex and co-educational independent day schools to provide a perspective on trends and patterns. More specifically, it sought to explore in depth some of the assumptions and findings of the existing research on parental choice of independent schools, and to seek to conceptualise and model some of the processes at work. The stimulus to undertake this research, though, also emanated from an interest in the possible impact of a number of important socio-economic and policy changes that were perceived as having potential to impact on parental choice of independent school. These changes were:

a   The removal of the Assisted Places Scheme (APS). The Assisted Places Scheme had been established by government in 1980, with the purpose of paying school fees for children from low-income families who could not otherwise afford independent school education. Its existence was a highly charged political issue (Whitty, Power, Edwards and Wigfall, 1998), and the scheme was eventually abolished in 1997. Its abolition was considered a threat to recruitment into the independent sector, particularly for those schools recruiting significant proportions of their pupils through the scheme (in some cases up to one third of their annual intake), and most schools developed strategies for seeking to make up recruitment shortfalls. Initial informal evidence was that the impact of the removal of the scheme had not been as great as expected, and few independent day schools reported any significant shift in the pattern or quality of their intake. There was a need to identify the impact of the demise of the APS on parental decision-making about independent education, and in particular on those who might previously have sought support through the scheme.

b   The introduction of university tuition fees from 1998. Prior to 1998 almost all students entering higher education had their tuition fees paid by their local education authority. From 1998, however, students were required to pay £1,000 per annum towards their fees, and it was perceived that this had provided an extra financial burden on parents within the total duration of their child's education. It was not clear whether this might impact upon decisions to pay for independent secondary education, and in particular whether it may have a negative effect on sixth-form recruitment.

c   Pupil loss at sixth-form entry. Loss of pupils at 16 who choose to move to alternative sixth-form provision for academic, social or financial reasons, such as sixth-form college, is an important issue for many schools. Understanding the choice process of parents and pupils in independent schools in relation to post-16 destinations was an important focus of the research.

d   The decline in the 'boarding sector' of education. Recruitment to the boarding sector has declined by some 30% during the last two decades, leading to the closure of some smaller independent boarding schools. This is not matched, however, by changes in overall demand for independent education, which has increased over the same period of time. There is clearly a changing perspective on what parents seek from their independent school, and there is a need to identify how far parents believe their schools are meeting those needs.

The study was based on detailed research with three selective independent day schools, each serving the 5–18 age range, in contrasting locations. The sample schools were all sited in university towns in south-east England, and demonstrated many similarities to each other but also some important differences. The Boys' School is located to the north of London in the Northern Home Counties. It has a co-educational pre-prep and sixth form, and its main competitors are a co-educational boarding school and several state sector comprehensive schools. The Girls' School is located to the south-west of London in the Southern Home Counties, and operates in a highly competitive market, competing with four mixed 11–18 state sector comprehensive schools and at least four independent day schools for girls. There were no independent co-educational day schools in the local area at the time the research was carried out. The Co-educational School is situated some distance to the south of London, and is in competition with two other co-educational independent day schools and several state sector mixed and single-sex comprehensive schools in the same city.

The research methodology adopted sought to use both factor analysis quantitative approaches and an ethnographic qualitative element. A questionnaire was sent via pupils to parents in each school, providing a total sample size of 900, and in-depth interviews were undertaken with a small sample of parents in each school, the Head of each school, and the senior member of staff responsible for marketing/promotion in the school.

From the analysis, a number of key aspects of independent school choice emerged in relation to:

- parental profile;
- choice factors and expectations;
- financial issues in independent school choice;
- attitudes to co-education;
- the nature of markets in independent education.

Parental profile

Who are the parents who are choosing in the independent day school market place, and how does this relate to stereotypical images? The research data shows that the profile of parents is strongly skewed to the more affluent and socio-economically advantaged groups within the community, although the range of parental profiles is large and shows that they are economically diverse but socio-culturally homogeneous. More than half of all parents were well-qualified professionals who had attended a selective school themselves, continued into higher education and gained a degree or post-graduate qualification. A high percentage of parents (90% of fathers and 87% of mothers) had undertaken full- or part-time education beyond 18. Half of the mothers and two thirds of the fathers in the sample had attended university, and 18% of fathers and 8% of mothers had attended either Oxford or Cambridge (Oxbridge) universities. The figures for Oxbridge education were higher in the Home Counties North region (26% of fathers and 13% of mothers) and lower in the South (10% of fathers and 2% of mothers). Under 3% of parents had qualifications below GCSE grade C or held 'no academic qualifications'.

The mean salary of parents in the study was £60,000 pa, although 21% of families were earning over £100,000, while 20% of families were earning less than £40,000 a year and 5% were earning less than £20,000 per annum. Mean annual family income in the UK at the same time was £18,000. There were more families in the South school's parental profile earning very low incomes (there were also more pupils supported by the Assisted Places Scheme attending the school). Over 95% own or are buying their own home, which is most likely to be a detached house with 3–5+ bedrooms (86%). Twenty per cent take a holiday outside Europe each year, although 20% take no holiday each year, and 75% of families own two cars.

Choice factors and expectations

On the basis of previous research into independent school choice, over 30 factors were included in a parental questionnaire, in which parents were asked to indicate how important those factors were in their choice of school. Academic issues emerged as the most important choice factor, with 'quality of teaching', 'academic reputation' and 'academic expectations' featuring as the most important individual factors. Overall, 'quality of teaching' was the single most important factor to parents regardless of the school their child was attending. Figure 4.1 shows the relative importance of each choice factor across the three schools.

Academic quality, though, is a concept that is an amalgam of a number of sub-themes. The interviews revealed a wide range of interpretations of the notion of 'quality of teaching' and it was clear that information about quality of teaching relied to some extent on feedback from other parents and via the child. Quality of teaching was linked to both individual support and academic progress, and was not necessarily based on an assessment of the *consistency* of

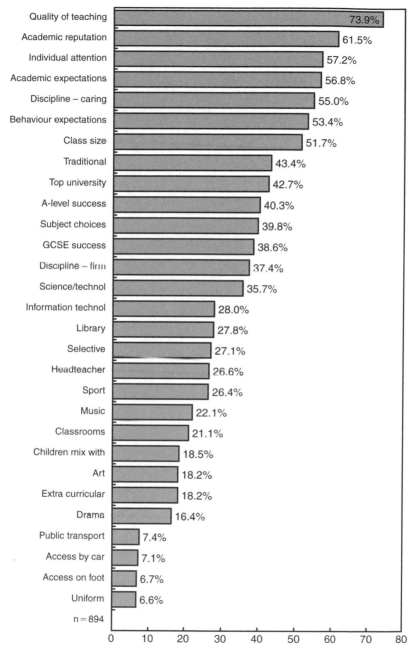

Figure 4.1 Factors influencing choice of independent day school (percentage of parents citing each factor as 'very important').

teaching strategies throughout the school. While parents were concerned that teachers at the school they had chosen should be 'good' or 'excellent' teachers, they rarely articulated in any detail what they meant by this, and attributes of 'good teaching' related to both academic and pastoral care issues.

Of some interest is the importance of academic quality to school choice in a highly competitive environment. While 'academic expectations' and 'academic reputation' were very important as a choice factor for parents overall, these factors gained less support from the Home Counties South parents. These parents explained that there were several equally good academic schools to choose from, and they had chosen the Girls' School in preference to a very close competitor girls' school which was perceived to be more academic, but with greater 'pressure'.

The factors which were least important to parents were related mainly to transport and travelling to school. This may reflect the affluence of the parental body and their access to transport by car. Although a high proportion of parents live in the same postal districts as their chosen school, especially from the Home Counties South and Home Counties North schools, the nearness of the school seemed to be relatively unimportant when making a choice of school in all three geographical areas. Parents from the South were slightly more concerned about access to school by public transport (11.4% regarded it as 'very important') but in the Southern co-educational school, the largest single group of parents answering the survey lived in a postal district several miles from the school, in an area where the local comprehensive schools were described by them as 'poor'.

A number of factors were more important to parents living in Home Counties South where there were more similar schools to choose from. Here class size and the headteacher were important factors, whereas GCSE success, A-level success, and getting into a top university were considered less important, largely because competitors were achieving similar success in these areas.

Detailed analysis of the data shows important differences in the factors influencing choice at pre-prep (ages 4–7), preparatory (ages 7–11 or 13), main school (ages 11 or 13–16) and sixth form (age 16+) entry. An important element in recruitment to independent schools is the continuity of pupils across the break points in the education system, and the study identified the factors that are important in persuading parents to stay in, or enter, the independent system at each of the break points.

Choice of pre-preparatory independent education

In relation to choice of pre-prep schools, factors which were of most importance related to both immediate and longer term concerns of parents for their children, such as gaining better qualifications (40%), making an early start on learning (43%), and gaining self-confidence (35%). The least important factors were the notion that parents might be able to continue to pursue their own careers more easily if their child attended a pre-prep, and the importance of gaining entry to a top university – although the latter of these factors was seen as being dependent on the factors that were being cited as the most important in the choice. This view was developed in the interviews with parents, who indicated that it was generally accepted that children would attend a nursery school and that attending pre-prep was a natural progression.

Choice of preparatory school

In relation to choice of prep school the influencing factors which parents indicated as most important are those related to making a good start in education, gaining qualifications, and developing good work habits, rather than a concern with social benefits such as ex-periencing a better lifestyle or mixing with other children. These responses match those of the pre-prep school parents, and suggest few differences in choice factors between the two phases of school-ing. Dissatisfaction with the maintained sector schools in the area emerges more strongly at this stage of choice, though, and was cited as a reason for choosing the independent prep school. Mrs Pam Chitty, who had two children attending the Boys' School in Home Counties North, explained that:

> We sent the oldest to the village school. At the end of infants we got feedback that he was doing very well indeed and had we thought of sending him to a prep. We thought that as he was doing so well we would think about a prep because he could obviously cope. The younger one we took out of infants because he had been moved ahead a year, he was doing so well. He had left his peers behind and was also going to have to re-do a year at some stage.
>
> (Mrs Pam Chitty, Parent – Home Counties North)

Independent senior school choice

In relation to choice of independent senior school, the factors which gained most support were similar in all three schools in the study – developing better work habits (55%), and having a better chance of going to a top university (46%). There were some differences when schools were compared. Gaining self-confidence was more important for parents choosing the Home Counties South Girls' School, and extra-curricular activities were more important for parents choosing the Southern Co-educational school. Factors which emerged as less important were social and lifestyle factors and enhanced opportunities of entering industry.

Parents were asked to list the other secondary schools they had considered, and the list was very extensive in each area. Two broad groups of parents emerged, based on their choice of school in relation to other alternatives. One group had considered an alternative independent school, usually one with similar fees. In Home Counties North this was more difficult because of the limited choice, although some parents had also considered a more expensive independent school, often a boarding school. In Home Counties South the fees were *not* viewed as important because fees were similar in the alternative day schools. One parent, Mrs Emma Sadler, confirmed that although they had looked at four girls' day schools in the area, the fees were not important because all four schools were charging virtually the same fees. One parent had considered a well-known girls' boarding school, but had rejected it not on the basis of the fees but because it required boarding.

Parents of children living in Home Counties North and in Home Counties South were not choosing on the basis of whether they favoured single-sex or co-education, because the selective schools in the independent sector were all single sex. Making a choice to join the independent sector was *de facto* a choice to go to a single-sex school. In the South, there was a choice for girls, but not for boys, and some girls were not happy to go to an all girls' school and had chosen the co-educational school. Some parents simply favoured co-education. Whereas there were parents of boys attending the boys' school in Home Counties North who would have preferred a co-educational school, none of the parents of daughters attending the girls' school in Home Counties South expressed a preference for a co-educational school.

The second group of parents were those choosing between their local maintained sector school and affordable independent sector schools – usually a selective independent school. In Home Counties North and the South the alternative for these parents, if their son/daughter did not gain a place at independent school, was to stay in the state sector. In Home Counties South parents of daughters were able to choose among a larger number of schools, usually at least two state schools and three or four girls' independent schools. Parents in Home Counties South often simply chose the school which offered them a place first, having applied to two or more girls' independent day schools in the area.

Sixth-form choice

In relation to sixth-form entry the factors which were most important to parents with a son or daughter already in the sixth form related to gaining the best academic qualifications, quality of teaching, and small classes. Variations between the schools were clear, though. Small classes were more important to parents choosing the Home Counties South Girls' School, for example, while parents choosing the Southern co-educational school emphasised the importance of gaining the best academic qualifications. Extra-curricular activities were very important to parents choosing the co-educational school in the South, especially when compared with parents choosing the Boys' School in Home Counties North. A better lifestyle, and gaining self-confidence, seemed to be more important for parents of daughters choosing the Home Counties South Girls' School, especially when compared with the choices of the Boys' School parents. Gaining academic qualifications to enter higher education and the professions were considered priorities by parents of all sixth-form students.

The importance of the sixth form as a factor in choice at all stages from 11 onwards was clear from interviews with parents. One parent, Mrs Alton, explained that they needed to have confidence in the sixth form of a school, even when making a choice for their child at age 11:

> We wanted an academic school and one with a sixth form. C ... comprehensive is our local school. We are both mathematicians and we didn't have any confidence in their maths staff at the school. They couldn't teach A-level there. They have a much higher academic focus at [the co-educational school].
>
> (Mrs Alton, Parent – the South)

Overall, the study showed that there is an important transition in the significance of key factors as parents move to each of the choice points in the system. The choice factors of importance through all the choice points were:

- developing good work habits;
- gaining the best qualifications;
- the quality of teaching;
- small classes;
- gaining entry to a 'top' university.

In relation to choices for younger children the importance of personal socialisation factors was considerable, linked to the provision of a sound base of learning. As the child becomes older this focuses into a specific concern for academic success, leading to higher education entry. Higher education entry is an important underpinning factor in the choice process throughout, though. With choice of pre-prep or prep schools it is not explicit, but this reflects not a lack of concern for this long-term outcome but rather an assumption by parents that this is the ultimate goal. The needs emphasised in early choices are the important foundations to ensure the long-term goal. By the time choice is made for 11 year olds and 16 year olds, however, parents believe that the foundations have been established and the principal purpose of the school is then to focus on the academic input to guarantee good GCSE and A-level results. Hence HE entry is expressed as the specific goal from age 11 upwards.

If these are the important factors in choice, how well are the schools delivering what parents seek? The study also investigated the level of satisfaction amongst parents with how well their needs were being met by the independent sector. The data shows that, on the whole, there is a good match between choice factors or expectations in relation to academic factors. However, although 'quality of teaching' was identified as the most important choice factor by 74% of parents, only 42% said that 'quality of teaching' was 'very good'. The factors which are closest to meeting parents' expectations, and which are considered important choice factors are 'academic reputation/standards' and 'sport'. Although only 40% of parents believed that A-level success was a very important choice factor, when asked how the school was meeting expectations, 51% said that A-level success rates were very good. When the schools are compared, there was little difference between them. The most important factors which were not up to expectations were 'individual attention', 'caring', 'class size' and 'quality of teaching'. Many factors were being met to a higher level than parents expected, and parents rated as 'very good' a number of factors which few parents had considered to be very important in their choice – in particular, GCSE success, A-level success, and some specific subjects, notably art, drama and music.

Financial issues in independent school choice

One of the most distinctive features of independent schools is the requirement for parents to finance the substantial fees over a period of several years. Sensitivity of parental choice in the market to changing patterns of personal and family finance was explored in this study in relation to a number of important issues – the effect of the newly emerging requirement of part-financing higher education fees; the impact of the demise of the Assisted Places Scheme; and the problems of meeting the costs of school fees.

Financing higher education fees

Opting into independent education is clearly seen as a long-term commitment to the sector for a child, and the financial implications of that, from the point of entry to the end of their educational pathway. Furthermore, it is a commitment to an academic pathway on into higher education, again with the financial commitments that this implies. A large majority of parents expect their son/daughter to stay in education and go to university – 99% of parents expected their son or daughter to stay in education beyond 16, 98% of parents expect their son/daughter to stay in education beyond 18, and 96% expect them to go to university. Almost all parents (89%) expected them to follow an academic route through post-compulsory education.

With a clear perspective from parents that an independent school is only one stop on the route to higher education, the study explored whether the introduction of university fees might affect the choices parents might make. None of the parents in interviews gave any indication that the fees would change anything in relation to choice of schooling or higher education destinations. Indeed, parents explained that one of the reasons for paying for their child's education was to help to secure a university place. One parent, explained that:

We pay more now than we would pay in university fees. Children cost money all the time. We are a new generation of parents, we expect to pay. We pay because we choose to, and it gives them a better chance of getting to university.

(Mr Robert Pook, Parent – the South)

Another parent remarked that:

University fees won't make much difference to us because we've been paying school fees – in some ways it will be easier, £1,000 is a lot less than we pay in school fees.

(Mrs June Munday, Parent – the South)

Parents clearly see independent education as a pathway to university and do not see changes in higher education finance as a concern within their accepted paradigm of buying education in the private sector.

The Assisted Places Scheme

The Assisted Places Scheme has been a small but significant element in independent school finance since its inception in 1980. Within the study there were 52 parents claiming school fees through APS, 22 of whom received 100% of the fees (18 of this group had children attending the Southern Co-educational School). Those awarded 100% of the fees were all earning less than £25,000 pa., and all parents claiming through the APS were earning less than £40,000 pa. A high proportion (86.5%) were earning less than £20,000 a year. The profile of the parents using APS, however, showed that apart from income there was almost no socio-economic difference between them and those parents not eligible for the scheme. Just over 84% are owner occupiers, and only three families (all from the South) were living in local authority owned houses. The main distinguishing feature was a higher occurrence of single-parent families or families where only one parent was in paid employment. One third held professional or semi-professional employment and 50% had a degree or post-graduate qualification. Only seven fathers were working in manual occupations and four were unemployed, of whom three were graduates and one was unable to work through illness.

The survey questions which asked parents to consider how changes in the Assisted Places Scheme might affect the opportunities of younger children were completed by 383 parents (those with younger children), 49% of whom said they had never considered the APS at any time. The data shows that about 16% of parents who had considered the Assisted Places Scheme (196) would be less likely or unlikely to send their child to an independent school without support from the Scheme. A bursary would seem to make a difference to only a very small percentage (2%–3%) of parents with younger children, who have considered, or currently rely on, APS. For those families eligible for the APS, however, the financial support it offered would make a substantial difference to their ability to support younger children through the school. There were 17 parents in the study who were claiming fees through the Assisted Places Scheme and who also had younger children. Without a bursary only 12% of these parents would be able to send their younger child to the school, but with a bursary 82% would be able to consider the school for their younger child.

Two groups of parents showed concern about the demise of the Assisted Place Scheme – those who wished to see a widening 'social mix' in the school and those who were benefiting directly from the scheme. Parents who showed most concern for the notion of a socially mixed school were those who themselves *could* afford to pay for their child to attend the school, but were concerned for those who they believed would not be able to attend the school in the future. Parents assumed that those who could not pay would be unlikely to be middle-class, yet the evidence of the study is that this is not the case. It is clear that the APS had the effect not of widening the socio-cultural mix of the school but simply of making the school accessible to those of similar social backgrounds whose economic circumstances prevented them from participating in independent education.

Meeting the cost of school fees

Meeting the cost of school fees is an important element in the choice of independent education. Despite the size of fees (typically £6,000–£8,000 per annum per child in an independent day school), there were no parents interviewed who thought they were making real sacrifices for their children by paying fees. Most parents were aware that they had made choices about how to spend any disposable income, though, but not in a way substantially different than choosing between, for example, having two cars and one holiday or two holidays and one car. As one parent indicated,

Something has to give. We tend to have an older car, or a
holiday in the UK instead of going abroad. But it's what we want
to do. We hope to see the results from our children doing well.

(Mrs June Munday, Parent – the South)

Long-term financial preparation also seems not to be a requirement
for most parents in relation to paying school fees. Despite the availability of a wide range of mechanisms for paying school fees (insurance plans, endowment schemes, etc.), the majority of parents
(80%) in Home Counties South paid 100% of the fees from annual
income. In Home Counties North this figure was lower (68%) and
parents claimed that the fees were paid from more than one source,
in particular by other members of the family (e.g. grandparents).
The most likely source of alternative finance for fees was from other
family members including an absent parent, or from the Assisted
Places Scheme. There were a few parents who paid part of the fees
through fees plans, lump sum investments or insurance.

The role of mothers' earnings in the payment of school fees provided an important insight into the mechanisms of financing
independent school choice. Twenty-eight per cent of families in the
South indicated that the mother's earnings effectively paid the
school fees, but this figure was lower in Home Counties North
(23%) and much lower in Home Counties South (14%). The interviews suggested that in many families engaging with independent
education the mother's earnings and potential earnings provide the
'cushion' necessary to fund fees. Only in a small number of families
was there an indication that income was potentially at its maximum
with both parents working in jobs which maximised their income.
Hence, in most families an increase in fees could be absorbed by
some change in the mother's working pattern. A decision to engage
in independent schooling, therefore, is essentially a decision about
the mother's economic activity levels.

Although fees were not of critical importance to these parents in
choosing whether to participate in the independent sector, their
level did, none the less, influence the shape of the final choices they
made. Parents paying fees for the Southern and Home Counties
South Schools tended to be those who had only considered
independent day schools with fees at a similar level. In Home Counties North there were several parents who, after rejecting state
schooling, had considered alternative independent schools including one local boarding school. For many parents, however, the
boarding school was out of their price range, and there were virtu-

ally no alternative schools which parents were happy with. In the South, although there were alternative schools in the area, parents argued that there was not much choice at the 11–16 stage and that the LEA schools were poor. For parents in Home Counties South and the South the fee level in this sense was not an issue with parents, for the alternative schools had similar fees, and they were not making decisions between particular schools based on fee levels alone.

Parents were asked about the impact of an increase in fees and almost all indicated that annual fee increases closely related to inflation would have almost no impact upon their decision to 'buy into' independent education. Most would pay the increases to enable their children to continue at the school, although a sharp increase in fees would be a concern for some – a variety of reasons were given:

- Many parents were already working full time and they had little opportunity to increase their income.
- Further 'sacrifices' would be needed to meet a more dramatic increase.
- Concern by some parents that other families would suffer although they themselves could afford the increase.
- Many women work to pay their children's school fees and would need to work more hours or become full time to meet the additional costs. Some mothers would begin work, although they were not currently working.
- There were alternative and very similar schools and these would have to be considered more seriously as an alternative for younger children (including good state sector schools if all independent school fees were substantially increased).

Attitudes to co-education

Strong allegiance to single-sex or co-education traditions is used by many independent schools as a distinctive marketing feature. Trends towards mixed sixth forms can be identified in the last two decades but few schools have sought to change from single-sex to co-education in the 11–16 age range. But how far might a change to or from co-education impact on a school's market and influence parental choice – and how far was that choice affected by opting for or against single-sex education? Parents with children attending the boys' school in Home Counties North were more concerned and vocal about issues related to co-education than parents attending either the co-educational school or the girls' school. In Home Counties South and Home Counties North the state schools were co-educational and the independent schools were single sex. In the southern town, the independent schools were co-educational or girls only, and the state schools provided a choice between co-education and single-sex education.

The study suggested that there are two main factors, 'socialisation' and 'distractions', used by parents both for and against co-education generally. Those in favour of co-education concentrated on the argument that co-education reflects the 'real world' and allows boys and girls to grow up together and relate to one another naturally. Those against co-education claimed that, especially between the ages of 11–16, boys and girls distract one another and there is a tendency for them to concentrate on their relationships with the opposite sex to the detriment of their studies. Parents also mentioned the problems of development and maturity rates of girls and boys, arguing that it was better to have single-sex teaching. Parents with daughters attending the girls' school had rarely chosen the school *because* it was girls, but they explained the benefits for girls of being educated separately from boys. During interviews parents were most concerned about retaining the ethos of the school and the academic emphasis. It seemed to be common knowledge that girls do better academically in single-sex schools and from this, parents calculated that there is little advantage in sending daughters to a co-ed school.

Overall, the study suggests that the issue of co-education v. single-sex education is an issue which is interpreted according to local circumstance rather than displaying generalisable factors that can be applied in all independent school markets. It is used as a strong justification for whatever choices are made from whatever options are available, but appears to be a factor which parents add to their list of *post-hoc* justifications rather than appearing on the list of primary objectives at the start of the choice process.

Markets, parents and choice in the independent sector

The nature of the market place in independent secondary education in the UK is shaped by the consumer choices of parents and their children. It is clear both from the Parental Attitudes to Independent Education Project and other earlier research that with the exception of a few of the most prestigious boarding schools there is no single national market, but rather a raft of overlapping local and regional markets responding to their own socio-economic and historical characteristics. Within each of these market places, the market both shapes and is shaped by the pattern of parental choice.

From the evidence of the choice process in the Parental Attitudes to Independent Education Project independent school market structures can be described under three headings:

1 *Supremacy markets* exist where there is only one provider of independent schooling in a particular phase of education (similar to a 'monopoly') and no other provision is available to parents in the local area.

2 *Competitive supremacy markets* occur where each school offers an educational service which in some way differs from its rivals, and so, in effect, does not have any substantial competition. The study suggested that in Home Counties North where there is only one selective boys' day school, and in the South, where there was no co-educational school in the locality, the schools were operating in this type of market.

3 *Rivalistic markets* operate where there is a market with a small number of key competitors (schools!) sharing a large proportion of the customers between them (similar to an oligopoly). They may offer virtually the same service, but they are mutually dependent and react to the decisions of the other schools. Because competition in the market tends to drive down fee levels, it is in the best interests of the schools to form a *micro cartel* which enables competitors to collude against the parents in the form of an agreement to keep fee levels similar. In the Home Counties South town the bursars of rival independent schools have come to an agreement about fee increases to avoid severe price competition. In 1999, for example, they all agreed to increase their fees by 5%. In this way the independent schools compete on factors other than fees, and fee differentials are not a factor within parental choice processes.

Other considerations come into play once fee levels cease to be an important factor in choice. In business markets 'non-fee competition' involves two major elements – product development, and advertising (Sloman, 1999). The major aim of initiating change and development is to introduce and enhance product differentiation to attract a significant number of customers. Schools in a rivalistic market need to be clear about why they are different from other competitor schools. This emphasises the need to be innovative in meeting parental needs and inform parents of the benefits through successful promotion. For schools in the independent sector this means that heads have to be innovative and imaginative and devise ways of improving the provision – for example, the head of the Home Counties South girls' school listed seven or eight new ideas to improve what was currently offered to pupils, including a new building programme, new curriculum subjects, additional visits and travel opportunities, and visiting students and staff from overscas. These all had cost implications, but it was not an option to allow any weakness to continue or to be content with the current provision. A school operating in a rivalistic market constantly needs to keep up with its rivals and try to get ahead of them. This strategy is essential in a rivalistic market but harder for a head to justify in a supremacy market. The claim that competition improves quality and that customer choice drives quality essentially relies on a rivalistic market model. Although the headteachers in the schools operating in competitive supremacy markets were also driving forward ideas for change and implementing programmes of continuous improvement, they were not driven by the conditions of the market constantly to address any weaknesses.

External influences on choice decisions in independent school markets

There are a number of factors, other than price, behind consumer behaviour in markets, which are referred to as 'external effects on consumption' (Bain and Howells, 1988). These effects appear strongly to influence the decision to participate in independent education and are used by parents to justify decisions to purchase the service of 'education' for their children rather than use the 'free' state education provision. Seven of these external effects have been identified in the Parental Attitudes to Independent Education study.

First, the 'bandwagon effect' occurs where parents send their child to the school because it becomes fashionable among the people they are in contact with. As more people send their children to the school, it becomes more acceptable as the norm. Without perfect information about the quality of all the schools in the area the school becomes accepted as the 'best' school because other parents have chosen it, and they are assumed to have some prior experience of the school which counts as privileged information.

Second, the 'elitist effect' is based on the idea that by choosing a fee-paying school parents can distinguish themselves from other people. This effect works particularly strongly where the main competitors of the independent school are state schools. The ability to pay for schooling rather than having to rely on free education enhances the effect, although this effect also works where some schools charge considerably higher fees than others. At low levels of income, people rely entirely on the 'free' maintained sector education system, but as their income rises they are more prepared to pay and transfer their support to more expensive education, thus relying less on the state system. As people's incomes rise the demand for (free) state schooling falls and free education is considered to have become inferior to fee-paying education. This effect may be compared with an effect which happens in commercial markets where cheap goods are perceived to be inferior as people's incomes rise (Beardshaw *et al.*, 1998).

Third, social norms and restrictions also have an effect. This effect is rather like a 'negative bandwagon effect' where people reject an option because no-one else is making that choice. Local maintained sector schools, or particular local state schools, become unacceptable choices because no-one within a particular social group has chosen to go there. This eventually gives the school an image of being inferior.

Fourth, an additional effect which seems to occur in independent education markets is the 'denouncement' effect. Once parents are able to pay for schooling, they have the option of rejecting the local free system of schools, especially when the academic achievement of those local schools is perceived to be relatively poor. They are also aware that this choice may not be politically acceptable, and so may justify their choice by denouncing or condemning the state sector schools within their locality, claiming they are inferior to their needs. The effect is also an attempt to deny the 'elitist effect', because it stimulates guilt about turning their back on their social conscience.

Fifth, the 'Veblen effect' (Bain and Howells, 1988) emerges from the idea of conspicuous consumption. With some expensive services the consumer may be interested in purchasing *because* it is expensive. The price is part of the attraction and a rise in price may also make it more attractive (Beardshaw *et al.*, 1998). Parents may pay for independent education because they believe other people think it is expensive. Participation in independent education is, therefore, viewed as an indicator of wealth and hence of success. The Veblen effect means that the higher the fees the more attractive the school becomes, although this tends to operate in the public boarding school sector rather more than in the day school sector. Similarly, a significant reduction in fees in an education market which was highly competitive could have the effect of reducing demand. Once parents have chosen a school with fees which they can afford, a reduction in fees is more likely to reduce demand on the basis that lower fees indicate an inferior service, which reduces the Veblen effect.

A sixth effect is the phenomenon of '*post-hoc* justification' which tends to shift attention away from the underlying reasons for choosing a school. *Post-hoc* justification is retrospective explanation of a choice which is the result of a complex decision-making process, and may involve some degree of self-deception to achieve self-appeasement (Hemsley-Brown, 1999a). Information provided by schools in their marketing information contributes towards *post-hoc* justification and helps parents to persuade themselves that they have made a good decision, as well as providing tailor-made reasons for the choice. This phenomenon highlights the importance of marketing and in particular 'marketing feedback'. Messages flow both ways, from parents to the schools and from schools back to the parents.

Finally, allied to *post-hoc* justification is the notion of 'conscience-salving'. Parents may have reached a decision with great difficulty after taking into account their political and social conscience. Parents, having made the choice of independent education, promote strategies and policies in the school that seek to demonstrate a reduction in selection or social elitism. Their choice may have run counter to the values and beliefs they have held in the past, and as a result parents may seek to promote ideas for greater inclusiveness to salve their conscience about the choice they have made for their own child. The Parental Attitudes to Independent Education study suggest that attitudes towards the APS, and pressure to limit fee rises are an attempt by parents to seek widening access to independent schools amongst non-participating socio-cultural groups and so salve their conscience about participating in an elitist educational system.

In summary

Independent education is the preserve of a small proportion of pupils in the UK education system. Parents opting for independent schools, however, are highly influential in shaping the nature of all schools by their decisions. They represent parents with high levels of cultural (and economic!) capital whom many state schools seek to attract through the organisational, curriculum and cultural systems they operate. In choosing independent schools they take those 'desired' attributes away from the state system. Their choices are based on a commitment to academic education as the pathway to higher education entrance and a career in high-status professional employment, and a long-term plan for their children's educational pathway towards this. Their decision is one that reflects the economic and cultural value they accord to education in the decisions they make about personal finance – they see education as an economic 'good' that they can purchase in the market place. Post-choice dissonance based on social conscience appears to be of significance in the *post-hoc* justifications that parents use, and a range of 'external effects' in choice, such as the bandwagon effect, underpin tenuous (and sometimes highly questionable) but strongly expressed negative comparisons to be made between state schools and independent schools. The importance of these comparisons in shaping wider community perceptions of state education in general and of specific schools in particular is an important area for future research.

5 Young people, choice and the further education market place

The further education market place

In the United Kingdom compulsory education ceases at the age of 16 and all young people must make the choice to remain in education and training or not. In the early 1980s the majority chose to leave education and enter the labour market, but as a result of changing societal expectations, changing labour markets, and the impact of government policy designed to enhance participation, by the late 1990s participation in education or training was the choice of 70% of 16/17 year olds. This has brought participation in this age group in line with international patterns of participation in education and training up to the age of 18.

The range of choices open to young people is enormous if considered at the level of specific programmes, courses and institutions. The choice of post-16 pathway by each individual student has two principal components, though – a choice of programme or activity (academic or vocational, full-time or part-time, etc.) and a choice of provider (i.e. a specific school, college, training organisation or employer). The two elements are not discrete, of course, and may indeed be inseparable where a particular pathway is only available through a specific provider. Broadly speaking, there are four main pathways and three principal institutional options open to 16 year olds, each of which may be available in full-time or part-time modes of study. The pathways are:

1 An academic pathway, involving the study of Advanced-level (A-level) courses, perhaps in combination with GNVQ (General National Vocational Qualifications) programmes.
2 A vocational pathway, based in an educational/training institution, involving some form of vocationally focused study. This

may involve following a GNVQ programme, or a focus on achieving some form of NVQ (National Vocational Qualification), and may include some workplace experience.

3   A training pathway, based in the work place with a particular employer, but involving some combination of work experience and training in a college or through a training organisation.

4   Entering the labour market direct without access to training or study.

The institutional options available for those choosing an educational or training programme are:

1   To stay in school and enter the 'sixth form'. Approximately 25% of young people choose to study post-16 in the school they have been attending up to the age of 16, usually to follow academic study programmes.

2   To study at a Further Education Institution (FEI). Within the UK there are over 400 FEIs, which range in size and programme provision. At one extreme, Colleges of Agriculture may be small and very highly focused in the programmes they offer. At the other extreme general Further Education Colleges may serve many thousands of students, including large numbers of adults, on programmes across the full range of post-16 provision. Between the two in scale are Sixth Form Colleges (SFCs), which focus mainly on academic programmes for 16–18 year olds, and Tertiary Colleges which focus on 16–18 year olds but cover a wider range of provision.

3   To undertake training with a training organisation or employer. Private training companies may specialise in a narrow or wide range of training programmes, often in collaboration with FEIs.

Choice at 16+ presents for the first time to young people the opportunity to opt for an education/training pathway which is highly specialised, with the choice traditionally couched in terms of dichotomous options – academic v. vocational, part-time v. full-time, employment-based v. institutionally-based, work-with-training v. work-with-no-training. A range of national government policies have sought to blur many of these divides during the last two decades, through, for example, the increase in participation rates post-16, the development of GNVQ qualifications, the introduction of a wide range of short- and long-lived programmes to promote vocational training (for example, the Training Credits Scheme in the early 1990s, and, more recently, Modern Apprenticeships), and the integration of vocational and academic pathways in Curriculum 2000 (DfEE, 1999). Despite these initiatives, however, the education and training landscape in England and Wales has a number of characteristics reflecting well-established gender and class patterns, and underlining the lack of parity of esteem between vocational and academic pathways (Davies, 1993; DfEE, 1995; Foskett and Hesketh, 1997).

i Almost two thirds of those opting to stay in full-time education/training post-16 express a preference for an academic programme rather than a vocational programme. Participation in A-level courses is, though, eventually less than 40% of the age cohort, which suggests that a significant number of young people are selecting vocational routes as a second best option at the final point of post-16 choice.

ii Participation rates post-16 are higher amongst young women than young men (75%: 67% in 1995/6), with females more likely to choose academic pathways. Amongst those choosing vocational pathways some 65% are young men.

iii Aspirations to full-time participation post-16 are higher amongst young people from middle-class backgrounds (85%) than amongst those from working-class families (72%), and these relative aspirations appear, too, in actual participation rates. The balance of choice between vocational and academic pathways, however, shows a strongly class-oriented pattern, with vocational pathways chosen by twice as many working-class young people than by middle-class pupils, while academic pathways show the reverse pattern.

iv Opting for pathways outside full-time education/training is strongly the domain of pupils from working-class backgrounds. Although the numbers choosing to seek employment directly or to follow a part-time education/training programme are small, employment is largely the option of working-class males, and part-time pathways are largely the choice of working-class females.

v The academic/vocational divide in choice is largely a social class divide, with vocational programmes principally the choice of young people from working-class backgrounds. This divide is hard to break down, for most young people are anxious to alienate themselves from one of the choices in favour of the other. As

Hemsley-Brown (1999a, p. 96) shows, on the basis of a longitudinal study of choice at 16+,

> Vocationally-biased students were keen to become adults and be regarded as wage earners (...). Working class vocationally-orientated students wanted to be treated as adults and rejected school which they associated with academic education. Upper middle/middle class students, all of whom chose academic courses, were unwilling to consider vocational training or employment at 16+ because they viewed this route as the choice of 16 year olds who had failed to gain good GCSE results.

In Chapter 1 we examined briefly the major changes in the policy and operational environment that have stimulated enhanced choice in the further education market place. Colleges have been charged by the Further Education Funding Council (FEFC) with rapid expansion of student numbers based in a funding model that has seen an annual reduction in the unit of resource. Hemsley-Brown (1999a, p. 84) suggests that

> the language of policy-making in further education is suffused with the rhetoric of the market, competition and choice – but 'the underlying objectives of policy have little to do with the promotion of market relations *per se* and much to do with increasing participation and reducing costs'. (Scott, 1996, p. 26)

Colleges have been faced, then, with choosing between expansion or decline/demise, and have been thrown into a highly competitive arena in which the choices of young people hold sway. Understanding choice processes is not simply an issue of academic interest, therefore, to the further education sector, for institutional competitiveness and survival are strongly driven by knowing how, knowing why and knowing when young people choose their post-16 pathways.

Although many institutions have undertaken market research on choice for their own strategic purposes, there are still only a few public domain studies of post-16 choice that exist. Early studies focused on specific aspects of choice in the post-compulsory market place, such as the market value of academic or vocational qualifications, the influence of some socio-economic factors, or the identification of labour market intentions (e.g. Roberts and Parsell, 1988; Roberts *et al.*, 1989; Gray and Sime, 1989; Fergusson and Unwin,

1996). More recently, though, research has built on the early initiative of Taylor (1992) and has sought to unravel a wider understanding of post-16 choice (e.g. Foskett and Hesketh, 1996a; Hodkinson and Sparkes, 1997; Maychell and Evans, 1998; Hemsley-Brown, 1999a; and Maguire, MacRae and Ball, 1999, 2000) in relation to the influence of a range of key factors and the process of choice in its social and cultural settings. This chapter and the one that follows will examine the key ideas that have emerged from this research. Within this chapter the focus will be on some of the generic issues in the choice process (the timing of choice, who chooses, and factors influencing the choice between vocational and academic pathways), and on young people's choice of college or school at 16+. Chapter 6 considers the specific issue of choice in relation to vocational pathways, with a particular focus on choosing in the arena of Modern Apprenticeships.

The timing of post-16 choice

While choice (perhaps more properly termed decision-*taking*) is a process that occurs at a specific point in time, the nature of decision-*making* means that choices may be formed and shaped over much longer periods. It is important to distinguish, therefore, between identifying the time in their school career when young people have made a choice about their post-16 pathway, and the time when they started to engage with the choice process. This issue was an important focus of the research in the Post-16 Markets Project (Foskett and Hesketh, 1996a, 1997), a national research project focused on the decision-making processes of young people in the transition from compulsory education at age 16 to the education, training and labour markets of the post-compulsory education environment post-16. The study used questionnaire surveys of 1284 young people in a range of schools in different geographical and socio-economic settings in the weeks prior to leaving school.

The findings of the Post-16 Markets Project suggest that by the point of completion of compulsory education 95% of young people have made a choice about their next step. In a minority of cases this was a firm decision, where the choice was not dependent on factors beyond the young person's influence – for example, those who had already accepted employment to start forthwith. For most, though, the decisions were provisional, depending upon the outcome of public examination results (principally GCSEs) that are not published until mid-August.

Identifying the timing of the initiation of choice is fraught with methodological issues, which have been discussed in Chapter 2. Identification of when the process began is subject to the limitations of accurate memory. In addition it reports the point at which the process became explicit to the individual, which, as we shall consider later in this chapter, may ignore the important developmental processes that are implicit throughout a young person's life. Few studies have sought to unpick this particular issue, but if we are to understand the choice process we must attempt to identify when it begins. The evidence suggests that the process can start at an early stage of a pupil's secondary school career, or earlier, for the Post-16 Markets Project shows that 42% of young people had begun the process of choice prior to the final year of schooling, and 5% had begun the process before the age of 14. In detail a number of differences emerge in this pattern of choice initiation in relation to gender, socio-economic status and intended pathway choice (Figure 5.1).

The data confirms a number of traditional hypotheses concerning post-16 choice. It suggests, for example, that girls start the choice process earlier than boys, and that those choosing an academic pathway start to choose earlier than those opting for a vocational pathway. However, the expected difference between children from working-class and middle-class backgrounds does not emerge strongly, and suggests that there is perhaps less difference in engagement with educational choice processes than traditional class-based models might predict.

Groupings

Timing	Age	Boys	Girls	Middle class	Working class	Academic pathway	Vocational pathway	Undecided pathway	Overall
Before Year 9	>13	5	5	6	4	15	7	8	5
Year 9	13/14	12	10	12	10	15	14	8	11
Year 10	14/15	22	30	25	27	32	32	23	26
Year 11	15/16	40	36	40	42	38	46	55	38
Not sure		15	15	14	16	11	8	15	–
No response		6	4	4	6	–	–	–	5

Figure 5.1 The initiation of young people's post-16 choice (%) (after Foskett and Hesketh, 1997).

The data may seriously underestimate the initiation of choice, for the reasons indicated earlier. Whether or not this is the case, though, the significance of the findings of early initiation of choice lies in its positioning relative to careers education and guidance (CEG) programmes in school and the promotional activities of FEIs. Almost all CEG is focused in Year 10 and 11 in most schools, by which time as many as 30% of those pursuing an academic choice of pathway may have already started the process of choice. Similarly, almost all promotional and communications activity by post-16 providers occurs in Year 11, by which time almost half of the age cohort may have undertaken part of the choice process. Post-16 decision-making may be occurring, therefore, in a partial information vacuum, and will be based on other sources of information than official ones.

Factors influencing pathway choice at 16

The Post-16 Markets Project examined the factors that appear to influence young people's choice of post-16 pathway (Foskett and Hesketh, 1996a). The study distinguished between *general influencing factors*, of which many may play a part in a young person's choice, and *specific factors*, which are those identified by individuals as the most important single factor in their choice. Amongst the general factors, those which emerge as the most important for young people are, in order of importance, the career prospects inherent in the choice, a desire to continue studying, improvement of their chance of university entrance, and the negative perspective of a desire not to leave education. In terms of specific factors, university entrance becomes the second most frequently cited factor, while a desire to enter the labour market and leave education/training emerges as the fourth most important factor.

When analysed in relation to the pathways chosen by respondents, however, a clear difference between the motivating factors for those choosing academic pathways and those choosing vocational pathways appears. While 'enhancing career prospects' is the most important single factor for both groups, the importance of university entrance is clear as a motivator for 'academic' choosers, while the motivation of earning money through employment appears as a significant general and specific factor for those opting for a vocational pathway. A number of interesting gender differences also emerge from this study. While enhancing career prospects is the prime specific and general factor for both girls and boys, girls place more emphasis on the inherent desire to continue studying than do boys (67%: 49% in terms of a general factor!), and also on a desire to enter university as an ultimate goal. Amongst those seeking employment directly, the motivation of earning money is more important for boys than for girls, whose motivation is more strongly influenced by a desire to leave school.

Factors influencing institutional choice at 16

The second element in the choice construct is that of the institution or training provider. The consideration of general and specific factors applied to pathway choice was also used by Foskett and Hesketh (1996a) to examine institutional choice. At a general level the most important influencing factors are 'the academic reputation of the institution' (cited by 47% of young people), the institution's prospectus (40%), proximity (38%), the 'impression created when visiting the institution' (34%) and the desire to transfer with friends (30%). At a specific level, however, the importance of these factors changes quite significantly. While academic reputation is still the most important factor (the single most important factor for 24% of young people), this is followed by 'the desire to stay in the sixth form of the current school' (17%), the availability of the chosen pro-gramme in only one institution (15%), proximity (14%), and the impression created by a visit (12%). The Post-16 Markets Project also showed how the nature of competition in the market place can distort the importance of these factors, though. In a market place with significant competition for post-16 provision the most import-ant factor in student choice is the academic achievement outcomes of the college, but in markets with few providers and little real choice proximity is cited as the key specific factor in choice.

While the broad pattern of the influence of factors at general and specific levels of choice is similar, several important ideas emerge from this data. First, for those choosing to 'stay on' in their current school the most important reason for choosing is the academic repu-tation of the school and its focus on academic achievement. This res-onates strongly with the findings of Foskett and Hemsley-Brown (2000) in relation to the decision to stay in the sixth form in independent schools, and suggests that a traditional school setting is seen as a stronger guarantor of academic outcomes than a college environment.

Second, frictions of distance and resistance to change emerge as strong *specific* factors. This suggests that distance and change may be strong frictional factors that must be overcome by the positive 'pull' of other factors, and that in many cases there is insufficient strength in those other factors to overcome this resistance.

Third, the role of parents as a general factor in choice is recognised by some 20% of young people, but their influence as a specific factor is recorded by less than 1% of pupils. An issue of some research interest in choice at 11+ is also relevant here – who, precisely, makes the choice, and what is the relative influence of young people and their parents? Although almost 80% of pupils reported that the choice was made by themselves, and only 2% indicated that their parents chose for them, the research shows that one fifth of young people, therefore, acknowledged the decision as a joint one between themselves and their parents. Of those indicating parental influence at the general level some three quarters were girls. By 16 the direct role of parents in choice has clearly been substantially reduced, therefore, in comparison to choice at 11, and particularly in the decision-making of boys. However, allowing for likely under-reporting, this suggests that the role of parents in the choice process is still of some importance, which may reflect the fact that the choice is made while the young person is still, in effect, a pupil in compulsory education.

Despite this initial observation of declining parental role in the choice, Davies (1994) suggests that the role of parents is still strong in choice at 16+, and this is confirmed by the findings of the Post-16 Markets Project. The notion of the 'framed field of decision-making' has been discussed in Chapter 3, and in the context of post-16 choice this conforms a process in which

> the decisions (young people) make are made within frames of reference defined, sometimes explicitly but more frequently implicitly, by their parents. Some options, whether of institution, course or career aspiration, will be excluded as possibilities by parents, but pupils will be able to make relatively unconstrained choice between non-excluded options. Thus the pupil's decision may not coincide with the parents' perception of the optimal post-16 trajectory, but will rarely be outside the parents' perception of an acceptable post-16 pathway.
>
> (Foskett and Hesketh, 1996a, p. 36)

We must not dismiss this as a process without conflict and dissonance, however, for divergence of preference may be quite strong between parents and their children. The tensions that may exist between parents and children in the informal development of choice is clear, and post-16 choice may be a condensation point for young people's pursuit of independence from their parents. The final placing of the choice boundaries may only emerge after extensive 'negotiation' between pupils and parents, and the public acknowledgement of the role of parents in this process by young people may be very limited as a way of emphasising their own independence. We should regard data on parental influence as recorded by 16 year olds, therefore, with some scepticism. This process, and the difference in attitudes between young people and parents, is well illustrated by comments from the marketing manager of a Tertiary College in southern England (quoted in Foskett and Hesketh, 1996, p. 36):

> You can't change parents' perceptions, but the kids you can affect – you can influence the choice of kids more than those of parents. If they want to come to this college, they will come to this college. Now what middle class parents would admit to that? (…). You know exactly what your average parent wants – there's three options; firstly they want them to stay in the school's sixth form, if its got one; secondly they want them to go to a sixth form college which is as close to a sixth form at school as you can get; and then, thirdly, they'll let them go to a rough and tumble adult-oriented FE college. For the kids you just invert what the parents feel!

The influence of institutional marketing on young people's choice at 16

The intensively competitive environment of further education recruitment means that young people are exposed to the influence of institutional marketing strategies in developing their post-16 choice. The Post-16 Markets Project demonstrated the importance of the institution's academic reputation in a rational analysis of choice, and most of the other general and specific factors in choice relate to the school or college's projection of its own image, provision and practice (e.g. the significance of visits to the institution by prospective students). The impact of marketing messages can be substantial. Hemsley-Brown (1996), in her study of post-16 choice in relation to a single market place in southern England, has shown how the promotional messages of the colleges are used *post hoc* by students to justify the choices they have made, even where the information in the message is palpably false. Where colleges cited 'small classes' as a positive feature of the institution, for example, students used this to justify their choice (and satisfaction) even where they were being taught in large groups, and friends at other institutions were being taught in much smaller classes. Perhaps of more significance, though, is the fact that none of the students in the study were able to give coherent reasons for their choices until after they had been exposed to the marketing information provided by colleges. At that point a wide range of 'rational' justifications for their choice emerged and were provided by the young people. Strong and timely promotional messages clearly have an important role in post-16 choice, but their use in choice justification questions the significance of rational, factor-based studies of choice at 16!

The nature of competition between institutions and the marketing strategies they use can be very important, therefore. Nicholls (1994) has shown how disinformation and information censoring processes are used in some markets by schools seeking to limit knowledge of alternative choices amongst their Year 11 pupils making post-16 choices, constraining the choices that individuals have. Hemsley-Brown (1994), in her study of the strategies used by an independent school to keep its pupils in its own sixth form, shows how their actions and information filters can distort the choice process. In this case it is clear that such strategies, if not managed effectively, can have the opposite impact to that desired – openness and information provision seem much more effective at persuading pupils to stay than does the use of covert information control strategies or negative publicity.

Identifying the sources of information that influence choice is an important issue for institutions and advisers seeking to shape the choices of young people, therefore. The Post-16 Markets Project identified the relative importance of the principal information sources. At the level of general choice of institution careers teachers and other teachers are the most important sources of information, followed by parents, with the promotional materials and events offered by further education institutions (FEI) providing additional important information. The significance of direct, person-to-person communication at this level of choice is clear. In relation to specific choice, however, the importance of promotional activities emerges more strongly, with the most important information sources identified as careers teachers (27% of pupils), open evenings at the FEI (18%), other teachers (15%), and FEI literature (11%). Here clear differences also emerge between those opting to remain in their current school for post-16 programmes, and those choosing to go elsewhere. For those intending to leave, FEI open evenings emerge as the most important single information source, and the influence of other teachers is small (7%). For those seeking to stay on at school, teachers are the most important information source (29%), followed by careers teachers (26%). Relationships between pupils and teachers in Year 11 of the secondary school may, therefore, be one of the most important factors for schools to address if they wish to retain their pupils into their own sixth form.

The intensification of competition in the post-16 market place has resulted in a marked enhancement in the quality and volume of promotional literature generated by institutions. This 'glossification' process is apparent in the nature of college prospectuses, and is based on a presumption that such documents are of considerable importance in the choice process. This assumption is open to serious question though, on the basis of the findings of the Post-16 Markets Project. At a general level of influence the prospectus was cited as a factor in choice by almost 40% of young people, but at the level of specific choice it is the key factor for only 6% of pupils. Its role is one of initial information provision, therefore, not of choice conversion, although it is also clear that the possession of a good quality prospectus is an essential permissive factor in entering the market. At the point of final choice though colleges must recognise that

> most people use (the prospectus) as a directory and say 'oh yes, they do a course I want to do', so at the end of the day it never can be used as a selling document, as a document which promotes sales. All it does is confirm that we do the course.
>
> (FE College Marketing Manager, quoted in Foskett and Hesketh, 1997, p. 313)

It is important to emphasise that knowing the factors involved in the choice, and even knowing their relative significance, does not provide any insights into the way those factors provide influence, either at a macro scale or for individual students. For example, it is not possible to identify how the importance of teachers as an influence on students choosing to 'stay on' actually operates. Do the teachers directly promote the advantages of staying into the sixth form, and if so how far is this a function of professional self-interest? Does the choice to stay on, alternatively, simply reflect the presence of excellent teachers, recognised as such by pupils, who estimate that teacher quality will be important to their achievement post-16? Or, do pupils simply provide a *post-hoc* justification for either a complex decision process or a choice to 'take the line of least resistance' and 'stay on' by citing teachers as an important source of influence and information? There is much scope for further micro-scale research on important questions such as these.

Guidance, choice and the problem of impartiality

Consideration of the marketing strategies of FE providers has raised an important ethical issue for many educationalists which relates to the tension between the needs and wants of the individual young person as 'consumer' and the institutional needs of the colleges, schools and training providers who constitute the 'supply side'. How far do institutions pursue as their principal objective the satisfaction of student need, and how far is their provision and guidance on choice driven by objectives relating to government funding policy and the inertia of simply providing what their traditions and existing resources suggest is suitable?

Gleeson (1996) and Watts and Young (1997) suggest that the quasi market in further education rewards institutions for recruitment through the funding methodologies employed by the FEFC, rather than for effective guidance, since most of the institution's income is dependent on the registration of students. Within institutions, the funding and resource models employed also result in the establishment of internal markets with competition between cost centres (e.g. subject departments, or different training programmes) for recruitment. Under such circumstances it is appropriate to ask whether impartial, student-centred advice can exist, and to question where the line can be drawn between guidance and marketing/promotion. The consequences of ineffective or poor guidance for an individual student can be substantial, for, as Martinez and Munday (1998, p. 82) suggest:

> Students on the wrong course are more likely to drop out and appropriate selection to courses by central admissions or specialist staff is of crucial importance to retention.

To address this issue of mis/dis-information, and hence to seek to reduce drop-out from FE programmes, Martinez and Munday have suggested a model of 'good practice in pre-entry guidance' for institutions. They suggest that the provision of information and admissions interviews should comprise:

1   An entitlement for applicants to unlimited specialist interviews.
2   Students who show interest in more than one course being interviewed by an independent admissions unit.
3   Designated admissions tutors in each department having formal links with central admissions guidance staff.
4   Admissions tutors providing generic vocational guidance and overseeing the consistent application of admissions procedures.
5   The introduction of accredited training in educational guidance for all interviewers.
6   The placing of students with minimal entry requirements on to diagnostic courses which are designed to enable them to demonstrate their academic and practical skills.

Even with such guidelines, though, Watts and Young (1997) question whether individual tutors can be expected to provide impartial advice when they have a vested interest in the student's decision. Watts and Young (1997, p. 149) define guidance as '... the range of processes designed to enable individuals to make informed choices and transitions related to their personal, educational and career development'. The emphasis is clearly on the needs of the individual, not on the needs of the organisations that they may choose to work with, yet the likelihood of impartiality varies with the sources of advice they may receive. Watts and Young suggest that there are three levels of impartiality, relating to different sources of guidance:

1   *Comprehensive impartiality*, which Watts and Young characterise as the guidance provided by the Careers Service. The traditional approach to CEG has been one based on impartiality and objectivity with a focus on responding to the identified needs and wants of individual young people. Directing young people towards particular career or education pathways has been strongly eschewed. Two issues arise from this perspective, though. First, it must be recognised that complete impartiality will always be a myth, in that CEG organisations and individuals have their own explicit and implicit objectives (and values) that will shape the nature of the guidance given. Organisational throughput targets for individual guidance may reduce, for example, the amount of detailed guidance that can be given to an individual. Second, complete impartiality may not be helpful to some individual choosers. While supporting the aspiration of young men to be professional footballers and of young women to be actresses may be impartial, pushing them towards

the development of aspirations that are more likely to make them successful in the job market may be more helpful to individuals.

2   *Intra-institutional impartiality.* Watts and Young exemplify this as the guidance services provided within a school or college. The guidance is impartial within the confines of a choice to attend that institution, but will not be impartial in relation to information about other programmes or options outside the institution. The degree of impartiality might vary, though, according to circumstances. There may be institutional policy to direct young people to high-income programmes or to programmes at risk of closure, for example. Higher levels of impartiality tend to exist where guidance is given to young people at a point where exiting the institution is a necessary choice. Research by Foskett and Hesketh (1996a, 1997) shows that the guidance given on post-16 choices by 11–16 schools is much more detailed, wide ranging and supportive than that given by 11–18 schools which have a vested interest in pupils remaining within the school for their 16–18 education. Nicholls (1994) has shown how such vested interests may seriously distort the operation of the post-16 market in a particular location to the disadvantage of young people. Disinformation processes, the censoring of promotional literature and the restriction of access to literature and individuals from 'competitor institutions' all serve to restrict the availability of impartial and objective information. FEFC/Ofsted (1994) have been highly critical of the impact of such processes on individuals, and suggest that increased impartiality CAN be achieved where institutions recognise their local guidance obligations and work through consortia or partnerships to provide appropriate choice information.

> Students had a better knowledge of the full range of provision available for 16–19 year olds in local institutions in areas where partnerships or consortia ... had been established; where cooperative arrangements existed between different providers; or where local careers services provided material describing the provision.
>
> (FEFC/Ofsted, 1994, p. 6)

3   *Low impartiality*, normally characterised by the guidance offered by teachers and lecturers on particular courses or programmes. For most young people there is a tension between the detail and

the objectivity of advice and guidance. Teachers and lecturers working in a particular career field will know a great deal about that field, with insights available often *only* to professionals in that field. CEG professionals cannot be expected to have such intimate knowledge of all potential fields. Counterbalancing this insight, though, is the risk of a lack of objectivity, a danger that information is outdated or only partial in its accuracy, and the likelihood that a teacher or lecturer will be proselytising for their field.

Recognising these degrees of impartiality is important for young people in their information and guidance search, for it may enable a richer understanding of the factors in their choice. Each of the forms of guidance has its place, and the three sources may provide important triangulation of ideas and choices. It is perhaps ironic, however, that the system established to create a market may result in poorer quality choice for the potential customers in the system, and an increased likelihood of dissonance and dissatisfaction in the choices that are made.

Pragmatic rationality and the process of post-16 choice

Following the analysis above of the factors that shape and influence choice, we must move to consider the process of choice itself. Rationality in the choice process is a presumed characteristic of most market-based models for education, but as we have identified earlier, the nature of that rationality is not clear from the research evidence that has emerged. Rationality in post-16 choice has been examined by Hodkinson, Sparkes and Hodkinson (1996) in their research on young people's engagement with choices of training programmes. Despite the rejection of rational models of decision-making, their research suggests that choice does have some elements of rationality within it, in that it is clearly not entirely 'non-rational'. Some components of the choice process involve making reasoned decisions in the context of the information that is available, while other components do not. Hodkinson *et al.* identify this process as one of *pragmatic rationality*, in that rational elements can be identified but their presence or their degree of absolute rationality is strongly tempered by pragmatism by the young people concerned. Here decision-making does not follow a linear sequence. Although there may be identifiable stages in the process, they do not necessarily occur in a particular order or over set time periods, and are often a response to

particular chance circumstances. The decisions made about elements of choice occur at particular moments and

> ... are determined by the external job or educational opportun-
> ities in interaction with personal perceptions of what was pos-
> sible, desirable or appropriate. Those perceptions in turn (are)
> derived from their culture and life histories.
>
> (Hodkinson, Sparkes and Hodkinson, 1996, p. 123)

The importance of understanding the sociology of educational
choice amongst 16 year olds emerges strongly from such a perspective, for it is clear that we can only understand individual choice by
considering its changing socio-cultural context over time. Recent
research has moved on from considering retrospective accounts of
decision-making set against choice factor analysis to longitudinal
studies of young people as they pass through the choice process.
Such studies reveal much about the dynamic nature, contingency of
choice and instability in decisions that characterise choosing educational and training pathways at 16 (Hemsley-Brown, 1999a; Hodkinson and Bloomer, 1999; Ball, Macrae and Maguire, 1999; Maguire,
Ball and Macrae, 1999).

The significance of these studies lies principally in their insights
into the thoughts and hopes, successes, failures, doubts, internal
conflicts and external discussions that young people experience in
their transformations from school to the post-school world. They
provide the micro-scale colour that emphasises the uniqueness of
each individual's choice, and show how young people are frequently
the victims of circumstances, chance events and their own life situations. Decisions fluctuate almost on a daily basis in response to new
perceptions and information and in response to the outcomes of
attempts to resolve the inherent contradictions and restrictions that
young people face day to day. The stories of Jordan and Luke
(Maguire, Ball and Macrae, 1999), of Toby, Wayne and Dawn
(Hemsley-Brown, 1999a), and of Liam and John (Hodkinson and
Bloomer, 1999) provide real insights into the challenges of choosing
for most young people.

Such longitudinal studies provide pictures of successes and failures in the choice process and in absolute educational achievement.
Failures, of course, are often more illuminating of the choice
process than successes, for they illustrate strongly some of the post-
choice dissonance that reflects the challenges of making those
choices in the first place. Recent research into the decisions of 'drop

outs' has helped our understanding of many of the substantive issues in choice at 16.

Non-completion, or 'dropping out', is a complex issue and is hard to define precisely. At its most simple level it describes the experience of young people who start a training/education programme but withdraw from it before the end of the course. Although typical figures for FE drop-out are between 12% and 20%, with higher rates on vocational programmes, Kidd and Wardman (1999) show how this does not provide a full and appropriate picture. Students may drop out at various stages – some may simply not start a course they have enrolled on, some may drop out in the first week or two, others may drop out at much later stages. Some may formally withdraw, while some may simply stop attending. Others may withdraw in the sense of ceasing active participation – their attendance continues but their engagement with the course in effect ceases. This may lead to 'counselling out' from the programme, but some may still survive to the end. Some may attend and engage, but the engagement may be sub-optimal – it may fluctuate across time, and may result in an outcome from the programme which is either failure or well below the potential achievement level of the young person. All of these forms of 'dropping out', though, contribute something to our understanding about the choice process that preceded enrolment on the programme. We shall consider seven important ideas that emerge from looking at drop outs.

First, it is clear that choice is a continuing process that does not end at the point where a decision is made to register for a particular course or programme. Beyond the compulsory phase of education persistence on a programme is a result of continuing decisions to carry on engaging. This has many time scales within it. At its most extreme for some individuals this is a daily decision – to attend college/work today or not. This in turn is set into the medium- and long-term decision context that most young people will continue to consider – how far does what I am doing today, tomorrow and next week continue to match my perceptions of my desired lifestyle now and in the future? Just as we now recognise that the beginnings of choice processes are hard to define, so it may also be the case that they have no formal ending, but merely continue at varying levels of priority in a young person's life.

Second, choices about education and training may not be the primary focus of a young person's concern. For many young people their life experience is constructed from their lifestyle, with its component elements of friendships, social life, social activities and part-time jobs, as well as an education/training life. The former occupies a much greater time proportion of their lives than the latter, and may assume greater importance amongst what Wyn and Dwyer (1999) have termed 'multiple commitments'. The decision to participate or to drop out of education may be a secondary consequence, almost a by-product, of a range of other life experiences and events. Hodkinson and Bloomer (1999) show how the conflicts between lifestyle choices outside education relating to personal and social lives and the demands of education (e.g. homework, projects, attentiveness in class) result in default decisions to discontinue. Similarly, events which impact adversely on an individual, such as those relating to broken relationships, make educational decisions relatively insignificant at the time for a young person. In such cases it is important to recognise that the decision to discontinue may lie largely outside the scope of the school or college to address.

Third, a decision to enter or drop out of a pathway may be part of a process of fairly frequent changes of personal direction. Hodkinson and Bloomer (1999, p.14) describe how young people

> reacted to pressures, be they college based or located elsewhere, by eventually backing off and escaping into another life. This pattern was repeated in their subsequent careers (… and was) followed by a cycle of frequently changing low skilled jobs and/or training programmes. (…) This pattern becomes a routine for the person concerned as it becomes their first, intuitive reaction to some of the problems that can beset either studying or working life. A part of this routinised transformation is the move from one career type to something completely different.

This suggests that decisions at any stage of the choice process may be short-lived, inherently lacking permanence, and simply waiting for a changing priority to emerge and displace them with a subsequent choice.

Fourth, Hodkinson and Bloomer (1999) have developed the concept of a 'learning career', which emphasises the evolution of young people's attitudes and disposition towards learning. The value and importance they attribute to education or training changes in response to influences both within school/college and outside in their personal lives. Learning may fluctuate between possessing high and low value over relatively short periods of time. Where a period of low value coincides with other pressures or the emergence of other opportunities then 'dropping out' or changing direction becomes easier.

Fifth, decisions to enter particular pathways are for many young people not the product of positive choice but a response to failure. Choices are made in the aftermath of a failure to achieve some other learning career ambition as they fail to meet entry requirements for the pathway of their choice. As Hodkinson and Bloomer (1999, p.15) suggest:

> In some cases ... students were not qualified for the courses they really wanted. Such students then start off with a twin or even a triple handicap. They have had their self-confidence dented by relative examination failure, they may resent being on a course they did not originally choose and, in some cases, they may be bringing poor studying habits and/or other problems that contributed to the disappointing results in the first place.

With such baggage at the outset of courses it may indeed be surprising that so few drop out.

This importance of failure in the choice process may relate both to actual failure and to self-selection by young people in which they exclude themselves from particular choice options by assuming they cannot meet the entry requirements. Cockett and Callaghan (1996), for example, suggest that a young person's final choice may be based on a deficit model of their own self-perception, i.e. it emerges from considering what is left in the range of choices after they have excluded those directions that their perceived 'inabilities' will not allow them to follow. Traditional careers guidance has emphasised the identification of areas of skill and knowledge to underpin career choice, but Cockett and Callaghan suggest that this may have established a culture amongst many young people of seeking to identify their own deficiencies. This idea of negative achievement underpinning career choice is one that needs to be investigated much further.

Finally, the research suggests that in understanding choice we must not underplay the importance of simply 'changing your mind' as an inherent part of the process. All decisions are provisional choices, for they involve choosing to embark on a particular pathway without having experienced the educational and training provision within that pathway and the lifestyle and personal implications that this brings. Pre-choice information is limited, largely second-hand, and imbued with the values and objectives of those providing it. Real 'lived choices' may be very different from a young person's perception of what that life will be like. Young people are at the same time experiencing very substantial personal, social and economic change as they move from adolescence into the role of 'young adult'. Set against all of these processes the emergence of contradictions, dissatisfactions, and reappraisals is not only unsurprising but may be seen as a positive dimension of the young person's development as an independent adult. The opportunity to 'change your mind' may, indeed, be a positive rather than negative outcome for the system as well as for the individual, for the generation of unhappiness and discord as a result of having 'square pegs in round holes' is destructive of the students, their parents and friends, and the educational professionals involved, as well as wasteful of resources. Although set in the context of HE, Hodkinson and Bloomer (1999, p. 13) illustrate this idea through the case of Charlotte who dropped out of university:

> The day after I left the course I think I felt relief and calm. I didn't get upset and stressed, I was just glad it was over. (...) I always thought when I was younger that I wanted to be in a high earning job, earning loads of money and wanted only the best. I wanted to be a career woman but things have changed now ... I've got myself a boyfriend and I'm settling down and I want to be getting a house and I want to marry in the future and I want to have children.

This would appear to be an entirely positive experience for the young person concerned. Unfortunately the education/training system is not designed to facilitate or reward failure as a positive experience. The existence of internal markets within institutions and the structuring of funding models to reward course completion mean that counselling and advice is not necessarily available in recognition that leaving a programme or changing your mind may be the right decision. Furthermore, as further education and higher education expand to provide for higher proportions of the age cohort, the social pressure to conform by entering or staying within FE may be substantial. In this way the process of considering dropping out may become yet another of the tensions and internalised conflicts that young people have to try to resolve for themselves. This may result, on occasion, in young people persisting when changing might have been a better alternative for them.

In examining the 'choice' processes of young people, the social context of their relationships with peers, family and teachers provides an important area for analysis. Just as this is a period in which they are seeking to identify their own individual *persona* in the transition from childhood via adolescence to youth to the status of young adult, so their decisions will reflect in part an attempt to establish or protect their position within these relationship groups. Hemsley-Brown (1999a) has described a 'model' that emerges from a longitudinal study of young people's post-16 choice process which incorporates the importance of self-image and group identity, and the use of psychological protection mechanisms to sustain them. Two important 'stages' are identified, although they are differentiated by their operation rather than by any exclusive temporal characteristics.

The *preliminary search stage* is dominated by parental and, particularly, peer group pressures, and brings together the young person's pre-conceptions of careers, pathways and institutions with the pursuit of a choice that will secure social approval in terms of maintaining self-esteem and peer group acceptance. In particular, it focuses on non-utilitarian factors. The protection of self-image and acceptance within the social peer group is an important element of the psychology of 15 and 16 year olds engaged in the choice process. The importance of choosing institutions and programmes which attract 'people like me' or 'people like I aspire to be' emerges as a strong theme within accounts of choice. Matching choices, too, to the choices of friends and peers protects the group identity and bolsters self-esteem. Hemsley-Brown (1999a, p. 89) shows, for example, how one working-class pupil in her study (Wayne) eschews the academic sixth-form college for the FE college where he feels the social class mix would enable him to fit in better. He comments that:

> From what I've been told I wouldn't go to the sixth form college. Well, it's the pupils who are in it. Well the people at the FE college are not like sixth form college students – there's a different group.(...) It stops me going there. I know people from the FE college and they're like what I'm like.

To protect self-esteem and peer group acceptance Hemsley-Brown suggests that young people use a range of psychological protection mechanisms in relation to their choice and its announcement. This involves bolstering the positive dimensions of choices they have made through distortion of the evidence, selective inclusion of evidence in announcing choice, and exaggeration of the positive reasons for choice. This process is described as 'self-appeasement' and Hemsley-Brown suggests that:

> This phenomenon is effectively retrospective or '*post-hoc* justification' of a choice resulting from a complex decision-making process, and may involve a degree of self-deception to achieve self appeasement.
>
> (Hemsley-Brown, 1999a, p. 92)

The second stage is the *refined search stage*, and is the period of active evidence collection through visiting colleges, attending careers sessions and reading promotional material such as prospectuses. Not all young people enter this stage, however, particularly those who have already chosen to leave school at 16 and enter employment without training and those who have committed themselves to stay in their school post-16. It is at this stage that young people actively consider academic versus vocational pathways and alternative institutional and programme options. The final choices and their justification, though, emphasise the sub-rational nature of the choice process. Hemsley-Brown (1999a) shows that important factors may not be considered until after the choice has been made, or the evidence quoted to justify the choice may be factually incorrect. Two students choosing film/media studies, for example, in post-choice interviews showed they had given no consideration to the quality of facilities in alternative colleges – and students justifying their choice of college as the one offering the best examination results were, in fact, incorrect in their assertions.

In summary

Choice at 16+ is not a simple process of weighing up alternatives and making a straightforward choice to follow a particular education/ training pathway. While at a macro-scale we can identify the most important factors which shape the broad patterns of choice, at the micro-scale of the individual it is clear that choice is a battleground in which the conflicts between developing self-esteem, the pursuit of domestic, social and cultural needs, and a rough and ready self-assessment of medium-term and long-term cost-benefit analysis create challenges and dissonance for young people. Despite the explicit recognition by many young people that they have choices it is perhaps unsurprising that many simply adopt the line of least resistance in those choices – staying on at school, or following the pathway that is the 'norm' for their peers and friends fro. socio-economic backgrounds. In this way replication of trao. patterns of post-16 'choice' are inevitable. In the next chapter shall consider this process in relation to young people's choices of training pathways at 16.

6 Choosing training pathways at 16+

Training choices and modern apprenticeships

Most of the research into choice at 16 in the UK has focused on progression into full-time, usually academic, pathways. The examination of choice of vocational and training routes has been less well developed, although a number of useful studies have emerged. Hodkinson and Sparkes (1994), for example, have focused on the decisions involved in the take up of training programmes, while Maguire, Macrae and Ball (2000) have looked at the process of choice in the wider context of the broad urban market place of London. Hemsley-Brown and Foskett (1999, 2000) have examined choice in relation to the take up of training programmes such as modern apprenticeships in two contrasting localities – Wiltshire, where the contrasts in economic character between the high-growth towns of the 'M4 corridor' and rural Wiltshire provide insights into sometimes contradictory choice processes; and inner London, where vocational training choice is made within a strongly multi-cultural, but working-class, community. In this chapter we shall examine choice in relation to vocational training, with a particular focus on choosing modern apprenticeships, to draw out some of the key aspects of training choice that distinguish it from academic pathway choice.

Modern apprenticeships (MAs) were introduced in England in September 1995, through a scheme financed and managed largely by the regionally based Training and Enterprise Councils (TECs). The development of modern apprenticeships since their inception in prototype form in 1994 has seen the numbers of young people engaged in them rise to almost 100,000 per annum nationally, with programmes in nearly 70 industry sectors available (Crequer, 1997). While the national picture is one of strong take up, however, substantial local variations may be identified, and their success across employment sectors is highly variable.

The success of MAs relies on support and enthusiasm on both the supply and demand sides – from employers, and from young people themselves. Houtkoop and Van der Kamp (1992) suggest that whilst vocational training is viewed as a way of raising the economic level of a nation it also has a significant impact on the relationship between labour supply and demand. There has been much interest in the possible rate of return for employers, as well as for individual employees, through participation in vocational education and training. On the labour demand side, 'employer involvement is vital to their success – but employers must come forward with places' (*Newscheck*, 1994, p. 4). On the labour supply side the success of MA relies on young people coming forward to take up places on the scheme, and government policy has been proactive in this direction in recognition of the fact that

> High quality careers guidance will be of strategic importance to the success of Modern Apprenticeship by allowing young people to make more informed choices.
>
> (*Newscheck*, 1994, p. 4)

Such guidance will always operate in the context of historical perceptions of vocational training programmes, though. In research into the aspirations of young people in 1992, prior to the introduction of MAs, Unwin (1992) found that there were two criteria used by young people to judge whether a job was worth taking when they left school:

1   that the job should be with an employer who would take you under his/her wing and teach you all you needed to know; and
2   that the job should give you the chance to get a qualification which an employer would recognise.

These features are the well-known characteristics of a classic apprenticeship model. Traditionally, the apprenticeship system remained in the control of employers and the trade unions and it could, therefore, be said to be an 'employer-led' system (Unwin, 1996). Gordon (1995, p. 278) further points out, however, that 'traditional apprenticeships tended to train craft workers in skills which they would *need* and *keep* throughout their lives' [emphasis added]. A modern workforce, however, faced with an ever changing work environment needs flexible, transferable skills such as communication, application of number, information technology and problem-solving (Gray and Morgan, 1998), a perspective well presented in the MA programme in the view from government that

> Modern Apprenticeships are designed to enable more young people to achieve higher level vocational qualifications and skills. They represent a fundamental long term reform of the country's training structures and an important step in improving Britain's future competitiveness, through a better skilled workforce.
>
> (Blunkett, 1998a, p. 1)

With flexibility and responsiveness seen as an important component of MAs it might be argued that their success may vary depending on the nature of the skills required for the particular occupational field, supply and demand in the labour market, retention and turnover, and the pace of change in the industry concerned. Each modern apprenticeship will be different, therefore, responding to the needs of its sector, but all have a number of common characteristics:

1   Employers select young people they believe can achieve NVQ Level 3 or beyond (regarded as the equivalent standard of achievement at A-level);
2   There is a formal pledge between young people and employer setting out each party's rights, obligations, and commitment to see the training through, all underwritten by the TEC;
3   The apprentice receives training up to NVQ Level 3, covering the core skills that the sector sees as essential as well as a broad grounding for his/her future career;
4   Training Organisations (TOs), either local or national, design the apprenticeships together with TECs, and delivery is arranged by the TECs under contract to the Department for Education and Employment (DfEE).

Against this background, though, how do young people make choices in relation to such training pathways? The expansion of vocational training through market mechanisms has placed the choices by individual young people at the heart of the system. Policy and financial support may provide incentives for young people (and training providers) to follow particular pathways, including modern apprenticeships, yet it is clear that young people's own perceptions of the nature and 'market value' of each option open to them will influence both their choice and their willingness to see programmes through to completion.

Choosing modern apprenticeships – the Wiltshire and Inner London studies

Our research into choices in relation to MAs involved two separate but linked projects, one based in the county of Wiltshire, characterised by substantial contrasts between a rural, agricultural economy and large urban areas experiencing rapid economic growth (e.g. Swindon), and one based in Inner London. The primary aim of both was to describe and analyse perceptions among young people of the nature, purpose and value of modern apprenticeships, and to explore the influence of these perceptions on choice. The research sought to provide a generic view of attitudes to MAs, but also focused on issues of particular relevance in each of the localities. In Wiltshire the research focused in depth on perceptions of MAs in two specific employment fields: an employment field with a tradition of training (engineering) and a field where training is a less well-established tradition (information technology). The aim was to explore contrasts in attitudes to MAs in different fields. In London the focus was on the relationship between attitudes to MAs and the socio-cultural background and experiences of the young people.

The research methodology in the Wiltshire project was qualitative in nature, working with young people, training providers, and employers in three localities (Swindon, Trowbridge and Salisbury), using focus groups/group interviews and face-to-face interviews to gather in-depth data. In each locality one secondary school was used for focus groups with Year 11 pupils, using a sample comprising five boys and five girls in each school. Across the localities in the study, six training providers were identified – two Further Education Colleges, and two private training providers operating in each of the chosen employment fields (engineering and IT). In each organisation a focus group was undertaken with eight young people following an MA programme. The focus groups operated in the same way as for the school-based young people. Trainees in IT were interviewed individually in a face-to-face situation because there were so few trainees. A telephone interview was also undertaken with a sample of five 'early leavers' from each of the employment fields identified from across the three localities. As part of the school-based data collection with pupils, the senior careers guidance professional in the school was interviewed, and four careers guidance professionals were interviewed altogether, two from the local careers service, and two careers coordinators in schools. In each of the training organisations, the senior member of staff with responsibility for managing the modern apprenticeship programme was interviewed, and from across the three localities a senior member of staff with responsibility for recruitment and training was interviewed in two large employers and two small employers in each sector.

The research methodology in the Inner London study was both quantitative and qualitative in nature and involved telephone interviews with careers coordinators and a postal survey of a sample of Year 11 pupils attending 25 Central London maintained secondary schools. A minimum of one school was selected in each of nine London boroughs, and the schools chosen included girls', boys' and mixed schools. In contrast to the schools in the Wiltshire study almost all schools identified were those with lower GCSE pass rates (below 30% A*–C GCSE, in 1998). Seventy per cent of questionnaires were returned to the research team, resulting in a sample of 1,413 young people, from 22 schools.

The research shows clearly how the interaction of the perceptions of young people, those of potential employers, and the attitudes of schools and training providers delimits the decision-making in this market place. In turn these interactions are shaped by the socio-cultural background of the young people, and by the significant contrasts between perceptions of modern apprenticeships in different occupational fields. A number of key ideas emerge from the research which will be explored below. These relate to:

- the limited knowledge of training pathways such as MAs amongst young people;
- young people's (and their advisers'!) perceptions of training as a lower status choice than an academic pathway;
- the significance of school background in training choice;
- the role of careers education and guidance in training choices;
- the contrasts between MAs in different occupational fields.

Young people's limited knowledge of MAs

Both studies showed only limited knowledge and understanding amongst young people of the nature of training programmes in general and MAs in particular. In Wiltshire only 35% of the young people in the focus groups had any substantive knowledge of MAs, and those who had decided to remain in full-time education had little knowledge of the MA route, or any vocational training route, regardless of their anticipated level of achievement at GCSE. One Year 11 girl, for example, predicted by her teachers to gain GCSE grades that would place her in the prime target group for MAs (3–5 good grade GCSEs), demonstrated this perspective about MAs:

> I don't know much about it. I'd rather go to college anyway. Better to go in the sixth form. Can't get a job for what I want to do. If you want to be a vet you have to go to university.

In London, three sub-groups within the whole sample were identified in relation to their knowledge of, or intention to participate in, MAs – 41% (581) of young people had heard of the MA, yet only 12% (165) said that they were interested in doing an MA, and only 2.9% (41) had already chosen an MA route. Amongst these groups a number of gender, ethnicity and social class patterns emerged. First, girls were almost twice as likely as boys to have heard of MAs, yet the ratio of boys to girls interested in pursuing MAs was 54:45, and amongst those who had chosen an MA was 61:32. Second, interest in and choice of MAs was stronger amongst white ethnic groups than amongst Asian and Black groups, with 32% of white students, but only 19% of Asian students and 21% of Black students expressing an interest in participating in MAs. No Asians chose MAs as a pathway to follow. Third, choosing MA emerges as an option for those from lower socio-economic groups, for while there are no significant differences between socio-economic groups in terms of who had heard of MAs, those interested in taking an MA were very substantially from families where parents had lower academic qualifications and lower status employment. The traditional view of training through apprenticeship as a pathway for white, working-class young men appears, therefore, to be replicated in the uptake of and interest in modern apprenticeships.

This analysis suggests that knowledge of and understanding about MAs may be a major constraint on their uptake as an option at 16+ for young people. The Inner London study explored this issue by identifying where young people had gained information about MA, and what the dominant images and perceptions were that emerged from the information they had received. Most young people who had *heard of* modern apprenticeship had gained their information from the school careers adviser, while more than a third of those who had *chosen* MA had heard about the MA from a careers service careers adviser. Nearly a quarter of those who had chosen MA had gained information through an employer. MA is clearly not a pathway at 16+ that young people are learning about from sources such as the media, parents or the community, therefore, and this may limit the extent of awareness of the programme amongst 15 and 16 year olds.

To identify the perceptions of training through modern apprenticeship, those young people who had heard of MAs were asked to indicate what the modern apprenticeship involves. Almost two thirds of those who had heard of MA knew that it was a paid job with training, and over half believed that the MA concentrates on skills related to a specific job. There were no significant differences in the perceptions of MA held by those who had heard of MA and by those who were interested in pursuing MA. Only a very small percentage of students (17%) believed that the MA would contribute towards the development of skills for a wide range of jobs. This suggests a broadly accurate perception of the nature of modern apprenticeship amongst those who had heard of it, and indicates that choices to follow or reject this pathway are based on an understanding of this form of vocational training. Despite this, though, only a small proportion of those who know the nature of MA were opting for this pathway.

When asked why they were not considering an MA the most common reasons given by young people were that they perceived that the qualification was not high enough for their career needs, or that the career they had chosen did not have an MA route. However, many other factors emerged from the students' questionnaire responses as important in dissuading them from MAs. These included:

1 They had decided to continue at college and were not interested in finding employment at 16.
2 They were only interested in doing an A-level course.
3 They did not know what they wanted to do, and, therefore, could not choose a vocational route which was highly specific in its training.
4 They believed that a vocational route was too narrow and that they should keep their options open at 16.
5 The job training route was not 'their thing' and they did not want to do the kinds of jobs available through this route.
6 They were hoping, ultimately, to study for a degree at university.

7 They did not believe an MA would help them to get the job they wanted, and MA was not available for their career choice.
8 Their parents would not support the idea of doing an MA.
9 They valued 'traditional', established qualifications, which meant following an academic route rather than a vocational route.
10 They did not know anything about MA and, therefore, could not choose it.
11 The MA route took too long to gain qualifications, which they could obtain more quickly by going to college on a full-time programme.
12 The qualifications have little market value in comparison with academic qualifications.

The theme of conservatism in choice emerges very strongly from these findings, for many of the perspectives derive from a valuing of traditional academic pathways and a concern about the medium- and long-term market value of vocational qualifications, particularly in a new format. This relates to the young people's own perspective, that of their peers, and the views of their parents. For a pathway to have real market value for choice it must have an established credibility with each of these constituencies. This reinforces the idea explored in Chapter 5 that choosing at 16+ is constrained and shaped by the socio-cultural environment within which choice is taking place, one element of which is an inherited historical view of the nature of choices available. The link between this issue and differentials in aspirations and expectations will be explored below.

High aspiration and the perception of training as a second tier choice

Both the Wiltshire and Inner London studies demonstrate high levels of aspiration and expectations amongst young people as they approach the end of compulsory education. In Wiltshire, prior to taking GCSEs, the majority of young people expressed the expectation that they would ultimately enter high-status professions requiring high academic qualifications (3–4 'good' grade A-levels followed by a university degree), even where teachers and career advisers had tried to lower their aspirations to match their GCSE predictions. As a result these young people were most unwilling to discuss vocational routes and training options. Those who expressed the wish to take an employment with training route, were usually those with the lowest qualification aspirations, or were choosing modern apprenticeship as a result of a negative decision (i.e. not to stay at school) and a decision to earn money while training. That MA offered young people the chance of securing a 'real job' at 16 was a key attraction for such young people:

> [I want to] earn money while I'm training. [I] want to leave school. It's what I want to do – money, independence, and I want to work with computers. Want to do MA – because there's a guaranteed job at the end of it.
>
> (Year 11 boy)

In London a very similar pattern emerged from the research. When asked to predict the number of GCSEs they expected to gain at Grade C or higher, young people's expectations for their examination results appear in many cases to be unrealistically high in comparison with statistics for the pass rates at each school (5+ A*–C grades in 1998). On average, 69.6% of the sample expected to gain 5+ GCSEs (Grades A*–C) but performance statistics for the schools involved in the survey suggest that this is unrealistic, for the average GCSE performance across all schools was 27% (5+ A*–C grades). For example, at Harriet Chatfield School, in a North London borough, in 1998 17% of Year 11 gained 5+ GCSEs at Grades A*–C, but 95% of the survey sample of students from this school expressed the expectation of gaining 5 or more A*–C GCSE passes. While no significant differences emerged in relation to gender, differences did exist between ethnic groups in terms of their GCSE expectations. Asian students had the highest expectations, for 77.5% expected to gain 5+ high-grade GCSEs. White students were far less optimistic and only 60% expected to gain 5+ good GCSE grades. The figures for Black students and for 'other ethnic groups' were 71.7% and 64.5% respectively.

The reasons for the optimistic expectations were explored in interviews with careers advisers in the schools, and a number of possible explanations can be considered. First, the desire to promote self-esteem, identified in Chapter 5, may cause young people to suggest a more optimistic outcome for their GCSEs than they really expect to achieve, particularly through the mechanism of an anonymous questionnaire. Second, the bolstering of confidence is a key strategy employed by schools in preparing their pupils for public examinations. Third, raising aspirations amongst their pupils is an explicit aim of many of the schools in the study, and the perspective expressed by young people may reflect the achievement of those aims. This aim is in part a result of aspirations for the young people by the school, but also reflects the use of GCSE and progression data as important performance indicators for schools. Teachers and careers advisers may be under some internal political pressure to promote aspirations to high GCSE performance and progression to academic programmes post-16 for the long-term financial and market profile benefits of the school, perhaps even at the expense of individual pupil needs. In reality, a mix of these explanations may account for the optimistic expectations young people hold. A number of important issues in relation to training choice emerge from this issue, though.

High expectations of GCSE results promote high aspirations in terms of post-16 pathway. The high proportion (70%) of young people expecting to gain 5+ good GCSEs hope to match the entry qualifications for embarking on an A-level programme at most of the local post-16 colleges, and 75% of young people in the study intended to proceed to college to follow a full-time programme in A-levels or GNVQ. The most popular single option route at 16+ was to study for A-levels (47.3% of the sample). The majority of young people were hoping to take a degree in the future (41%) and 24% were continuing even though they were unsure what course they might eventually pursue. The percentage of young people who were not interested in studying was very low (2.8%) and only 8% were intending to take a vocational training route, rather than full-time education. The findings relating to those who were *interested* in MA shows that even amongst this group one third of the students were expecting to take an A-level course, and a third were hoping to take a degree in the future. MA was clearly an option of second choice. An important issue arises from this pattern of high expectation and aspiration, however, for the consequence of the mismatch between GCSE expectations and the reality of likely performance levels will be that most young people will need to pursue a much lower preference choice of pathway post-16. Dissonance, dissatisfaction and dismay may be the outcome for many as a result of this mismatch.

Entwined with this issue are the implications for training pathway choices, including modern apprenticeships, for these will be perceived as the choice of those with low expectations and aspirations when choices are made pre-GCSE, and the second (or lower) tier choice of those who opt for MAs after GCSE results are known. The Inner London study examined the expected GCSE results of young people who had expressed an *interest* in MAs. Their expected GCSE performance was lower than the average for the age group, in that just over half (53%) expected to gain 5+ good GCSEs. The analysis also examined the GCSE expectations of young people who had *chosen* MA. They were much less optimistic compared with the sample as a whole, for only 21.6% of this group expected to gain 5+ A*–C grades at GCSE. Those aspiring to MAs clearly have lower expectations of their GCSE results than other young people, although this may reflect that they are the young people who can make a more realistic assessment of their likely achievements rather than those with a less optimistic view of the world. Teachers suggested in interview that it is students who are expecting to perform poorly at GCSE who are more likely to be interested in vocational training routes and to be persuaded to consider a vocational alternative to full-time college courses. The political imperative of achieving appropriate institutional performance indicators, however, may mean that only those with almost no chance of approaching 5 good grade GCSEs are engaged with such discussions by careers teachers.

A third implication of high aspiration and expectation relates to career choice. Optimistic views of career pathways mean that many young people aspire to careers where modern apprenticeship or other forms of training would be inappropriate, but where academic pathways are essential entry routes. In contrast, those who had *chosen* MA were more likely to have chosen a career in 'fashion and beauty', 'sport and leisure' or 'maintenance/manual' work than the survey sample as a whole. The 41 students who had chosen MA listed target occupations such as hairdresser or beautician, footballer, or carpenter, or a job in the building trade such as plasterer. These aspirations show a number of interesting gender and ethnicity patterns. Analysis by gender and ethnicity shows that it is male Asian students who are most interested in careers in finance, IT and engineering and both male and female young Asians were interested in law and medicine. Among Black students, it was females who were most interested in becoming a doctor, a lawyer, or going into business, and males who were interested in sport, engineering, finance and IT. There were almost equal numbers of male and female Black students interested in a career in art and design, but more girls were interested in the performing arts. Among White young people, girls were more interested in pursuing teaching, law, or fashion and beauty, and boys were more interested in sport, finance and IT. There were almost equal numbers of White boys and girls choosing all the arts careers, in Art and Design, TV/film/theatre and the media.

In summary, it is clear that young people were rather over-

optimistic about their expected performance at GCSE, when compared with the expected pass rates for the school they were attending. Young people's resultant high expectations for themselves
contribute to their decision-making about post-16 options, and to
their hopes for a future career, which were also ambitious. Unfortunately, a significant consequence of such optimism is that many
young people will enter modern apprenticeship either as a low aspiration pathway or as a second (or lower) choice.

The significance of school background in MA choice

Analysis of knowledge about and take up of MAs both in Inner
London and in Wiltshire suggests that the school a pupil attends is
an important influence on their choice of, and interest in, modern
apprenticeship. This is not a straightforward link for in the Inner
London study as the percentage of young people in a school who
know about MA rises, the percentage of young people showing an
interest in MA does not necessarily increase. Indeed, in some schools
a high level of knowledge resulted in low interest, for example in
girls' schools and in schools with high achievement levels at GCSE.
The schools with the highest percentage of students with knowledge
of MA have some of the lowest interest in pursuing the route. Three
factors seem to have an influence on the pattern identified – the
nature of the school in relation to gender and ethnicity, the academic achievement levels of the school, and the character and
organisation of CEG.

In relation to gender there is some *prima facie* indication that it is
boys' schools in which uptake of MAs is greatest, for schools where
there was more interest in MA were all boys' schools. In the seven co-
educational schools surveyed, no regular pattern emerged in relation to interest in MAs. In four schools there were more boys
interested than girls, in two schools there was an even division of
interest, and in one school there were more girls interested than
boys. However, it is the girls' schools which showed most knowledge
of MAs amongst their pupils despite the low uptake of MA programmes. This suggests that the pattern is more a function of gender
patterns of interest, knowledge and uptake than in the gender status
of the schools concerned.

An analysis of the data on ethnicity and on school performance at
GCSE suggests a similar finding. While significant differences exist
between schools, the differences can be accounted for in terms of
the choice patterns of different ethnic groups, and also in the

uptake of MAs amongst higher achieving pupils. The principal difference between the schools appears to be accounted for mainly in differences in approaches to careers education and guidance. This will be explored below.

The role of careers education and guidance

The nature, organisation and quality of careers education and guidance provided varies from school to school. Interview data reveals that the three schools with the highest percentage of young people who had heard of MAs were schools with careers teachers in senior roles within the school, as Deputy Head or Curriculum Manager, and where the careers input was taught entirely by a small specialist team of teachers. The schools with the lowest level of knowledge were schools with an ethos of non-specialist tutoring, where personal tutors carry out all the careers work, with no specialist input, or where the careers service input had been significantly reduced. There is some support, therefore, for the possibility that input from careers specialists, rather than from non-specialist form tutors, increases knowledge of MA, although this factor may have less impact on choice and interest in MA. The main differences in CEG between the schools in the two studies which link most strongly to patterns of knowledge and uptake of MAs are:

1   the careers teaching arrangements;
2   the work experience arrangements;
3   the experience of the careers coordinator;
4   the personal knowledge of the careers coordinator;
5   the networking capabilities of the careers coordinator;
6   the educational philosophy of the careers coordinator;
7   the ethos of the school.

Contrasts between schools in relation to these factors can be illustrated with reference to two schools in Inner London, Powys School and Clwyd School. Clwyd is an 11–18 boys' school with a 31.8% Asian population, which had low levels of interest in and uptake of MAs. In contrast Powys School, an 11–16 mixed comprehensive school with 10% Asian pupils and 25% Black pupils, had 20% of its pupils who had expressed an interest in MAs, with 6% already committed to an MA programme. Although schools vary in terms of how careers education is delivered and some schools rely on a few specialists, both Powys and Clwyd rely on non-specialist tutors to deliver the programme, within a PSHE (Personal, Social and Health Education) programme. The programmes are blocked (a number of weeks are allocated) so that approximately one hour a week is spent on careers education, with larger blocks of time during Years 10 and 11. The work experience programmes vary among schools, with some schools relying on the LEA to provide work placements, and other schools arranging all their own work placements. Most schools relied on a mixture of both systems, and both Powys and Clwyd relied on this system of work placements. Both careers coordinators were anxious to improve links and both said that they needed more information in this respect.

There were, however, significant differences between the two careers coordinators in terms of their experience and knowledge of careers generally and MAs in particular. The careers coordinator at Clwyd had been appointed recently and had no formal training in careers education. She admitted that she knew nothing about vocational routes and was only just gaining information about GNVQs. Her knowledge was limited to the academic routes through full-time college A-level programmes. The careers coordinator at Clwyd also had very little personal power, as a newly appointed coordinator. She was not in a senior role in the school, and yet had complete responsibility for careers education, through the tutorial system. The careers coordinator at Powys, however, had been in post for a number of years and was very experienced and knowledgeable. He was able to access any information he needed through a range of sources he had built up over a long period. If a young person wanted to pursue an MA in a particular field he was able to turn to a range of sources for the information and had shown considerable ingenuity and determination in this respect. However, both coordinators complained that they were not given sufficient information about MA early enough, and this influenced the number of people who could be introduced to the MA route. The coordinator from Powys explained that the information about specific opportunities was too vague and too late and the information they received was about MA generally rather than particular opportunities.

The coordinator from Clwyd had not had any opportunity to gain much needed training in careers education before taking on the role. The reaction to this lack of experience, knowledge and information was to concentrate on the route she knew well – full-time academic courses in colleges. She explained that she advised most young people to go on to the college to do a full-time course, and A-level courses were the most likely choice (even though the 5+

A*–C pass rate was only 17%). Links with colleges, however, were made exceptionally easy for all schools because the colleges were very anxious to attract students so that they could secure funding through the FEFC. Colleges begin their marketing very early and are prepared to offer a place to all students who apply, to join one programme or other, at least on a conditional basis.

Limitations in the guidance available in relation to MAs merged as an important factor in the Wiltshire study, too, where different attitudes and knowledge by careers advisers about MAs in engineering and IT impacted on the information available to young people on which to base their choice. Here there were marked contrasts in the guidance available about MAs in engineering and those in IT. Trainees claimed in interview that schools were unable to advise them about pathways into IT, and recommended full-time academic routes. Trainees on IT MA claimed that teachers in schools were totally unable to grasp the notion of a non-graduate career in IT.

> They didn't know about this sort of job at school. They didn't know about doing the training and getting a job as an analyst. They were negative about IT at school and more interested in using IT to do academic work. They said 'do what you're good at', but they didn't really do things with computers.
>
> (IT trainee, aged 20)

All IT trainees on MA programmes, without exception, were 'computer enthusiasts' with IT as a serious hobby prior to choosing a career in the field. All had experienced discouragement at school, however, when they suggested taking a job-training route in IT. They were strongly encouraged to take the A-level route, and one was told that the job training route was 'only for school-drop-outs'.

> At school they discouraged me from going to work, they said it was only for drop-outs – it was a bad move.
>
> (IT trainee, aged 20)

> I wanted to do IT at school but they didn't think I could do it. So I had to do something else. They wanted you to do IT at A-level and they said my maths wasn't good enough, so I couldn't do it. I love computer programming and I wanted to do a job in it, but they said I couldn't.
>
> (IT MA trainee, aged 20)

School careers coordinators were also aware that when advising young people, it would be in the interests of the (11–18) school to encourage young people to remain in the sixth form, and IT represents a field that is available as a traditional A-level programme.

> We have our own sixth form, so we don't want to shoot ourselves in the foot – we have IT here at A-level. We advise on an individual basis. We would like them all to come back here, but some of them want to leave.
>
> (Careers Coordinator)

A further important element in the role of CEG for young people is the importance that they place on choosing post-16 pathways that link to school subjects. Young people often make choices based on their experiences of school subjects rather than their knowledge of career areas. For example, although their experiences of both IT and Design Technology varied widely, in all cases the emphasis had been on creativity, resulting in young people wanting to be, for example, 'computer games designers' or 'car designers'. Many were also very influenced in their choices by what they perceive to be the 'typical' route into a chosen job. For each job there is a 'known' way in – e.g. for computing 'you go to university', for engineering 'you get a job in a garage', etc. Many young people believed that the most likely route into IT was through an academic pathway and A-levels. However, they associated engineering, hairdressing and retail with the vocational training route:

> ... if you're working in a shop, you can do retail Modern Apprenticeship. You do a college course as well while you're working.
>
> (Year 11 student)

In engineering young people were fully aware that they needed training, or a job with training to work in the sector. In IT, however, young people believed that there were jobs available which did not rely on on-the-job training. IT jobs relied on qualifications gained in full-time education:

> You need A-levels to do computers. You need to use computers at home.
>
> (Year 11 boy, Albury School)

The advice pattern was further handicapped by the fact that young people were very reluctant even to discuss training if they had not chosen this pathway or subject area. They were wary of volunteering information about anything they had not chosen. While the day-release system of job training was well known by those who were considering modern apprenticeship, most young people were unaware of other patterns of training, and tended to call all forms of job training 'the modern apprenticeship'. They were unaware of the difference between MA and traineeships, for example.

The educational philosophy of the careers coordinator and the ethos of the school (which in many cases are linked) also influence the careers education pupils received. The careers coordinator at Clwyd explained that she believed young people should make their own choices and that she should not try to influence them. She relied on the student indicating what s/he was interested in, and provided information accordingly. Foskett and Hemsley-Brown (1997) have described this approach to careers education as 'information on demand' and have found (Foskett and Hemsley-Brown, 1999, p. 2) that many 'teachers have a liberal child-centred view which tends to result in a reluctance to influence what is viewed as a personal choice'. The careers coordinator from Clwyd School in Inner London also believed that pupils would not listen to advice. The careers coordinator from Powys School, however, was much more prepared to intervene by offering a range of vocational options to the young people he worked with.

Schools also vary in ethos. Some schools have a more liberal approach to education generally, and to 'choice', than others, and some schools are more reluctant to help students to be 'realistic' about their career aspirations than others. The ethos of the school and the personal teaching style of the careers coordinator (and other teachers), therefore, influence the choices of pupils. In some schools, pupils who are hoping to pursue a career in medicine, for example, but are unlikely to achieve appropriate GCSE results, might continue to believe that they can become a doctor until their GCSE results are published, while in other schools such pupils may be pushed to consider alternatives at an earlier stage, when they might begin to consider other options – even if only as a second choice.

More specifically, the attitudes of careers teachers, and their schools, to the range of choices open to young people at 16+, and their implict and explicit allocation of value to those choices, will be important in influencing and shaping choice. Without exception, careers teachers assumed that a high percentage of their Year 11 students would be staying in full-time education, and would attend a college of further education, or join a sixth form, with an expectation that they would study advanced or intermediate GNVQs and A-levels. When asked about those who may not continue in full-time education, it was clear that these young people were generally viewed as those who were 'dropping out' of education. Even though teachers were aware that pursuing a modern apprenticeship would not be 'dropping out', these young people tended to be grouped together with those likely to 'drop out' or who were unambitiously looking for a low-skilled job without training.

The dominant view amongst careers advisers was that there are no jobs available for 16 year olds and 'a good job with prospects' no longer exists for young people at that stage of their careers. Therefore, all 16 year olds should be going to the next level – which means full-time college education. Some schools acknowledged that there were some bright students who want to go directly into employment, especially those who believe they can't afford to go to university. However, teachers were anxious that all young people – especially those expected to gain five or more GCSEs (A–C) – should be staying in education full time.

Such issues of emphasis and value are underlined by a conflict between the MA application system and the system of applications to colleges post-16. Teachers pointed out that information on MAs is extremely difficult to find, especially during the autumn term when young people are making choices. The young people who are eligible for MAs are also the ones who could be going on to advanced courses, and they make their decision in November, when colleges are most actively promoting their full-time courses. The choices young people make are very strongly influenced by the courses now available in local colleges, and students make these decisions very early in their Year 11. Schools discourage young people from making late decisions because of the need to concentrate on examinations from January of Year 11 onwards, and yet the modern apprenticeship literature is not available until April when many young people have made their decisions. MAs, therefore, may be second in the information race and the promotional activities of the colleges may by then have drawn young people into choosing full-time academic programmes.

School differences in support, approach and CEG appear to us, therefore, to be of considerable importance, in shaping the nature of advice given to young people about vocational pathways, which, in turn, feeds through into the choices they make. The key factors which varied when Clwyd School was compared with Powys School, were related to the experience, knowledge, and personal approach to CEG of the careers adviser, and to a lesser extent, the ethos of the school and its willingness to influence young people's choices more directly. This is confirmed by our findings from the Wiltshire study that:

> Recruitment on to MA was to some extent controlled by the 'gate-keepers', the teachers and careers coordinators in schools. Access to information is often restricted to a pre-selected group of young people.
>
> (Hemsley-Brown and Foskett, 1999, p. 64)

Contrasts between MAs in different occupational sectors

The research demonstrates clearly the problems of seeing recruitment into modern apprenticeships as simply the operation of a single market place. Each occupational field in each local market is distinct. For example, the long history of apprenticeship training in engineering significantly influences every aspect of the MA in this occupational field. Similarly, the tradition of employing mainly those with qualifications and experience in business, administration and secretarial fields has significantly influenced the implementation of the MA in the IT sector. History and tradition, and the essential skills needed in the industry, impact on the operation of the MA in each sector and affect perceptions of MA, the communication of information, links between employers and others, and the attitudes of those already working in the field. The views of training providers are highly influential on the shape of the market place. Recruitment on to an MA with a training provider, whether in Engineering or IT, relies on employers demanding trainees and providing employee-status training places, and hence on their perceptions of the types of individuals suitable for MA. Young people's experience of the recruitment process, therefore, varies depending on the occupational field. There was a difference, for example, in the age range of typical recruits in the two employment sectors in Wiltshire. Whereas engineering firms were quite used to recruiting the youngest trainees of 16 or 17 at the most, IT firms were less likely to find an appropriate candidate among the youngest applicants.

We only take one or two onto the MA. We would be looking for someone of 18 from a full-time course. By the time they reach Level 3 they have to be able to work with graduates.

(CAD company)

We were not looking for anyone of 16. We needed someone who knows about IT. They had to have a driving licence and be able to speak to customers on the telephone.

(Logistics Firm, who employ an IT trainee)

We take 16–17 year olds, no older. The ones who are older haven't usually done anything in the meantime. They are often unemployed and are not a good bet.

(Motor Retailer)

We need a 16–17 year old who has been to college for one year. They need to be bright though.

(Engineering Firm Manager)

As a result, there is a clear difference in the employee profile of the two sectors. A computer firm in Swindon admitted that they had traditionally recruited graduates with experience in the business and they had very little experience prior to 1996 of recruiting young people. In engineering it was clear that employers had always relied on the apprenticeship tradition to provide the workforce. Most employees had themselves undertaken an apprenticeship, often with the same company, at some time in the past.

Figure 6.1 illustrates these contrasts by providing a summary comparison between Engineering MAs and IT MAs.

In summary

We have examined modern apprenticeships as an example of the process of choice in relation to training and vocational pathways post-16. At a national scale their success is evidenced by the take up of MA placements, but such headline figures mask significant differences in uptake between sectors and localities and may hide important variations in completion rates. The complex range of influences on choice, and the nature of perceptions of modern apprenticeships, emphasise the complexity of understanding choice at the level of micro-markets and of individuals. The teachers interviewed in Wiltshire and Inner London were able to provide a rich picture of

Engineering	IT (Information Technology)
'Well-trodden path' – ways into engineering are well known	Still at the pioneer stage – training routes and providers are not well known and employers are new to vocational training
Employers are already in close contact with training providers	Employers are not volunteering and training providers need to be proactive
Traditionally has an apprenticeship route	Perceived to be mainly a graduate route occupation
School experience provides some experience of similar skills	School experience is patchy so far and does not provide installation or repair experience, only the use of some software programs. Relies on personal interest/IT as a hobby
Known as a route for non-academic – image is practical not intellectual	IT perceived to be for the academic – and image is an intellectual one
Training alongside colleagues is well established	Training in the workplace is new and work colleagues are unfamiliar with this role
Team working with other trainees well established	IT tends to be an individual activity and the notion of watching and learning is new and problematic
At technician level engineers are solving old problems in traditional ways	Few tasks require technicians to solve old problems. New problems are emerging all the time
Engineering relies more on the notion of 'this is how we always do things'	IT relies more on the notion of 'can you find a way to solve this new problem?'
Engineering is visible – the tasks and processes tend to be visible	Much of the work of IT is intellectual and some processes are non-visual – is therefore 'invisible'
Engineering has a tradition of taking the young and turning them into adults	IT has relied on taking adults who have proven skills and maturity
The routes into engineering are known by most people including many parents. Young people are directed towards a training provider from many different starting points	Routes into IT are emerging all the time and there is no history of job training in IT
Commitment to a long career with an employer is accepted as the 'norm'	IT is a fast-moving business and it is accepted that employees will move on quickly

Figure 6.1 Engineering and IT modern apprenticeships – a comparison.

the issues facing young people in considering MAs, which helped to explain in part why many young people were not choosing to pursue a modern apprenticeship route:

- Teachers believe that employers don't offer jobs for 16 year olds, because the kind of 16 year olds who want to go out to work have so little to offer in the workplace. There are now very few good opportunities in the workplace for someone of 16, and it is no longer possible to work your way up in a job to reach a high level. This suggests that any work opportunity offered to a 16 year old must, therefore, be a 'dead end' job.
- Teachers believed that young people now do GNVQ courses if they are interested in a vocational route, often simply because colleges talk to them in early November of Year 11 before they are given any information about MA opportunities. Contracts for training providers are not awarded until April, which may be too late to influence the choice process. Most young people are under pressure to make arrangements about their post-16 destination before March.
- Employers and training organisations involved in the MA scheme tend not to be visible at careers fairs. Training providers often change from year to year, and the lack of continuity means that teachers and careers advisers are unable to give clear advice about where students should go to secure a modern apprenticeship. Most employers involved in the scheme only take one or two MAs and so it is not appropriate to promote the scheme for such small numbers.
- There is now considerable pressure on all pupils to stay on in full-time education, and any other option is now considered to be 'dropping out'. Only those who are very assertive will make a choice different from those of their peers and insist on getting a job or a job with training. As a result teachers and careers advisers only put pressure on academically very weak students to consider vocational routes such as a job with training. However, because only the academically weak are considered suitable for a vocational route, there are unlikely to be any young people in this group who could meet the requirements for entry on to an MA.
- Training schemes of all kinds are viewed sceptically by teachers, parents and young people because of the poor reputation of Youth Training (YTS) schemes in the 1980s, where young people were not given employment status. Parents are particularly

sceptical about the value of training programmes for they perceive they have a reputation for exploiting young people.

- Modern apprenticeships are still viewed by teachers as training opportunities within traditional (gender-specific) fields, such as engineering and manufacturing or hairdressing. However, many teachers believed that there were few businesses in London or Wiltshire offering opportunities in these fields, particularly in manufacturing, although they acknowledged that 'some girls still wanted to be hairdressers'. As one London careers teacher said ...

> I think that London children think apprenticeship has something to do with factory work or greasy jobs. Parents think it's working in a garage. It's a simple view, but that is the perception. Apprenticeships equals dirty male job.

- Pressure on colleges to increase growth, especially among 16–19 year olds, has prompted them to increase their marketing and promotion to include students from a wider range of ability and social background. Students are also more aware that they could gain a place at most colleges if they chose to – it is a 'buyers'' market. The 'norm' amongst 16 year olds is now to stay on in full-time education.
- From 1999 statutory entitlement to careers guidance is only available in a one-to-one situation for those young people at risk of leaving full-time education. As a result, fewer young people are given any individual guidance, and it is assumed that they will go to one of the local colleges or stay in the sixth form.
- It is now generally accepted by young people that they will need the best qualifications they can achieve. Qualifications are assumed to be academic qualifications, or at least qualifications achieved in full-time education. Training routes are considered, therefore, to be the choice of those who are unable or unwilling to stay in full-time college education.
- Teachers feel they don't know enough about training organisations and the quality of training. In consequence they distrust them and are reluctant to recommend them. Teachers need to know that some of their own students have succeeded through this route.

This summary of careers coordinators' views of training routes and modern apprenticeship provides a rich picture of the range of explicit and subliminal messages that young people are exposed to as they consider their options at 16+ in relation to training pathways. It is also evident from the two research studies presented here that one of the most important influences on vocational pathway choice is the nature of the guidance and support provided by the careers service within and outside school. Whether or not the list of constraints described above is an accurate picture of the nature of the modern apprenticeship market place, as the views of careers coordinators it will be *de facto* the perception that young people absorb. The role of careers coordinators, and the impact of their attitudes and values, and those of the schools they work in, is an important area for further research in relation to post-16 choice.

7 Choosing higher education
Reaching for anticipated futures

The context of higher education

The expansion of higher education participation has been an important feature of the educational environment in the UK during the last decade of the twentieth century. Age participation rates of 18 year olds have increased over the decade from 15% in 1989 to 31% by the year 2000, and further expansion to the year 2005 will mean that almost one in two young people continue their education beyond 18 into undergraduate study. Foskett and Hesketh (1995) have shown that some 60% of young people consider applying to HE in the UK, and some 40% actually do so. Internationally the picture of high age participation rates in higher education is now a common feature of most advanced economies (e.g. USA 45%; Australia 35%; France 28%). The shift from an elite system of HE, available to the few, to a mass system of HE, accessed by a high proportion of young people, has been apparent in many OECD countries, premised on the presumed link between higher education participation rates and national economic performance.

To talk of higher education as if it is a single unified commodity would be highly misleading, for university level education is characterised by huge diversity, both within and between countries. Despite the shared international view of the importance of HE, the organisation and structure of HE and the funding models both for institutions and students that underpin it are highly diverse. In the United Kingdom two separate systems exist, one which is in effect common to England, Wales and Northern Ireland, with a separate system in Scotland. The traditional model in England, Wales and Northern Ireland is of entry to highly specialised, often single-subject, three-year undergraduate degrees at age 18, while in Scotland entry has normally been at age 17 into four-year undergraduate degrees starting with a broadly based programme before specialism in later years.

Contrasts in the basic system are complicated by considerable diversity of institution. Within the UK, for example, a range of HE institutions can be distinguished, which provides significant potential for differentiation in the market place:

a   The traditional research-based universities, including the ancient foundations such as Oxford and Cambridge, the civic universities established in the nineteenth and early twentieth centuries (e.g. London, Leeds and Manchester Universities) and more recent foundations which espouse the same traditions, e.g. Southampton, Warwick. Here the institutional aims are based on the centrality of research and its dissemination into teaching and consultancy.

b   The post-1992 new universities, mostly former polytechnics established during the 1960s and 1970s where the tradition is of degree level teaching with a lesser emphasis on research, and with degree programmes often more focused on direct vocational relevance, e.g. business studies degrees.

c   The Colleges of Higher Education (CHEs). Most of the CHEs are derived from monotechnic institutions, often teacher-training colleges, that have diversified their range of degree level programmes. Some remain as strongly focused colleges in terms of their range of academic programmes (for example, colleges of art and design).

Within these broad groups, though, there are also significant variations in the nature of institutions according to size, location, ethos and reputation (both generally and in relation to particular subject disciplines), and also in relation to performance indicators of, for example, graduate employment rates, completion rates, research ratings, student degree performance, etc. These differences impact upon supply and demand for places in each programme and institution which is demonstrated in the market by variations in the entry requirements imposed. Amongst the highest demand institutions and courses entry requirements of three grade A A-levels may be common place. At the lower end of the market entry is possible with very substantially lower prior achievement (e.g. two grade E A-levels). The HE market place in the UK, therefore, is highly diverse.

Higher education has two further important characteristics. First, it can be segmented by the level of programme that students study. While participation in undergraduate programmes is by far the largest element in the market place, higher degrees at Masters level and doctoral level, or in relation to professional qualifications are an important part of the course portfolio of many universities. Second, higher education is an international market place. Some 400,000 students engage in the international HE market place each year (the UK's market share is approximately 17% of this), which is an important element not just in the economies of individual institutions but also in terms of national economies in the international arena of trade. An important issue for policy-makers in higher education must be the recognition that understanding choice in international contexts is different than understanding their own national setting. It requires an understanding both of the national setting in which the choice is made and the interaction of that system with the international market.

Participation in higher education is not compulsory, of course, although economic and social pressures to participate in some countries and amongst some social groups are often very substantial. In consequence a market for HE has always existed and the patterns of participation that are observed are the outcomes of the decision-making processes of potential students. In essence potential applicants must choose a higher education 'package' in relation to a number of choice fields:

a   The nature of the course or programme in terms of its subject content and approach to teaching and learning.
b   The location of that programme in terms of the institution or organisation through which the programme is delivered.
c   The mode of participation, in terms of a choice between part-time and full-time programmes, or between distance learning or face-to-face modes of delivery.
d   Socio-economic decisions relating both to the direct costs of participating in HE (fees, travel costs, living, expenses, etc.) and the longer term economic and social benefits of a university degree.
e   Personal lifestyle decisions relating to the short-term and long-term implications of participating in HE.

Although participation rates in HE in the UK have increased substantially during the last decade, there are still a number of clear differences in participation rates across social groupings and between different universities. Data from the Higher Education Funding

Council for England for university entrance in 1995 (Major, 1997) shows that the highest participation rates are found amongst Asian students, rates which are higher than those for white students, and considerably higher than those for Black students. There are more women than men at university, and have been since the mid-1980s. While university is still strongly dominated by students entering straight from school at 18, the age group with the second highest participation rate is those aged over 60. This hides, though, a number of participation patterns linked to ethnic and social groups – students from ethnic minority backgrounds or working-class backgrounds are much more likely to be at one of the 'post-1992 new' universities and to enter as mature entrants than white or middle-class students, and the 'old' universities are still the preserve of white, middle-class 18 year olds.

It is clear that the complexity of the market place is enormous, but that understanding student choice and decision-making is important in the development of policy and practice in the arena of higher education participation. This chapter focuses on the evidence relating to choice in the largest broad segment of the HE market, admission to undergraduate programmes.

Higher education choice – the research evidence

Research into higher education choice has not been extensive, and has been stimulated principally where institutional need to understand the process has become important. In the UK the period prior to the late 1980s was characterised by a significant excess of demand over supply of HE places, so little pressure for research emerged. In the USA, in contrast, the more competitive environment which has traditionally existed has stimulated more market research by HE institutions, but it is clear that the specific nature of education markets mean that many of the findings are not directly transferable between different national settings (Barrett, 1996). This economic pressure to understand the market place, though, has now emerged in the UK and the volume of research has increased in recent years. Amongst the earlier studies was that of Roberts and Higgins (1992) which investigated the key factors in HE choice amongst undergraduates in the UK, a study replicated and extended in 1997 (Roberts and Allen, 1997) which has enabled some measure of changing patterns of choice to emerge. More recently a number of studies of choice at 16 have investigated ambition and perception in relation to higher education entry at 18 (e.g. Foskett and Hesketh, 1996a). A comprehensive study of undergraduate choice by Connor, Burton, Pearson, Pollard and Regan (1999) provides the most recent general investigation of university choice processes. Alongside these broader studies, a number of smaller research projects have investigated specific facets of HE choice. These include research on gender (Stables and Stables, 1995) and ethnicity (Modood and Shiner, 1994) in HE choice, the choice process of 'non-traditional' students (Hogarth *et al.*, 1997), the significance of family and school/college contexts in choice and aspiration (Reay, 1998b), and the role of student finance in HE choice (Callender and Kempson, 1996; Winn and Stevenson, 1997).

Modelling higher education choice

The broad parameters of HE choice models have been considered by a number of researchers. Watts (1972) sought to develop a theoretical model of the university choice process at a time of expansion of HE but when participation rates were still small. Watts acknowledged himself the limitations of the model in demonstrating the complexity of the choice process in reality, and its ideas are limited in transferability to the current context. Connor *et al.* (1999) suggest that choice is the product of the interaction of two key influences – students and their advisers on the one hand, and the education system on the other. These represent the demand and supply sides of the market place and the precise form the market takes results from their interaction. This idea of the interactions builds on the model developed by Bredo *et al.* (1993), which suggests that not only are these two elements interacting but they are themselves both subject to external social, economic and political influences. We might conceptualise the higher education choice arena, therefore, as the interaction of three dimensions (students, HE and the external environment) with each impacting on the others to create a dynamic arena for choice.

Developing aspirations for higher education

Within the United Kingdom the formal process of choice of higher education is focused through a centrally managed system (operated by UCAS, the Universities and Colleges Admissions System), and occurs during the year prior to university entry for most students. The choice process requires applicants to narrow their choices through a process of selection from the eight to which they can apply, to the two from which they can hold conditional offers in anticipation of public examination results in August. The final decision is then taken within a very small time frame in August each year when institutions decide which students they will admit and young people decide finally whether to accept an offer of a place at university.

This process of final choice must be seen as the culmination of a long but accelerating process of decision-making, the roots of which can be traced into the early years of secondary school and before. It is important to distinguish here a decision to seek entry into higher education (the general decision) from the choice of specific course and institution. The evidence for early decisions to enter higher education is strong, and is present in most of the research studies identified earlier. Connor *et al.*'s 1999 study of the higher education aspirations of 1894 students in the final year of compulsory education (i.e. one or two years prior to entering higher education) shows that at that stage of their school career 62% of pupils indicated they were 'very likely' or 'fairly likely' to go into HE to study for a degree, diploma or HND, and only 22% said they were 'unlikely' to do so.

A number of patterns can be identified within pupils' HE aspirations which suggest differences between important groups within the school population:

a   Aspirations to enter HE are higher amongst girls than boys. Connor *et al.*'s study (1999) suggests that 69% of girls compared to 56% of boys expect to enter HE. This aspiration is reflected in the HE enrolment trends from 1995 to 1999 in the UK which show a small increase of female participation but a 9% decrease in male enrolment.

b   Strong regional contrasts exist, with higher aspirations amongst Scottish children (69%) than English or Welsh children (61% and 58%) respectively. This suggests that low or high levels of expectation of participation within different socio-cultural groups may be an important influence on HE choice.

c   Significant differences exist between pupils of different ethnic backgrounds. Connor *et al.*'s study (1999) indicates higher levels of aspirations amongst ethnic minority children (71%) than white children, although this may reflect the high proportion of children of working-class families in their sample.

d   More children from higher socio-economic groups (72%) have HE aspirations than those from lower socio-economic groups (56%). This is reflected in the high proportion of HE entrants (18%) from an independent school background. (The *Guardian*, 26 May 2000)

The motivation for entering higher education falls broadly into three linked but discrete areas – the study of a subject of interest, the pursuit of a particular career, and the pursuit of improved economic gain. Connor *et al.*'s study of 15/16 year olds suggests little significant difference in the importance of these groups of factors across the population as a whole, but indicates that there is a greater focus on economic and career gains amongst boys than girls, and amongst pupils from ethnic minorities than amongst white pupils. This pattern is more strongly emphasised by research by HEFCE (Major, 1997) with university entrants in 1995 which suggests that there are clearly defined contrasts between the motivations of different socio-economic groups. Their conclusion is that:

> Students from white middle class backgrounds raised some concerns about lack of money, but regarded university as a process of 'natural progression'. But entering university for black students was much more about self-esteem, widening career opportunities and enhancing earnings.
>
> (Major, 1997, p. i)

Developing aspirations for higher education do not start for many young people in the year or so before the formal choice process begins, though. The roots of HE awareness can be found in the knowledge and ambitions of young people throughout the primary and secondary phases of education, and amongst parents the ambition for their son or daughter to enter HE is for many a basic assumption from when the child is very young. Foskett and Hesketh (1995, 1996b) undertook a study of HE knowledge and awareness amongst a sample of 247 Year 10 pupils (age 14/15) and 260 Year 8 pupils (age 12/13) in a range of secondary schools in southern England. The study was extended to Year 6 pupils (age 10/11) in the work of Hemsley-Brown and Foskett (1997), with a sample of 274 pupils in primary schools.

An important feature of the data emerging from the studies was the relatively high level of aspiration for HE entry (Figure 7.1), with little variation between the boys and the girls, but a clear decline in intention to participate across the age groups in the study. Because the studies were approximately synchronous and not a longitudinal study of a single cohort it is not clear whether this reflects steadily increasing aspirations amongst young people in the education and training system, or a decline in aspiration as children get older.

Two other important findings emerged from the three studies,

		Year 6	Year 8	Year 10
Intending to enter HE	Overall	65	61	59
	Boys	65	56	59
	Girls	65	66	59
Undecided about entering HE	Overall	31	34	29
	Boys	31	37	29
	Girls	31	31	29
No intention of entering HE	Overall	4	5	12
	Boys	4	7	12
	Girls	4	3	12

Figure 7.1 Higher education aspirations amongst Year 6, 8 and 10 children in Hampshire (figures are percentages).

which show some strong consistency across the age groups. First, there is a strong link between HE aspiration and family experience of HE. Where a parent or sibling had attended university/college the aspiration rates increased to 74% amongst Year 6 pupils and 61% amongst Year 10 pupils, with no significant change in the number of children choosing not to go into HE. Children from families with HE experience, therefore, appear to have firmer intentions of entering HE. Secondly, there appears to be a strong class-based link with aspiration for HE. Amongst the Year 10 pupils, for example, 71% of middle-class children had decided to enter HE, with only 3.7% rejecting the idea, whereas amongst children from working-class families these figures are 54% and 12% respectively. Although this contrast between socio-economic groups is clear, what is particularly significant is the high level of aspiration that still exists amongst children of working-class families. Compared to class-based participation rates in the late 1990s of 45% amongst classes ABC1 and 20% amongst social classes C2DE, this data suggests a large but untapped aspiration for HE amongst working-class young people.

The motivation for participation in HE amongst young people identified in the Hampshire pupils study is strongly driven by long-term economic and personal benefits. Figure 7.2 shows the relative importance of key motivating factors in HE choice amongst the Year 6, Year 8 and Year 10 pupils. The 'pull factors' of economic motivation are strong across the pupil groups and appear much stronger than 'push factors' such as parental pressure. The increasing importance of the choices of friends begins to emerge more strongly

Motivation for HE	Year 6	Year 8	Year 10
Better job after HE	63	83	76
Better pay after HE	45	61	52
Chosen career requires HE	62	62	47
Parents wish me to enter HE	29	33	23
Enjoy studying	*	15	10
Friends will go to HE	14	6	22
There will be no 'good' jobs at 16/18	*	31	23

* Factor not included in the study.

Figure 7.2 Motivations for applying to higher education amongst Year 6, 8 and 10 pupils (figures are percentages of sample mentioning the factor as important).

amongst Year 10 pupils, but of note is the limited importance of the intrinsic stimulation of study as a motivation to enter HE.

Sources of information about higher education

Understanding the sources of information that young people access to facilitate their choices of HE is important both for potential applicants and for institutions. From the applicant's perspective, this can enable key information channels to be used to ensure information reaches them in the right form in the right time to enhance their choice process. From the institution's point of view, the same process can ensure that their marketing and promotional strategies are enhanced in a competitive arena, and, at the very least, failure to use the right channels in the right way will disadvantage their performance in the market place.

From the work of Roberts and Higgins (1992), Roberts and Allen (1997) and Connor *et al.* (1999) it is possible to identify a number of groups of information sources that are important to potential HE applicants in the UK:

1   *Primary publication sources.* These include the UCAS handbook and the prospectuses and course booklets of individual universities. The students in Connor *et al.*'s study indicate that such publications have a high level of influence on their choice, with prospectuses being the single most influential factor in the choice process.

2   *Direct contact sources.* These include visits to universities and colleges, attendance at careers conventions and fairs, or attendance

at school visits by university representatives. Amongst the sample in Connor *et al.*'s study the importance of a visit to a university or college in terms of its influence on choice was the second most important factor after prospectuses, and was slightly more important for women than for men. Two other issues emerged as important in understanding the shaping of decision-making in relation to direct contact. First, although HE fairs and conventions are a source of ideas and information for almost 70% of applicants, their value is not seen as particularly high, especially amongst older applicants. This may reflect the limited personal contact that actually occurs at such events. Second, visits from a university representative to a school or college are more useful to older mature applicants and to Black applicants. This may in part be a result of the targeting of contact on such groups by widening participation programmes, but may also reflect the greater importance of personal contact in persuading those who may see themselves as non-standard university students to consider applying to HE.

3 *Secondary publication sources.* These include the use of interpretative publications on HE entrance, including newspaper and commercial 'guides', and published league tables of teaching or research ratings. The importance of published quality assessments shows some interesting differences between groups, in that they are

> ... used slightly more by men than women, and also more by younger than older applicants, by ethnic minorities as a whole, by higher social class groups, by applicants from independent and grammar schools and by applicants with some family experience of HE.
>
> (Connor *et al.*, 1999, p. 33)

Such a profile parallels the model of active choosers in the choice of secondary school, and suggests that vigilant choice may be most developed amongst such sectors of the community at all stages of education and training choice.

4 *ICT based sources*, including both videos and electronic communications such as CD Roms and websites. The use of such sources was recorded by Connor *et al.*'s study as more important amongst men and amongst those applying to science courses, although there was no significant difference in the use of the

Internet amongst younger and older applicants. A comparison of the Connor *et al.* study and the work of Roberts and Allen (1997) suggests a decline in the use of CD Rom and video sources in the period between the studies (1995 to 1998) but a substantial increase in the use of the Internet over that period, from almost no use in 1995 to use by 28% of students in 1998.

The importance of different information sources is subject to change as the nature of communication technology progresses. While we can identify access to information as an essential require-ment in a young person's search for an HE programme, it is not clear how important such information is in the final decision that they make. As with choice of post-16 programme, information sources may serve simply to confirm the characteristics of an institu-tion and course – persuasion to convert that interest into choice may be much more dependent on the wide range of social and cultural pressures acting upon the choice process.

Young people's knowledge of higher education

Decision-making in relation to choice at any stage of an individual's education/training pathway is a process of adding to pre-existing perceptions and knowledge with new and developing knowledge, and matching the new understandings with short- and long-term personal aspirations. Understanding the models and perceptions that young people have constructed by various stages in their lives provides both a benchmark of the developing process and a starting point for establishing knowledge deficits or errors that may be addressed by enhanced information provision (or by promotional activity). In particular it helps to answer an important research ques-tion – how do young people form and develop their personal models of higher education and their own relationship to it?

A number of studies of perceptions of higher education amongst different age groups have been undertaken. Within the ages of com-pulsory schooling, Foskett and Hesketh (1995, 1996b) and Foskett and Hemsley-Brown (1997) have examined the aspirations of young people at ages 13/14, 15/16 and 10/11 respectively towards further and higher education, and the pattern of knowledge that underpins those aspirations. Closer to the final decision-making point, Roberts and Higgins (1992) and Roberts and Allen (1997) have examined perceptions amongst Year 12 students, a group aged 16/17 who will embark on the formal choice process in the following school year.

Roberts and Allen's study of 600 Year 12 students shows that the detailed knowledge they have of the HE system is limited and may have declined in terms of detail and accuracy since the study by Roberts and Higgins in 1992, although the broad parameters of HE seem to be well understood. An interesting contrast in knowledge between genders emerges from the study in that female students had a more accurate and wider knowledge of the details of HE and the applications system than did males, and indicated that they might apply to a more diverse range of institutions and courses. Male applicants exhibited a stronger traditional view of the nature of HE and, overall, were more likely than females to:

– hold traditional views of the established university sector and the 'gold standard' of A-level qualifications as an entry qualification to higher education.

– agree or strongly agree that a first degree from an established university was more academically challenging than one at a new university or college of higher education.

– disagree or strongly disagree that a degree from a new university or college of higher education is regarded by employers as having equal value to one from an established university.

(Roberts and Allen, 1997, pp. 70–1)

Roberts and Allen attribute the decline in knowledge about the HE system to the rapid expansion, which has multiplied many times the number of available options and the amount of information available in the system for young people. They conclude that

There is too much communication, to the point where it could be defined as 'noise' ... (and) (t)here is too much choice ... perhaps beyond the threshold of comprehension and rational evaluation.

(Roberts and Allen, 1997, p. 3)

Perhaps more important, though, is the change in the numbers and the social mix of those participating in post-16 education and aspiring to higher education. The differences identified by Roberts and Allen may be no more than the inclusion in the study of a swathe of social groups not represented substantially in the 1988 study. There are, nevertheless, important implications of the levels of understanding portrayed in this study. In particular, Roberts and Allen express concern about the impact of young people's limited understanding on the ability of policy-makers and institutions to stimulate rapid change in the nature, or societal expectations, of higher education. Although young people recognise the high participation rates (indeed they overstate them, with the average response being that 48% of the age cohort will attend HE), their knowledge as portrayed in the study is highly conservative and traditional, eschewing substantially recent changes in the system. The image of higher education they portray is one of traditional academic subjects, delivered by traditional teaching strategies in well-established 'old universities'. Developments in the role of colleges of higher education, post-1992 universities and HE within FE seem largely unknown:

> Whatever the causes, young people appear to have only a superficial understanding of higher education. Knowledge facilitates choice in a market situation, and in markets where consumers are well informed new developments and change are often more readily considered, whereas in the situation we describe this is less likely as consumers revert to what is known; they play safe, relying on accepted norms and conventional wisdom.
>
> (Roberts and Allen, 1997, p. 3)

The studies of HE knowledge amongst Hampshire schoolchildren, undertaken by Foskett and Hesketh and by Hemsley-Brown and Foskett (op. cit.), shows similar patterns to those identified by the Year 12 study of Roberts and Allen. Across the age range in the research there was a clear increase in general knowledge of the nature of higher education, but this was limited to the broad principles of understanding. In contrast there was a consistent level of detailed knowledge, with some 25% of the pupils knowing the length of university courses and the types of educational qualifications (e.g. A-levels, GNVQ) necessary to enter HE – this level of knowledge appeared to change little even following careers education programmes that the Year 10 pupils had experienced.

Even in the absence of specific detailed knowledge, however, young people expressed a positive image of the higher education experience, with a clear and consistent pattern of generally very positive lifestyle perceptions emerging. Most pupils believed that they will need to work hard while at university (51% of Year 6s and 58% of Year 10s believe this to be true), but they have a strong positive perception of the independence they will have as a student and that student life will be challenging but exciting and fun. Concern about financial issues, however, increases across the age groups, with 13% of Year 6 pupils, 25% of Year 8 pupils, and 39% of Year 10 pupils believing that participating in higher education will be financially very difficult for them. Of particular significance, though, is the consistency in the shape of these perceptions irrespective of gender and social class – the lifestyle model of higher education appears to be largely independent of these key personal characteristics, and there is only a small difference in perceptions of the financial implications of HE participation between middle-class and working-class children.

Sources of influence

The importance of a number of groups of people in influencing the choice process has been recognised by much of the research on higher education choice.

The Hampshire study sought to identify the major sources from which young people had acquired this knowledge, and across the age groups five particular sources emerged as important – parents, teachers, careers teachers, siblings and television. The importance of each varies across the age range (Figure 7.3), in a pattern which appears to reflect the growing input from school-based staff about HE as the children progress through the school system. The large decline in parents as a source of knowledge may reflect their displacement by other sources, or may, of course, simply reflect the increasing unwillingness of adolescents to acknowledge the influence their parents have upon them. The importance of television in shaping their knowledge and image of HE raises significant implications in relation to career choice that will be explored in Chapter 8.

Roberts and Allen (1997) and Connor *et al.* (1999), for example, show that a wide range of groups of people are consulted by over 60% of applicants to HE – parents, friends, subject teachers and class

Source of information	Year 6	Year 8	Year 10
Parents	72	74	57
Siblings	19	32	30
Teachers	34	61	68
Careers teachers	*	4	40
Television	40	39	*

* Not included in the survey.

Figure 7.3 Percentage of children in the Hampshire schools study mentioning each source of information about HE.

teachers (by over 80% of applicants), school/ college careers advisers, HE staff and current HE students (by over 70% of applicants), and siblings. Potential applicants clearly draw on both 'formal' sources of advice (e.g. careers teachers) and informal sources (e.g. friends), and the relative importance of each of these groups varies between different segments of the applicant pool. In general, formal advisers are more important to those who represent groups relatively 'new' to the HE arena – students from vocational or access course backgrounds, applicants from lower socio-economic groups, Black applicants, and those without family experience of HE. Of significance in this analysis by Connor *et al.* is the observation that older applicants find many of the formal sources of advice are not available to them because of their pre-application education and training histories, and this may be a major impediment in initiatives to widen access to HE amongst mature applicants. Clearly those seeking entry to HE from employment rather than from school or FE college may find accessing careers service advice problematical from a practical perspective. Furthermore, such individuals may have a personal educational history of failure, associated with poor perceptions of the attitudes of the school system towards them. Under such circumstances such formal sources of support may appear unapproachable.

The role of informal advisers varies between different groups of potential applicants. The importance of parental advice is greater amongst younger applicants, female applicants and those from higher socio-economic groups or where there is parental experience of HE. Amongst different ethnic groups, Asian applicants are more likely to consult with the extended family network and not simply with parents, while Black applicants are the least likely of all groups to consult parents. Consultation with employers is not seen, overall, as being of great importance, or of particular influence where used, except in the case of applicants in the 21–24 year old age range and amongst those applying to study business studies or engineering/ technology courses. This may reflect the high vocational focus of such courses and the need for mature applicants in particular to be confident that their choices will lead to sound employment opportunities on graduation.

The importance of the influence of family and friends on choice is clear from a range of the research evidence. Connor *et al.* (1999) show that in their study of 15 and 16 year olds

. . . although there was a relatively broad social spectrum, half of the sample had a parent who had been to a university or college, one third had an older brother or sister who had done so, and only 17 per cent had neither a parent nor sibling who was a 'graduate'.

(Connor *et al.*, 1999, p. 9)

The significance of personal advocacy in relation to a general choice to enter HE is enhanced in the choice of specific institution. Caplen (2000), in a detailed case study of a single HE institution in southern England, shows that a very high proportion of new entrants had a friend, brother or sister who had previously attended the institution.

Data on the influence of advisers is, of course, open to important questions about reporting by respondents. First, influence has many components. It may be pro-active or reactive, and may provide new information or opinion. It may seek to constrain choices very substantially or simply provide very broad parameters for choice. It may be explicit or implicit, and it may be based on knowledge or ignorance. It is clear that no advice or guidance can be wholly objective and, indeed, one of the important skills that careers advisers may be able to provide to potential applicants is the ability to be appropriately critical (or even cynical) about the information and guidance that emerges from different sources. Second, *post hoc* self-reporting of influence by applicants is limited by the constraints of memory or of the ability to recognise the nature and importance of influence. What will be reported is what the individual believes was the nature of the influence, but this may or may not be a reflection of the processes that actually operated. Third, respondents are socially situated individuals responding to explicit and implicit social forces. The importance of parental influence, for example, as reported by Connor *et al.* (1999), is very large, yet may be under-reported in the sense that much of the influence on choice by parents is long term and is inherent in the values, attitudes and perspectives that the young person is subjected to over many years. The difference in parental influence reported by males and females in the study, too, may also reflect a greater tendency for young men than young women to eschew the influence of their parents on their lifestyles and choices.

Factors in HE choice

Identifying the influence of a range of factors on the specific choices made by individuals about HE has been the focus of much of the existing research in the field. Concerns about the implications of research methodologies that ask individuals to prioritise predetermined lists of factors in *post hoc* situations have been explored in depth elsewhere in this book. The importance of recognising the unique suite of influences for each individual applicant cannot be overemphasised, and the necessity to distinguish macro-scale patterns from micro-scale individual needs is clear. Against these 'health warnings', though, it is possible to identify the relative importance and influence of a number of key factors at the micro-scale on the basis of consistent patterns in the research evidence.

The primacy of subject choice in the process of HE selection is clear from all the research. Choosing a subject is the key limiting factor in an initial information search, and for the vast majority of students choosing an institution is constrained by the availability of the subject and the nature, reputation and organisation of the courses in that subject. Choice beyond this limiting factor is then defined by a wide range of influences, and it is possible to identify a number of groups of factors that appear influential:

1   factors relating to learning experiences at the institution – for example, teaching reputation and academic support facilities;
2   factors relating to entry requirements, including the competition for places;
3   anticipated lifestyle factors, including social life in the institution and in the local area, the availability of accommodation for first-year students, and safety and security;
4   output factors, including graduate employment prospects;
5   geographical factors, including distance from home and the institution's locational characteristics.

These factors are, of course, not discrete. They overlap, they reinforce or contradict each other, each may be interpreted in a negative or positive light, and between them they create an overall image or impression of the institution or course. High entry grades, for example, may create a positive image of quality and good employment prospects, but a negative image of competition and of a strong academic but poor social experience. A metropolitan location may be attractive from a social perspective but unattractive from a safety and security point of view. What is critical, therefore, is the individual's perspective on each of these factors and the balance between them.

Connor *et al.* (1999) suggest that overall the second most important factor after subject choice is the 'overall image of the university/college'. This makes little contribution to understanding the choice process, however, since it is in effect a summative term for the process itself, and gives little indication of the component factors within that image. More helpful is their identification of 'teaching reputation', 'graduate employment prospects', 'entry requirements', 'location' and 'academic support facilities', and 'social life', as factors of almost equal importance. Variations between different groups of applicants in the importance of these factors, though, is important in understanding choice within particular communities or socio-economic groups. Each of the factors is more important to some groups than others, and Connor *et al.*'s summary of the key influencing factors (after subject choice) in different social groupings is particularly helpful in describing this process (Figure 7.4).

The differences described in Figure 7.4 are essentially differences of emphasis, although it is clear that a number of generalisations can be made. What the data does demonstrate, however, is that the 'natural constituency' of an HE institution will influence the factors that are important for students and should be emphasised in promotional strategies. Similarly, changing the constituency, for example in promoting the widening of access, will require changes to the emphasis both in provision within the institution and in the marketing programme that is used. For example, the important influences on choice that need to be considered will be very different for a metropolitan, teaching-focused university drawing a high proportion of its intake from ethnic minority, working-class or mature applicant groups than for an elite, research-led Russell group university with a national profile of recruitment dominated by white, middle-class 18-year-old applicants with high level academic qualifications.

Finance and higher education choice

For the majority of entrants into higher education the decision they are taking includes active consideration of a number of financial issues for the first time. These include:

1 the decision to forego immediate income by not entering the employment market, or, for mature entrants, leaving the labour market temporarily;
2 the recognition of the direct costs of fees and maintenance and the need to ensure sufficient income to sustain these over a period of 3–6 years from gifts, loans, grants and earned income; and

Applicant group	Most important factors in choice
By gender	
Males	Overall image, social life, teaching quality, employment prospects, entry qualifications
Females	Overall image, teaching quality, employment prospects, entry qualifications, location, academic support
By age	
Young (<21 years)	Overall image, social life, teaching quality, employment prospects, entry qualifications
Young mature (21–24)	Teaching quality, academic support, employment prospects
Older mature (25+)	Attitude to mature students, teaching quality, academic support, distance from home
By prior qualifications	
Academic Qualifications	Overall image, teaching quality, employment prospects, social life, entry qualifications
Vocational/access Qualifications	Teaching quality, academic support, employment prospects
Highly qualified Entrants (21+ points)	Overall image, teaching quality, entry qualifications, social life, employment prospects, accommodation for 1st years
By ethnicity	
Black	Teaching quality, academic support, employment prospects, overall image, attitude to ethnic minorities, location, entry qualifications
Asian	Employment prospects, teaching quality, entry requirements, academic support, distance from home
By social class	
Middle/upper class	Overall image, teaching quality, employment prospects, social life, location
Working class	Employment prospects, teaching quality, overall image, academic support
Other groups	
Scottish domiciled	Employment prospects, teaching reputation, overall image, entry requirements, academic support, facilities, location

Figure 7.4 Influences on HE choice amongst different applicant groups (adapted from Connor *et al.*, 1999, p. 44).

3   an estimation of the long-term benefits of higher education over the employment lifetime of the individual.

Student finance must be considered an important factor in HE decision-making by young people at two levels – its influence on their decision to attend higher education at all, and, if they decide to enter HE, its influence on their choices in relation to course, subject, location, mode of study, etc. In the UK, student funding in HE has changed rapidly during the last decade to move a higher proportion of the financial responsibility to the individual student. This mirrors an international trend that seeks to widen participation in HE without a proportionate increase in public expenditure, and also reflects a view that it is the individual as well as the state which benefits from HE participation. Changes in the UK during the 1990s have included:

- the freezing, reduction and demise of student maintenance grants;
- the introduction of maintenance loans, repayable from income when the student crosses specific income thresholds in the labour market;
- the introduction of top-up fees for most students.

The effect of these changes has been to defer the financial burden of HE participation to young people and their parents, and to move them more strongly to the role of direct consumers in the HE market place. Debate on the future funding models for HE students continues and consideration of the charging of differential fees by universities will diversify the higher education market place. Whatever the outcome of this development, though, finance is clearly a major issue in the choice process of young people in relation to higher education.

Research into the impact of financial issues on student choice has not been extensive. Connor *et al.* (1999) examined the impact on the choice process of financial issues amongst those who had, nevertheless, decided to enter higher education. Their survey suggests a wide range of responses, and it is possible from their results to identify a number of strategies used – the figures in brackets indicate the proportion of Connor *et al.*'s sample indicating they had considered the strategy:

a   *Cost reduction strategies,* including applying to universities or colleges closer to home (50%), either to reduce travel costs or to enable a young person to live at home, or choosing an institution in a location with lower living costs (34%). A significant contrast between young and mature applicants emerges from Connor *et al.'s* data in relation to a willingness to reduce costs by living at home, for some 58% of applicants over 25 were willing to live at home, while only 29% of those under 21 were willing to take this course of action. For 18 year olds there is a strong perspective in the UK that going to university is also a process of developing the independence that comes from living away from home.

b   *Short-term earning strategies*, such as seeking part-time employment, taking a course part time rather than full time (3%), seeking sponsorship or applying for a bursary (20%), deferring entry by a year or more to earn sufficient funding to support their time at university (24%), or taking a loan. Almost all applicants indicated a willingness to undertake paid employment during the holidays, and 71% were willing to work during term time to enhance their income. While almost three quarters of students were willing to take a student loan, significant differences emerged between socio-economic groups and ethnic groups, with students from low income families and those from ethnic minority groups less likely to take out a student loan.

c   *Long-term earning strategies*, such as choosing courses or institutions with better long-term employment prospects (40%). The importance of institutional graduate employment records and of vocationally-focused programmes in post-1992 universities is recognised as a key element in expanding participation rates from lower socio-economic groups and from ethnic minority groups.

d   *Non-participation* (19%). It is clear that the financial implications may be sufficient to deter young people from participation, particularly amongst lower socio-economic groups and amongst young people from family backgrounds with no history of university entrance.

These strategies are simply those considered and there is no evidence of the strategies actually used by the potential applicants. The data also hides a number of significant differences in the importance of these strategies between groups. Amongst older mature applicants (25+) the two main strategies considered were attending an HE institution closer to home (66%) and not applying at all (39%), and 13% considered a part-time course. Amongst young applicants (under 21 years old) only 48% considered an institution closer to home, and only 17% had considered not applying at all. Contrasts between those from high-income and low-income households are also very clear from Connor *et al.*'s study, with much higher proportions of those from low-income backgrounds considering a part-time course, living closer to home or not applying at all. Overall, therefore, it is clear that for most young applicants the increased financial burden of HE is not sufficient to deter them from applying, but amongst lower socio-economic groups and mature applicants the financial implications are more likely to precipitate a decision not to apply to university or college.

Foskett and Hesketh (1996b) and Hemsley-Brown and Foskett (1998) have considered the impact of financial issues on the higher education intentions of younger people. Amongst Year 6, Year 8 and Year 10 pupils there was, not surprisingly, little detailed understanding of the financial processes underpinning participation in HE. There was, however, a clear recognition that, unlike school and 16–19 education, the responsibility for financing HE would fall upon themselves and their parents. The notion of HE as a consumer good appears to be recognised by young people from an early age.

Modelling the process

Identifying the sources of information in the choice process, though, needs to be treated with some caution without understanding the precise process by which choices are made. It is also important to distinguish the processes by which general choices are made from the final conversion decision, in which a student chooses a particular course at a specific institution. A number of distinguishable components of the choice process can be identified, which, while neither comprising discrete stages in the process nor suggesting a linear and sequential trajectory in their operation, may make different demands on a potential applicant's information needs. Each of the stages in the model outlined here may result in a decision not to participate in HE or to return to an earlier stage of the model.

1 Entering the game. The decision to consider applying to higher education, and to complete an application form, is an essential first stage. For many this may simply be an assumption that has been present from the earliest stages of their education pathway. West *et al.* (1998), for example, have shown how choice of independent primary school occurs in some cases before a child is born, and that the decision is predicated on assumptions about the need to provide a pathway for the child which leads to university and on into the professions or into a senior role in business. For others this decision to enter the game is a more pro-active step. Connor *et al.* (1999) suggest, for example, that for many mature HE applicants and for some Black students the impetus to participate in HE arises from meeting existing HE students or staff. Between these two extremes lie a full range of other situations.

Information needs at this stage will vary according to precise circumstances, but will tend to be at a general level focusing on the potential benefits (personal, social and economic) of higher education set against the risks that individuals will identify for their own circumstances. Woodrow (1998, p. 3), in a consideration of the widening access debate in relation to higher education, suggests, for example, that '… increasing participation by young people from lower socio-economic groups has become one of the last frontiers'. The gap in aspiration to HE between higher and lower socio-economic groups is well established by research, although this gap is narrowing. Increasing the numbers of young people from these groups who consider HE, or who 'stay in the game' in the later stages of the choice process, depends on understanding the fears and concerns they or their families may have. Woodrow (1998) presents a number of case studies of strategies by HE institutions and other stakeholders to raise aspirations and widen participation amongst such groups, and identifies a key success criteria as

> firm targeting of access strategies towards these young people, with clear criteria for identifying and concentrating resources on those most in need of support. 'Catch all' approaches directed towards 'non traditional' students in general are not attracting this group.
>
> (Woodrow, 1998, p. 6)

The need to identify and counter individual fears and concerns is clear from Woodrow's research.

2 Scanning the options.   A second stage in choosing an HE place involves scanning the options at a general level in terms of the range of subjects an individual may study and the types of course and institution that may be appropriate. At this stage detailed knowledge of HE is not necessary, for the individual is considering general messages about HE programmes and considering them against their priorities for and perceptions of their own personal abilities and aptitudes, lifestyle ambitions and long-term economic and social objectives. As with choice at all other stages of education and training pathways this choice will be sub-vigilant and sub-rational in the process that is undertaken.

3 Focusing the choice. This is the stage at which firm potential subject/course choices emerge. Within the UK system it is the stage at which the UCAS handbook and generic guides to HE may be most important and which are used to derive a long list of course/institution options. It is here that individual HE prospectuses play their part and when Internet and CD Rom sources of information come into play.

4 Shortlisting. Shortlisting is the stage of applying and requires a clear choice of a number of institutions and courses.

5 Prioritising and preferencing. This stage is the developing of a priority list on the basis of detailed information and direct contact with institutions. Course handbooks, visits to the universities chosen, and more vigilant pursuit of focused information about the institutions and their social, cultural and economic environments are key elements in this process.

6 Conversion and decision-taking. The final stage is that of conversion and decision-taking. For most HE applicants this involves a potential decision, since it will be dependent on the achievement of specific entry requirements. In this case there are two sub-stages – potential conversion, and final choice. The latter of these occurs where the individual decides to register at a particular institution for a specific course. During this stage the principal information needs are associated with reinforcement processes, confirming in the mind of the chooser their confidence in the decisions they have made, and enabling the announcement of choice to be undertaken in the context of optimising self-esteem. This parallels strongly the process of preserving self-esteem and group identity described in relation to post-16 choice (Chapter 5).

The model outlined here provides a broad conceptualisation of the processes at work in selecting an HE programme. The research evidence is clear, though, that its exact form and nature will vary from individual to individual, and is a highly subjective, socially situated process influenced by a unique set of information sources and socio-economic pressures. The process involves acquiring information and triangulating the ideas that emerge with other sources – and the continuous matching and testing of the emerging images with the changing self-perceptions and awarenesses that develop. The role of particular influences or information sources will be highly variable, therefore. We can suggest that the influence of parents is strong overall, for example, and that we might expect their influence to be strongest in the first stages of the model. For some, though, their influence will be almost nil, while for others parents may be intimately involved in the final choice in Stage 6.

Within the literature on choice in general the notion of vigilant decision-making emerges as an important concept. It is unlikely that any individual will undertake a process of information collection which approaches any objective definition of 'vigilant', but some will be more vigilant than others. The research of Connor *et al.* (1999) and others suggests that vigilance is greatest amongst a number of specific groups of potential applicants to HE – females, those in higher socio-economic groups, those with family histories of HE participation, those with higher academic achievements prior to the HE admissions process, those applying to study science-based courses, and applicants from independent or selective schools. This pattern certainly reflects no single reason for increased vigilance, for it may be explained by personality traits, the development of skills of logical and systematic investigation and an emphasis on rationality in choice, wider experience of consumer choice in professional services markets, or a recognition of the complexity of factors involved in making choices that are as good as possible. It does stress, however, that the higher education market place is by no means homogeneous and is in practice a highly segmented market.

In summary

Choosing to participate in higher education is no longer restricted to an elite minority group of 18 year olds but has become the choice of a significant proportion of young people. Going to university may soon become the norm rather than the exception. Despite these changes in participation rates, though, some of the traditional patterns of participation in relation to socio-economic background have persisted. This reflects the contiguous nature of the values implicit in HE participation and the values and aspirations of middle-class young people. Although we have been able to demonstrate the range of factors and influences on choice of HE within this chapter, this is an arena where there is a substantial need to research the process of choice at the level of individual young people, to explore the interaction of influential factors and their developing image of themselves within the social, cultural and economic worlds they inhabit. In particular, we must identify how far the tensions and dissonance present in FE choice are found within, and shape, HE choice.

8 Choice or chance?

Career decision-makin
processes of young pe

Career choosing, education, training and the labour market

In our analysis of young people's decision-making so far we have considered the processes of choice in relation to significant transition points within education and training pathways – entry to primary school and secondary school, and choices about entering further and higher education. At each stage the impact of earlier choices constrains, in some way, the options that are available, and so, ultimately, shapes the choices that a young person can make as s/he moves from education or training into the labour market as the first formal step in their economic working life or career. The ways in which young people make active or passive choices that lead to career entry are the central theme of this chapter.

One of the key outputs from education and training markets is the supply of new employees to the labour market. From an economic perspective the provision of new entrants with the right skills and knowledge at the right time in the right place would provide the sort of 'just-in-time' system that would increase efficiency and responsiveness for business and for service providers. The education and training system is, of course, a long way from meeting such 'just-in-time' demands, as a result of the differences in time scales of change between the two environments of education/training and the labour market. Labour market needs can change on very short time scales of months or one or two years. In contrast, the response time of education and training in identifying needs, and establishing and delivering programmes, operates on a much longer cycle traditionally measured in years. The net result is often a mismatch of supply and demand in the labour market. Even on the longer time scales that education and training systems operate within, the changing

arket has raised fundamental questions about policy
s in education and training systems. Some of the recent *meta-*
s in the labour market for young people have been described by
oberts (1995) and include:

a   The entry requirements for jobs at all levels have risen, with the graduatisation of some jobs that were once open to school leavers. Qualification inflation has the contradictory characteristics of raising demand for education and training while at the same time reducing its market value.

b   In some employment fields increasing numbers of young people have been unable to find jobs for which their qualifications are required or where their certificated abilities will be used. Rather than finding themselves in high demand, some young people have been experiencing what Roberts terms the 'great training robbery', with employers able to select on the basis of qualifications that may bear little relationship to the job's technical requirements.

c   In other employment fields, and in areas of rapid economic growth, demand for labour has challenged traditional training needs. In the IT field, for example, and in retail and service sectors in regions like the 'M4 corridor', excess labour demand has reduced the pressure on school leavers to pursue education and training by creating relatively high wage levels and a guarantee of almost full employment.

d   Jobs in manufacturing have been in decline since the 1950s, as a result of new technology and improved labour productivity, and now account for less than 25% of jobs in the economy. At the same time employment has expanded in the service sector, which now accounts for two thirds of all jobs. Traditional training and education needs have changed significantly, therefore, and continue to do so at an accelerating rate.

e   A range of gender-related patterns can be identified. Traditionally male-dominated employment sectors are those in decline (e.g. manufacturing), while female school leavers now attach the same importance to occupational careers as males. Despite these changes, traditional gender patterns persist in employment, with males dominating management and high-status professions, and women dominating lower-status and lower-paid sectors.

f   Throughout the 1980s and 1990s unemployment, compounded by qualification inflation, has been a major factor in persuading 16 year olds to continue in education and training. The penalty for educational failure today is often no job rather than poor quality employment, and the social and economic contrasts between those in work and those who are unemployed have been expanding.

Set against this background of change, labour market planning at a macro-scale requires a clear understanding of how young people make career choices. While a rapidly changing labour market can seriously compromise quite valid career choices made by individuals in the past, understanding the process of career choosing may enable careers education and guidance systems to support more closely the balancing of the needs of individuals and of society and the economy.

Careers education and guidance

An important component in the interaction of the education/training market and the labour market is Careers Education and Guidance (CEG), for it represents one of the ways in which the two inter-dependent worlds may be brought into closer alignment. Howicson and Croxford (1996, p. 3) stress how CEG is 'increasingly recognised as important not only to individuals but also to the economy', and that as a result '(CEG) now has greater prominence in the public policy agenda', with the publication of *Skills for Choice* (SCAA, 1996), *Routes for Success* (CBI, 1993a), and *A Credit to Your Career* (CBI, 1993b) raising the profile of CEG within schools. Careers education and guidance (CEG) is now a statutory element of the curriculum for all pupils in maintained schools in the UK. The 1997 Education Act requires that schools provide a programme of careers education to all pupils between the ages of 14 and 16, and work with local careers services to 'ensure that pupils have access to materials providing careers guidance and a wide range of up-to-date reference materials ... to help pupils make informed and realistic choices about their future' (OFSTED, 1999, p. 10). This prioritising of CEG has stimulated the most recent policy initiatives by government in relation to widening participation and enhancing lifelong learning, in response to the *Learning to Succeed* White Paper (DfEE, 1998), which has established an entitlement to effective guidance to all young people through the Connexions system (DfEE, 2000). While Maychell and Evans (1998) show that there is a significant statistical relationship between experience of CEG in schools and staying on rates post-16, Howieson and Croxford (1996) suggest that the benefits of CEG to pupils and students is not always easy to demonstrate. It is not easy to identify, for example, whether the relationship identified by Maychell and Evans shows that those choosing to 'stay-on' are more likely to seek, follow or even remember careers education and guidance than those who do not, or whether it is the experience of CEG by pupils which pushes them towards continuing in education or training after 16.

The pattern of careers advice within the education and training system in England and Wales is currently characterised by a concentration on careers advisory programmes in Years 10 and 11 of compulsory schooling, with little explicit advice at an earlier stage than this. In primary schools formal careers education is largely absent, even where opportunities arise naturally within the curriculum. Hemsley-Brown and Foskett (1997), in their study of career perceptions and higher education aspirations amongst primary phase children, observe that there appears to be

> ... no inclusion of job-related or careers-related components in the curriculum (...). The absence of formal 'careers' elements (...) was not perceived by either senior management or class teachers as a matter of concern. Information on specific careers was seen to be the responsibility of the secondary school. . . .
>
> (Hemsley-Brown and Foskett, 1997, p. 3)

The Dearing Review of Qualifications for 16–19 Year Olds (Dearing, 1996) was also critical of the careers guidance offered within existing structures, suggesting that students making choices at 16 feel they are doing so in an information vacuum. Dearing goes on to emphasise in his Recommendation 184 that:

> Excellent, independent careers education and guidance should be provided to all young people on their choice of pathways and their potential level of achievement. . . .
>
> (Dearing, 1996, p. 14)

Despite this concern, Dearing provides little evidence of analysis of the informational requirements of young people as they progress through their compulsory education into FE, other than observing that careers information should be available to 14–19 year olds. However, research on career choosing (Kelly, 1989; Keys and Fernandes, 1993; Keys *et al.*, 1995; Foskett and Hesketh, 1995; Foskett and Hemsley-Brown, 1997) shows that occupations and career intentions are chosen at an early stage. Delaying careers advice until upper secondary school, therefore, may miss the important stages of conceptual development and choice which occur in the upper primary or lower secondary school.

Career choice and decision-making

Two main theoretical approaches to occupational choice have dominated CEG in the last four decades. Structural, or personality matching theories, suggest that individuals select work environments which represent a 'way of life' and are consistent with their personalities. In this way a choice of occupation is an expression of that person's motivation, knowledge, personality and ability. Holland (1985), for example, identifies six dominant personality types in relation to occupational choice:

* realistic – dealing with specific objects, tools or machines, e.g. mechanic, farmer;
* investigative – investigation and enquiring, e.g. designer, engineer;
* artistic – work in creative, ambiguous, unsystematised fields, e.g. writer, artist;
* social – working in systems with and for people, e.g. teacher, social worker;
* enterprising – manipulating resources for economic or political gain, e.g. politician, sales;
* conventional – systematic manipulation of data and records, e.g. accountant, administrator.

While such a trait model perspective has been important within CEG, research by Moir (1990) suggests that there is little evidence for such a close relationship between personality and occupational choice. While not entirely deterministic in nature this model places little importance on the role either of the individual's personal and psychological development or his/her choice-making potential. Developmental models (e.g. Ginzberg *et al.*, 1951; Super, 1953), on the other hand, present occupational choice as an unfolding maturational process involving an individual progressing through a number of stages to the point where they can make realistic choices. Ginzberg's Advanced Development Theory suggests young people pass through three stages (fantasy, tentative and realistic stages) leading towards a final occupational choice. Super developed these ideas further by emphasising the importance of the development of the individual's self-concept in the later stages of the process, drawing strongly on their home and school experiences. Such structured developmental models paralleled the stage models emerging at the same time in relation to children's learning (e.g. Piaget, 1953), and their appropriateness has been challenged as too prescriptive. Moir (1990), for example, failed to identify such a clear-cut development, with no linear process apparent, and 'choosing' at any age drawing on both fantasy and realistic models of occupations and reality.

Super's recognition of the importance of developing concepts of self, however, is an element of career choosing that has been of value. Vondracek *et al.* (1995) link vocational development to the wider arena of personal identity development, drawing on the ideas of Erikson (1968). Erikson (1968, p. 15) suggests that the young person develops a personal identity which represents an interaction between what the child 'has come to be during the long years of childhood, (...) that which he promises to become in the future, (...) that which he conceives himself to be and that which he perceives others see in him and expect of him'. Beven (1995) draws on ideas from Personal Construct Theory to emphasise the individuality of the development of such ideas. Personal Construct Theory (Kelly, 1955) suggests that individuals make sense of the world around them in different ways, and that the ideas they develop reflect their own personal models of the world, or constructs. Beven suggests that

> to try and give guidance to a pupil without taking account of their interpretation of events, their terms of reference and (...) what is important to them can lead to making assumptions about motivation, values and choices, and the subsequent guidance given may not be particularly appropriate.
>
> (Beven, 1995, p. 2)

The concept of developmental models has been developed further by the work of Hodkinson (1995), and Hodkinson and Sparkes (1993, 1997) which is encompassed in their theory of 'careership'. Hodkinson and Sparkes identify significant discrepancies between the career decision-making implicit in both trait and developmental models and the reality of how students actually 'choose'. Traditional perspectives have placed an emphasis on a technically rational view of career decision-making. As Bennett *et al.* (1992) indicate:

We assume that, knowing their capabilities and other personal characteristics, individuals form an estimate of expected earning resulting from each education, training and labour market option, and taking into account their taste for each, choose the stream which offers the greatest utility.

(Bennett, Glennester and Nevison, 1992, p. 13)

Hodkinson and Sparkes (1997), however, suggest that while students may give rationalising reasons for their 'choices', creating the impression both for themselves and others that their decision was rational, in reality decisions are pragmatic, opportunistic, based on partial information, and highly context-related. The importance of chance personal contacts and experiences, of family background, culture and the pupils' own life histories, and of highly personal and individual feelings and emotions cannot be underestimated. From this analysis Hodkinson and Sparkes suggest a new model of career decision-making, which they term 'careership', in which three components interact with each other to 'generate' career choice. The three dimensions are:

- pragmatically rational decision-making, i.e. decision-making that *is* rational within the confines of the individual's limited knowledge and their *habitus*;
- interactions with other people, both other choosers and others with whom they are socially situated;
- the chance outcomes that arise from the 'location of decisions within the partly unpredictable pattern of turning points and routines that make up the life course' (Hodkinson and Sparkes, 1997, p. 33).

From this developing understanding of career 'choosing', two important ideas emerge strongly. First, the long-term formation of ideas, perceptions and images that lead to choice is now well established. The roots of career choice lie not in the teenage years but at much earlier stages of each child's personal development. Second, within this process, perceptions of reality rather than any objective reality are of fundamental importance. It is the individual's development of a complex set of internalised images which 'forms' the making of decisions and choices. There are several of these images. The image that pupils or students hold about themselves and their own desires and capabilities is one element of this perception. Their image of the nature and 'value' of each of the alternative education and training pathways available is a second. A third is the image they hold of the nature of the jobs and careers that they may see as the possible outcomes of different pathways. The fourth is the image they hold of their own broad role within the economy and society. These images are, of course, subject to restructuring and re-clarification in response to the input of ideas and information, but underpin decisions that need to be taken about career choice at any particular point in their career, education and training pathway.

The CEG system in the UK is still largely underpinned by traditional career matching approaches. While in recent years there has been more emphasis on the chooser, on the integration of work roles with other life roles, and on broader issues of lifestyle choices (Herr, 1997), most CEG still operates a relatively systematic and mechanistic approach to guidance, based on assumptions about the rationality of choice. Such an approach is contentious in the context of the recent emphasis on individual choice within both labour and education/training markets. Choice, whether free or constrained, is dependent on a range of highly individual facets, including personal history, life experiences, and perceptions and interpretations of explicit and implicit socio-cultural and economic pressures. These will be experienced by a young person throughout their life in contexts ranging from personal experience, to the family environment, to school, and beyond to the social environment he or she participates in and the wider environment portrayed by the media (Hawthorn, 1995a, 1995b, 1996). These inputs are then subject to processes acting over short or long periods of time, which involve the development and re-working of ideas and images. Understanding this interaction of images, perceptions and career decision-making has been the focus of a substantial research project, whose findings are explored in the next section.

The 'CAPDEM' Project

The Career Perceptions and Decision-Making (CAPDEM) Project (Foskett and Hemsley-Brown, 1997) took as its baseline the notion that it is in the formation of young people's perceptions of careers that the roots of their career, education and training choices are to be found. By examining perceptions at a number of important transitional points in pathways through school and college the project sought to model the ways in which career perceptions emerge and develop and then influence the choices the young people make. The Project, undertaken during 1997, used questionnaires and focus groups to identify the perceptions and knowledge of specific careers held by pupils aged 10 (in Year 6, the final year of primary education), aged 15 (in Year 10, the penultimate year of compulsory education) and aged 17 (in Year 12, in the period prior to starting the formal higher education application system). The sample of pupils was taken from two contrasting socio-economic environments, one in the West Midlands and one in south-east England, and investigated pupils' knowledge and understanding in relation to:

1 their perceptions of the careers education and guidance they had received;
2 their perceptions of the career they currently aspired to;
3 their perceptions of two other specific careers (nursing and engineering). Nursing was chosen for focus as an example of a career which has become increasingly a graduate field, and where gender stereotypes and media images may play a significant part in external perceptions. Engineering was chosen because of the contrast but potential confusion between technician and professional career pathways, and its traditional gender and image stereotyping;
4 the impact of those perceptions on their recent and forthcoming decisions in their learning career.

From the study three main groups of findings emerged in relation to: young people's career choice mechanisms and choice criteria; their perceptions of careers and work; and the nature and influence of CEG.

Career choice mechanisms and choice criteria

Young people almost all have enough knowledge of the world of work to have a view of the career area they aspire to, at whatever age they are asked. Amongst younger pupils, where we might expect limited knowledge of career fields, only 3% were unable to say what career they had chosen. Amongst the older pupils, where we might expect greater hesitation in choice, 14% indicated they had not chosen a career area. In terms of the specific choices indicated, well-established patterns related to age, socio-economic background and gender emerged quite strongly:

1 Overall, the most popular choices were jobs within arts and the media, including acting, television presentation and journalism, with 18% of young people aspiring to work in this field.
2 Amongst the youngest pupils the 'fantasy stage' of career choice was strongly apparent, with high levels of aspiration to work with

animals (in almost all cases as a vet) (19%), to work in the arts and media, principally as an actress (19%), or to work in sport, most frequently as a professional sports man or woman.

3   Amongst the older pupils the focus had moved away from such fantasy choices to employment in the professions. Medicine and allied professions emerged as the principal ambition area (18%), followed by employment in the arts and media (15%), with employment in financial services (11%) emerging as the third most important career field.

4   Gender differences appeared most strongly amongst younger pupils where the fantasy aspirations of girls were to work as a vet or an actress, while for boys it was to work as a professional sportsman. Amongst older pupils the emergence of engineering and finance services as strong employment aspirational areas reflected the shifting choices of boys.

5   Class differences emerged, in that sport and employment in the armed services were very strongly the choices expressed by pupils of working-class background, while medicine and management were predominantly the domains of young people from middle-class backgrounds.

6   An analysis of the influence of parental occupation on a young person's choice demonstrated little *prima facie* linkage. While the pattern of parental occupations represented a realistic guide to the kinds of jobs available in the labour market, young people were choosing both 'fantasy jobs' and higher status jobs in proportions that bore little resemblance to real employment patterns. The only strong link between parental occupation came in relation to choosing careers in business and management, where two thirds of young people choosing this career had a father working in the field – and almost all of these young people were from middle-class families.

These key findings in relation to career perceptions and ambition lead to the emergence of a new categorisation of career choice amongst young people, based on job status and the realism of the choices made in comparison to the main features of the labour market. Three groups of jobs emerged within this model:

Lottery jobs

Lottery jobs are high-profile jobs, frequently attracting very high salaries, but with very limited opportunity for entry. Entry is dependent on the possession of a very specialised talent or ability, and entering the profession is dependent on chance and being 'talent spotted'. They include jobs such as professional sportsman or sportswoman, actor or actress, and unique jobs such as a television news reader, and are distinguished by the fame that accompanies the role and, normally, the high incomes they attract. Like taking part in a lottery, the chances of success are very small indeed, but despite this limitation such jobs were the target of 28% of young people in the CAPDEM study. Amongst the youngest pupils 45% aspired to a lottery job, compared to 25% of 15 year olds and only 20% of 17 year olds. While such declining numbers might be expected, it is still clear that by the time key *decisions* on careers are being taken many young people have a highly optimistic view of the career they will end up following.

High-status jobs

High-status jobs are those which are typically professional careers such as doctor, dentist or barrister. They are characterised by high potential earnings and status, but also by a highly selective entry process that requires high academic qualifications and a long and demanding training. Just over 20% of young people in the CAPDEM study had chosen a high-status profession as their target, although only 5% of mothers and 14% of fathers were working in such fields. Amongst pupils from middle-class backgrounds a quarter aspired to high-status jobs, while only 15% of working-class pupils had such aspirations.

Customary jobs

Customary jobs are those which are available in larger numbers within the labour market, and which provided employment for three quarters of the parents of the young people in the study. They include jobs such as teacher, nurse, engineer, manager, news journalist, administrator, production worker, or those involving domestic work or manual labour. Only 40% of young people aspired to such jobs, predominantly as teachers or nurses.

The CAPDEM study examined the factors which young people believed had motivated their choice of career. Although pupils cited a wide range of factors, 'enjoyment' was the main reason given for their career choice, a factor which was independent of gender. The importance of enjoyment as a factor was strongest amongst those choosing 'lottery' and 'high-status' jobs, and the emphasis on enjoyment in career choosing may skew the career options towards these particular job fields. The second most important factor was the idea of 'helping', whether in relation to people or to animals, and the third most cited factor was financial gain. This third factor was strongly associated with career choosing amongst boys, and amongst older students, and lead in most cases to a decision to enter a career in finance, business or law. The idea of 'helping' emerged much more strongly amongst the girls in the study.

Beyond the simple notion of influencing factors, though, the study investigated ideas associated with particular careers through a technique in which young people were asked to list five key words they associate with the careers of their choice. The increase in cognitive maturity between the younger pupils and the 17-year-old students was demonstrated in the pupils' choice of words. Younger pupils associate careers with concrete objects and tasks (e.g. 'fixing cars'), while the oldest group of young people were more likely to use abstract concepts such as 'challenge', 'security', and 'respect'. Between the two groups, the 15 year olds emphasised emotional responses to their choice, using words such as 'interesting', 'enjoyable' or 'frightening'. While this pattern is not surprising in the context of the process of maturation, it has important implications for choice in education markets. For the very young the abstract concepts that are important elements of many jobs in the economy are incomprehensible, yet decision-making in relation to key choices may be well under way by the time children leave primary school. Some career fields may have been rejected as a possibility by young people before they can realistically be aware of the true nature of those jobs.

Young people's perceptions of careers and work

So, how do young people form their perceptions of careers, and from where do they obtain the ideas? What models do they create of the labour market and the processes within it? The questionnaires and focus groups in the CAPDEM study enabled a number of important conclusions to be drawn out in relation to:

- image construction and reconstruction;
- job visibility and invisibility;
- an holistic lifestyle view of careers.

Image construction and re-construction

Whenever a child comes into contact with a job or career field, whether through direct experience or from second-hand information, they will develop some form of image and perception of the nature, characteristics and status of that job. New information, whether from careers education or further life experiences will simply add to, extend or modify the existing models in the child's mind. Three sources and types of image can be identified:

- *Contracted images* are those that come from direct personal experience, such as the image a child has of the job of a teacher. In addition to experiences through everyday life, as part of CEG most pupils gain some direct experience of the work place through work experience. OFSTED (1999) suggest that 95% of 14–16 year olds are involved in work experience. Despite OFSTED's contention that 'for many this is their first encounter with the workplace and its demands' (OFSTED, 1999, p. 12), Hobbs, Lindsay and McKechnie (1996) provide a summary of research evidence on work experience that suggests that as many as 75% of children have some experience of paid employment by the age of 16. It is clear, therefore, that most children have experience of the work place that will have given them insights into the three domains of work-related experience that OFSTED (1999, p. 1) suggest are important:

  - learning *about work*;
  - learning *through work*;
  - learning *for work*.

- *Delegated images* are those passed to the child by adults. They are second-hand, in that they are images mediated by the adult's experience, and further re-worked by the child as the image is formed. A child's image of the work of a bank manager or of a Member of Parliament will be a delegated image. The strength or detail of the image will depend on the adult's experience – the engineer's daughter will have a more insightful and detailed view of engineering as a career than will the crofter's son, while the crofter's son will have an intimate knowledge of employment opportunities in a marginal rural environment.

- *Derived images* are those conveyed by the media. Television, for example, or children's books, convey impressions about the nature of particular jobs, and also about how certain jobs are perceived and valued by society as a whole.

These images, whatever their source, are not simply received and stored, but are subjected to filtering, re-working and re-construction by each young person operating explicitly or implicitly as a critical, selective and reflective individual. What is taken and used from the incoming image and is added to the existing perceptual models in the child's mind will be unique to each child, influenced substantially by their position as socially-situated individuals. Their personal life histories and their current social, economic and psychological environments will act as lenses and filters through which the image is focused and formed. The same information may, of course, be interpreted negatively or positively by different individuals, emphasising that there is no simple causal link between information or images that are inputs to the perceptual system and the value-laden constructs that emerge as outputs into the individual's consciousness.

Job visibility and invisibility

Some careers are more visible and create stronger images than others. Jobs may be described as visible when they have a component of performance which is publicly seen. The supermarket checkout assistant's job, for example, has a high level of visibility through those elements that involve interacting with customers. All jobs, though, have important invisible components – those elements of the job that occur out of sight of the public (for example, the shopkeeper's work in stock taking or completing accounts), or those which are essentially intellectual rather than practical. Some jobs are largely invisible, in that much of the work is intellectual. Such invisibility, though, may hide considerable differences between jobs. In a solicitor's office, the solicitor, the legal administrator, and the secretary have a shared visible component, in that they are office-based and involve working with documents, a model which might be seen by a 12 year old as 'boring office work'. The three jobs, though, are enormously different, in that the training required, the intellectual challenge of the jobs, and the skills and abilities needed to operate in the jobs are quite different.

A number of types of invisibility may be identified. *Inherent invisibility* describes those elements of jobs which are 'invisible' even to those outsiders who come into contact with the job, as for example, with the planning of patient care by a nurse. *Stage invisibility* exists where a job does not come into the natural experience of a particular age group. Many jobs, for example, might be seen as adult-world jobs (e.g. insurance broker), and are unknown and therefore invisible to young people. The third form of invisibility is *conceptual invisibility*. This characterises those jobs which can only be understood at the end of a long period of education, training or induction for a particular career field, and might be exemplified by the work of an actuary.

An holistic lifestyle view of careers

In examining the descriptions young people provide of the careers they are attracted to or have rejected, a strong theme is the indivisibility of jobs from the sort of people who do those jobs, the circumstances they work under, and the lifestyle associated with the job both inside and outside the work place. This holistic view is a summated model, and seeking to separate out the component parts is difficult, for the image developed may be synergistic. Understanding such an holistic lifestyle view of careers is important, though, in that it means that promotion of particular jobs requires developing in young people an understanding of 'how (people) spend their time at work and away from work, how they have progressed to their present position, (and) what their concerns, joys, successes and fears are' for young people are 'actually interested in the sum total of work, personal life, income and relationships that constitutes the concept of lifestyle' (Foskett and Hemsley-Brown, 1997, p. 72). We may surmise that this emphasis on lifestyle is exacerbated by the importance of 'style' in the western culture of the late twentieth/early twenty-first century, but we must also conclude that such lifestyle perceptions have always played a significant part in the personal value attributed to particular careers by individuals.

From these ideas three important conceptual models of career choice and perception can be identified, relating to:

- profiling perceptual components in career fields;
- entry and progression in the labour market;
- a defaulting model of occupational choice.

Profiling perceptual components in occupational fields

The constructs of image development, invisibility, and the holistic lifestyle view of careers provide a set of career perception components that enable a profile of particular careers or occupational fields to be built up. The nature of this profile will vary from career area to career area. The CAPDEM Project examined nursing and engineering as specific career areas, and Figure 8.1 demonstrates their contrasting profiles. Nursing has a strong presence through contracted images for most young people and all adults. Its derived image, as portrayed in the media coverage of hospital drama, emphasises an image of 'caring', while media coverage of pay issues presents a negative derived image for many young people. The images, of course, relate to the visible components of nursing, yet many of the managerial and intellectual components of the job are invisible. Engineering shares some elements of the profile of nursing in that much of the managerial role is invisible. Its delegated image, derived from the direct experience of most adults, relates to a technician view of engineering (for example, of a car mechanic or a washing machine repairer), however, and much of the intellectual and creative demand of graduate entry professional engineering is invisible. Like nursing, its dominant visible component is linked strongly to relatively low-level job activities. Neither field has a strongly developed image in terms of an holistic lifestyle view of the career.

Career perception

Component	*Features of nursing*	*Features of engineering*
Contracted images	Direct experience for most young people	Limited direct experience for most young people
Delegated images	Direct experience for all adults	Limited direct experience for most adults of professional engineering. Strong image of 'technician' engineering
Derived images	Caring image. Media coverage of pay disputes	Limited, dominated by extremes 'Oily rag' v. 'Tomorrow's World'
Inherent invisibility	Management, organisation and leadership roles invisible	Technician role visible, all others invisible
Stage invisibility	Familiar at all life stages	Technician role partly visible, professional engineer role not visible
Conceptual invisibility	Management roles invisible	High invisibility
Holistic lifestyle view	Some media images, but generally not developed	Not developed and possible negative image

Figure 8.1 Image profiles of nursing and engineering as careers.

Entry and progression in the labour market

A second model developed from the CAPDEM Project relates to young people's perceptions of the organisation and structure of a career field in terms of their expectations of entry points and progression within the career. Whether a career field is large or small, we might conceptualise its structure as pyramidal, with most jobs towards the base of the pyramid with relatively modest salaries, and few jobs at the top occupied by the highest earners in the field. Some 'career pyramids' will be very tall, some small but broad based. Entry to most will be at or near the base of the pyramid. The perceptual image demonstrated by young people in each of the age groups in the CAPDEM research was, however, one of an inverted pyramid, or of a highly asymmetrical diamond. Most expect to enter, providing they obtain *some* relevant qualifications, some way up the pyramid, and believe that the number of opportunities and jobs will increase as they move up through promotion. Only in the very highest echelons of a career field (e.g. in the sphere of Managing Directors) do they expect a narrowing of the field again.

This perceptual model may be explained in part by the invisibility of many senior management roles. Where a career area is seen only in terms of its visible characteristics, young people see a job undertaking those visible roles as being close to the top of the career field. Becoming a doctor or a teacher is seen as close to the top of the field, with only a limited recognition that there may be a few more senior roles to 'manage' the organisation of the professional work involved. While demonstrating the significance of invisibility, it also shows a lack of awareness of the operation of the principles of demand and supply in influencing potential entry points in the job market. Increasing graduate output means some graduates will end up starting in jobs that were not traditionally graduate roles. In overcrowded job fields, such as the theatre, the highest entry point for many may be very low down (perhaps as a box office clerk), thus elongating progression and promotion pathways. In fields where there is under-supply of new entrants (e.g. in engineering) entry points may be higher and promotion pathways may be shorter.

A default model of occupational choice

Defaulting is the process of downward revision of career aspiration, normally as a result of either a failure to achieve entry to a desired occupational field or a reassessment of anticipated achievement.

The process can happen at almost any stage of a young person's career choice pathway, and occurs in two distinct forms. First there is defaulting into a different career field. This frequently involves defaulting from a high-status or lottery job ambition to a customary job ambition, and might include, for example, the aspirant actor accepting a job as a personnel manager or a teacher. Second, there is defaulting into a related field which makes lower entry demands on the individual. This may be in recognition that the higher level aspiration is no longer achievable, or it may be to gain entry into the field at a lower level but with a retained hope or intention of achieving the original higher status target job. Fifteen and 17 year olds expressing an intention to become a PE teacher may, for example, have had earlier aspirations to be a professional sportsman or woman, and those pursuing journalism as a career may have had (and may still harbour) ambitions to be a television presenter. In many career fields, defaulting simply places the career entrant further from the top of the field, but does not fundamentally prevent progression back to the top. In other areas, linked careers may have no 'ladders and bridges' between them either up or down, so defaulting must, of necessity, involve a change in career ambition. The 10 year old with ambitions to be a doctor may have defaulted to a nursing career by the age of 17, and progression then into medicine is no longer possible. The 10 year old with ambitions to be a news presenter may enter employment on a local newspaper but can still, in theory, progress to the highest levels of the profession.

The nature and influence of careers education and guidance

The important message from the findings of CAPDEM in relation to CEG are that effective careers education and guidance is dependent on working with young people's perceptions. Two important aspects of this may be identified. First, developing images and changing perceptions must start from the existing perceptions and understanding that young people have. Ausubel (1958) has shown how 'meaningful learning' will only occur where the teacher understands the pre-existing models and concepts that individuals hold in their mind and then sets out to extend or re-model those ideas. Second, it is important to understand the processes by which these images 'naturally' change over time, for if CEG programmes are to be most effective they must ensure that they can access the young person's learning at the right time and in the right way.

The CAPDEM Project investigated the nature of careers advice which young people had experienced, and examined how that advice and guidance had contributed to the decision-making process they had undertaken. This was identified from the pupils' own explicit accounts of their experience and the contribution of CEG. Recognising that young people may not always see the influence of particular sources of ideas, or may choose not to give them appropriate credit even if they recognise the contribution made, this contribution was also examined through the implicit evidence of the pupils' accounts and responses.

While the importance of CEG in helping to shape pupils' ideas has been identified in much of the research on choice at 16+ and beyond, we must not overemphasise its influence. Formal CEG begins for most pupils at age 14. If choices are intuitive and shaped over many years throughout childhood and adolescence, influenced significantly by what Hawthorn (1996) terms *subliminal* factors such as television images, then

> careers advisers and teachers are entering the process of decision-making at a very late stage, and they are severely disadvantaged in terms of influencing the decisions young people make. Careers education cannot compensate for social and cultural disadvantage however much we would like it to do so.
> (Foskett and Hemsley-Brown, 1997, p. 87)

Howieson and Croxford (1996, p. 24) suggest that 'personal and social characteristics (are) the major influences on young people's outcomes after 16, and Careers Education and Guidance can only have a limited effect'. This limited effect is in part a result of the perception that young people have that careers guidance operates as an *information on demand* system. They perceive that if they express some interest in a particular career then much of the energy of the formal careers system is directed into satisfying information needs in relation to that preference. This is reinforced through the widespread use of computer-based careers guidance programmes which pupils believe start from describing the subject areas they are already interested in and then seek to narrow down choice options quite quickly within the guidance programme. Overall, young people see the CEG system as designed to expedite single career choice.

This view conflicts with the explicit aims and perceptions of CEG professionals. While recognising that the behaviours identified by pupils are common issues, they assert quite strongly that CEG 'should help (pupils) gain confidence in decision-making but should not foreclose on careers decision-making before they are ready for it' (Rule, 1992, p. 5). The mismatch of CEG aims and pupils' perception of CEG may lie in two issues. First, CEG starts formally at a stage when the social pressures experienced by young people push them towards narrowing choice rather than exploring options. An earlier start to CEG when ideas about careers and the labour market are more pliable may enable wider ideas about, for example, career decision-making or the key characteristics of changing labour markets, to be explored. Second, the late start of CEG, the anxiousness of young people to narrow choice, the often unreal expectations many young people hold about their own future achievements, and the predominance of 'enjoyment' as a key choice criteria makes them *selectively deaf.* Only those ideas that reinforce or bolster their thinking at the time of consultation are considered. Their information seeking is strongly convergent rather than divergent, even where they explicitly recognise that pursuing another career/education/training direction might provide them with a better chance of a job. Most appear to believe that their own determination, or the operation of positive chance factors, will enable them to overcome any barriers to the achievement of their goals.

Employability and consumerism in the labour market

At the macro-scale of understanding the operation of labour markets, the CAPDEM Project identified an important perceptual issue providing friction in the CEG system and in the connection of young people with the needs of the labour market. This is the self-perception of young people as consumers in the labour market, which has emerged both from the increasing emphasis on individuals as consumers in society at large and the focus in CEG on individuals making choices based on interest and enjoyment.

The outcome of these two pressures is that young people perceive employers as the supply side of the labour market, meeting potential employees' demand for secure, well-paid employment. Young people may recognise that their choices can increase or decrease their chance of employment, but they are rarely prepared to compromise on their prioritisation of enjoyment as the key factor in job and career choice. They make decisions about subjects to study, and further education and training options, as if they are consumers in the market. Indeed, in education and vocational training markets students have increasingly been formally awarded sovereignty as consumers through both market forces and statutory requirements.

While in some sectors and some localities this model may be a realistic view of the labour market, overall this is not how employers view the world. More frequently, employers see themselves as the demand side of the job market, requiring potential employees with the right skills and available at the right time at the right price. Young people are not viewed as customers in a labour market, even though they have been elevated to the position of customers in education. They have been forced, by changes in supply and demand to become *providers* – providers of skills to meet the demands of the labour market.

Significant within this view of contrasting perceptions in the labour market and the education/training market is the idea of 'employability'. Rajan *et al.* (1997, p. 60) suggest that

> the concept of 'job security' is being replaced by 'employability' (...). The idea is that employees will forego traditional job security for high quality training in transferable skills that will stand them in good stead after the current job.

Implicit within the idea of employability is the view that an individual must provide him/herself with the skills and attitudes that enable them to compete as the supply side of a highly competitive labour market. The importance of 'employability' as an idea emerged in the CBI's paper *Towards a Skills Revolution* in 1989 (CBI, 1989), in which the importance of individuals maximising the skills they have to match the demands of the labour market rather than focusing on their own particular interests is stressed. However, the emphasis on interest and enjoyment in career choice demotes the importance of 'employability'. For example, although an individual may understand that 'computer skills' are in demand, he/she may still choose on the basis of what they are *interested in*, because they cannot foresee a situation where they would want to work with computers. The notion of *employability*, however, means that young people need to understand through CEG how to invest in their own skills to meet the demands of the labour market. While they are expected to behave as *consumers* of education and training, they are the providers of skills in the labour market. This provides a significant challenge for careers education and guidance systems for:

> Unless young people and their parents are helped to understand the notion of employability and life long learning as a replacement for life time job security, future cohorts of young people

will continue to search for non-existent jobs and career pathways, based on their own agendas.

(Foskett and Hemsley-Brown, 1997, p. 101)

The evidence from the CAPDEM study is that amongst those 17 year olds with aspirations to enter higher education there is a growing recognition of the need for self-investment. Increasing awareness of the significance of developing portfolio careers, and of engaging in continuing education (lifelong learning) as a response to the increasing rate of change and demand for greater flexibility of the job market, is emerging, with an understanding that typical careers may require several job changes and re-training. Amongst younger pupils (age 10 and 14) and amongst those 17 year olds aspiring to a vocational training pathway, however, there is still only limited recognition of this expectation. There is still a clear need, therefore, for an emphasis in CEG on 'a development ethic which builds on entitlements and responsibilities' (CBI, 1989, p. 21). Overall, CEG professionals recognise this imperative, but are constrained by resources from developing this understanding with young people at the ages and stages at which they will be responsive to it. We must, therefore, identify how far these important ideas may pass to young people through other sources – their teachers (other than CEG teachers) and their parents.

The role of teachers in careers education and guidance

The evidence presented in most of the chapters in this book is that teachers play a pivotal role in the careers, education and training decision-making of young people. Their role is explicit, in that young people perceive them as a validated source of information and guidance. It is also implicit, though, in that they help to shape young people's perceptions of careers and pathways through their own attitudes, values, beliefs and prejudices. Careers teachers, of course, play a central formal role, but young people are much more exposed to the influence of their class teachers. More importantly, formal careers education and guidance is absent until upper secondary school, and so misses the important stages of conceptual development and choice which may be occurring in the upper primary or lower secondary school. As Foskett and Hemsley-Brown (1997, p. 1) suggest, 'by late primary school most pupils have rejected most jobs on the basis of perceptions'.

Implicit within these findings is the belief that teachers can and do play an important role in shaping pupils' careers education, all the more so if the process of career perception development is diffused throughout school experience and is also occurring from the point where each child enters school. Resource constraint will always mean that most careers education will be informal and will occur through a range of 'normal' curriculum activities conducted by teachers who are not careers specialists. The work of careers specialists will serve to refine and focus this informal work at key stages in young people's education/training pathways.

The importance of teachers' roles in CEG is also likely to be enhanced by current developments in secondary schools which raise the profile and status of the 'work-related curriculum', particularly for those who are perceived as having least to gain from academic programmes in the upper secondary school. The growth of alternative curriculum models involving general national vocational qualifications (GNVQs), and national vocational qualifications (NVQs) (Butterfield and Chitty, 1997) means that many pupils will be making specific career commitments (or excluding some career possibilities) at the start of Key Stage 4, aged 14. Butterfield and Chitty's research into the planning by schools to manage these Key Stage 4 changes suggests that most secondary schools recognise that teachers will need staff development in terms of teaching GNVQ or NVQ, but few recognise the impact in terms of CEG staff development:

> Only 15% of schools recognised (careers education) as an area for (staff) development. It would seem reasonable to hypothesise ... that schools are in the main underestimating the impact of curriculum choice post-16 on individual decision-making, and therefore the kinds of support needed by students and the expertise needed by staff in ensuring that separate pathways do not become the right and wrong side of the tracks.
>
> (Butterfield and Chitty, 1997, pp. 12–13)

Understanding what contribution most teachers can and do make to careers education is, therefore, an important starting point in considering future plans for CEG in schools and colleges. Recent research (Foskett and Hemsley-Brown, 1997) shows the role of teachers in shaping pupils' knowledge of specific careers and their characteristics is important – what pupils know or do not know about careers, training and entry requirements in part reflects what their teachers know or don't know. Gaining an insight into the images they hold and the knowledge that they have, therefore, provides an important perspective on the shaping of career perceptions amongst young people.

Foskett and Hemsley-Brown (1999) have examined the perceptions of careers and of education and training pathways held by teachers to try to identify the ways this may shape the formation of young people's perceptions. Their study, involving teachers in a sample of eight primary and secondary school clusters in southern England, used individual interviews to identify teachers' knowledge and understanding of recent and current developments and trends in the labour market, further education and higher education, together with their knowledge and understanding of the characteristics of three specific career areas – engineering, nursing and law. The principal findings of the study relate to teachers' involvement in CEG and their perceptions of career opportunities and pathways beyond school.

Teachers' involvement in careers education and guidance

Teachers recognise that they have an influential role in the education of children about the world beyond school. Amongst those working with secondary phase pupils almost two thirds had been formally involved in some element of CEG, normally through tutorial work or programmes in PSHE, or through supervising older pupils on work experience placements. Few primary phase teachers believe that they have been involved in any element of careers education, though, and amongst the study group many respondents indicated they believed CEG was not appropriate with younger children. In both secondary and primary phases, teachers expressed concern about their own limited knowledge of 'careers' and their ability to offer any form of guidance or support.

Teachers' perceptions of careers opportunities

To identify the origins of their understanding, teachers were asked to indicate the sources they had relied on for information and knowledge about careers. The pattern that emerges is very similar to the models describing how young people acquire their ideas. The principal source of information is 'friends', with 90% of primary teachers and 79% of secondary teachers using ideas derived from personal friends. Other significant sources of ideas are 'personal experience' (76%), 'the media' (63%), 'own observation of the world of work'

(62%) and 'direct work experience' – over half of the sample had worked for more than six months in a career other than teaching. An important difference between primary and secondary teachers was in the use of careers information in publications or on video, for while many secondary teachers cited these sources of personal information, almost none of the primary teachers used these sources.

The expansion of further and higher education participation rates has been both a sign of and a stimulus to a changing culture of educational and training expectations amongst young people. These changes in post-compulsory education appear to be fairly well understood by secondary school teachers, with half of the teachers in the study demonstrating their understanding that some 70% of 16 year olds will proceed to FE. Amongst primary school teachers only 25% recognised the high post-16 participation rates, however, and almost a quarter believed participation rates to be less than 40%. The concept of mass participation is only slowly gaining ground in the awareness of primary teachers.

In terms of specificity of knowledge, both primary and secondary school teachers were more confident in the knowledge they have of academic pathways beyond school than in their understanding of vocational routes. This, of course, largely reflects the traditions of the educational systems in the UK and their own personal career pathways to becoming teachers, but it means that the images and aspirations they may convey to young people are not balanced. This vocational/academic imbalance was strongly reflected in the teachers' knowledge about entry pathways into the three specific career areas chosen for focus in the study – nursing, engineering and law. Most teachers were more aware of the existence of graduate entry pathways into each career area than of vocational pathways related to NVQs, but the level of accurate knowledge was quite variable between the careers – for example, while over 80% of the teachers were confident that entry into law careers required a degree, less than 20% believed that nursing is a graduate entry profession. Overall, knowledge about entry pathways was based on an understanding of career pathways that were in place when teachers were themselves making career choices, and the addition of information into that framework of understanding was quite limited – in the case of primary teachers there was almost no current career pathway knowledge added to their historical understanding.

An important feature of the findings of the study was the

recognition by the teachers of their limited knowledge and their unwillingness to be placed in the position of providing formal CEG to most pupils. In terms of their detailed knowledge, for example, over 70% of all the teachers indicated they had little or no knowledge of the nature of careers and jobs in engineering.

All this may at first sight not appear to be major issue – teachers recognise their limited knowledge of careers and do not wish, therefore, to engage with careers education and guidance. However, it is in the implicit and subliminal messages from teachers, and in the attitudes and values they portray, that much of the careers education they provide takes place. It is informal and implicit, not formal and explicit. Identifying the teachers' perceptions of careers is important, therefore, if we are to recognise the delegated images that are being passed to pupils. The images teachers have of careers are macro-scale images, lacking differentiation and detail, often rather dated, and based on recognisable stereotypes. A strong image amongst most of the teachers for example was of law as a high status, high salary but less secure career, while nursing was perceived as low status, low salary but secure. Law is characterised in perceptions by images of confidence, intelligence, strong communication skills, high pay and work in law courts. Nursing is characterised by perceptions of dedication, patience, caring, calmness, low pay, and hospital-based work. Engineering is characterised by images of problem-solving, mathematical skills, mechanical skills and attention to detail, and as a male-dominated environment involving working with machines. There is also an explicit link between the teachers' perceptions of pupils' likely achievement in relation to school performance indicators and their suitability for particular careers. Law is seen as a career for high achievers, engineering is for average achievers and above-average achievers, and nursing is for average achievers.

It is clear from the picture painted here that teachers' knowledge and perceptions of specific careers is highly constrained. There is a tendency for teachers to re-affirm stereotypical images of careers and those who enter them, and there is a substantial lack of confidence in their own knowledge about non-academic pathways. The world of vocational education and training is *terra incognita* to most teachers. This in turn leads to significant issues which impact on teachers' unrecognised role in shaping young people's perceptions.

First, teachers seem to treat the term 'careers education' as being synonymous with 'careers guidance'. In this context there is a predominant view that:

a   Pupils below the age of 14 are too young to receive careers education.
b   Young people should have made some form of decision about their career before any careers education is provided.
c   Careers education requires detailed and expert knowledge.

The importance of developing understanding of the world of work and careers from an early age, even in primary school, is not recognised by most teachers, for careers education as a prelude to careers guidance is not recognised as an entitlement for young people.

Second, teachers are a biased sample of adults and this may be reflected in the images of careers they portray. All have chosen, for example, not to enter (or have chosen to leave) the private sector, industry, or non-teaching related careers. Many are subject oriented in their outlook, and may know little about careers beyond teaching even in fields related to their own subject discipline. For many teachers in the study, it was important that a career should emerge from a school subject or subjects that a child enjoys, but most school subjects are not vocational. A strong finding from the study, though, was that most teachers are not very positive about careers other than teaching (and many were not very positive about teaching either!). There was a strong perception of hostility towards law because of the 'money making' image, towards engineering because of a 'boring' image, and towards nursing because it was perceived as a job for those who are 'kind and caring' but who need to work hard at a physically demanding job for little financial reward.

A fundamental social and cultural shift is required to meet the need for highly skilled and educated individuals in the twenty-first century. Young people trust and rely on a number of key adults such as teachers to provide them, formally and informally, with up-to-date knowledge, analysis, interpretation, and 'street guidance' to help them make the informed choices about their future. Most teachers, however, are unaware, for example, of variable working patterns, have limited knowledge of vocational qualifications, and hold strongly stereotypical views of specific occupational fields. Although secondary teachers may be knowledgeable about academic routes and qualifications, about A-levels and about subject specific degrees, in other fields the images and guidance they can provide may be little better than those which young people gain from the media and from parents. This is of importance because teachers have a disproportionate role in influencing the views of young people over significant periods of time.

In summary

Choosing a career is the final outcome of the processes of choice that young people experience as they travel along their personal education and training pathway. For some this career will be in the form of a lifelong commitment to working in a particular field and progressing to positions of higher status, responsibility and achievement over time. At the opposite extreme, for others it may involve a 'career' of many and diverse jobs, perhaps with periods of unemployment. For some it will be an outcome linked to the pursuit of long held ambitions and positive choice. For others it will be the result of failure, second choices and defaulting. We have explored in this chapter how the 'choices' individuals make are shaped by their perceptions of jobs and careers that emerge from their personal experiences and lives, and which they acquire from those adults they spend most of their younger lives with – teachers and parents. It is in the details of those images that ambitions are nurtured or modified, and careers planned or reconstructed.

9 Choosing futures
Issues and implications

Continuity, interaction and choice

Within this book we have followed the decision-making pathway of young people by focusing chronologically on the main decision points that emerge within the education and training system of England and Wales. At each stage we have considered both the range of factors that are influential in choice which emerge from macro-scale analysis of decision-making, and the process of choice as experienced by young people (and their parents) in relation to those decision points. This latter analysis has helped to draw out the micro-scale individual experiences and challenges of choice in education and training markets. A strong theme which underpins our view of choice, though, is that in reality these choice points are not discrete, unique experiences but are simply part of a complex web of choice and decision-making that links every choice and decision from birth to labour market entry. While there are specific emphases and issues at particular choice points, there are also many common themes and linkages between them. Furthermore, decisions at each point can at least shape, and may ultimately strongly determine, the opportunities that fall into the individual's choice environment in the future. The traditional research approach in student choice of focusing on only one choice point, while providing a useful part of the picture, simply contributes to the jigsaw puzzle. We feel that there is now enough evidence from those jigsaw pieces to enable us to gain some understanding of the whole jigsaw picture. We are also keenly aware that within this book we have arbitrarily chosen to limit our analysis of choice up to and including higher education entry/labour market entry at 18, so that the focus is on decisions taken while young people are at school or college. This is another choice point rather than a fundamental boundary, and it is clear from the issues that emerge that many of the factors in, and processes of, choice will continue throughout individuals' lives as they make education, training and employment decisions.

Within this final chapter we shall draw together some of the emerging ideas by examining the patterns and themes in choice that have emerged; the models of choice making that can be inferred from the analysis; and the implications of the ideas for some wider policy issues that emerge from our understanding of young people's choices and choosing.

Choosing futures – patterns and themes

From our synthesis of ideas relating to choice throughout and about education and training a number of themes have emerged which weave together both the process of choice and the outcomes of decision-making. These relate to the emergence of choice over time; the role of the family in choice; the social context of choice; the role of teachers, schools and colleges in shaping choice; the primacy of academic pathways in choice; the importance of perceptions and images; the psychological dimensions of the development, reinforcement and protection of self-image; the role of failure, defaulting and dissonance in choice; rationality and sub-rationality in choice; and the tensions between stability and instability of choice outcomes.

The emergence of choice

The evidence from each of the key stages of the education/training pathway demonstrates that choice is a dynamic and emergent concept at all times. It originates in the attitudes, values, perceptions, images and beliefs of a young child's family and their circumstances, before evolving in the young person's own emerging values and perceptions. By the beginning of adolescence many of the fundamental attitudes to particular pathways and careers have been firmly established, either as negative or positive attitudes, built from the influential ideas transferred implicitly and explicitly by parents, teachers and the media. These provide the principal conceptual framework of a young person's understanding of adult life, and of its economic and related social constituents. While these can be modified, added to, or developed by the active experience of adolescence and life as a young adult, the fundamental structures and components seem to be established by the age of 11. Choice is not an instantaneous or even short-term period of decision, but a momentary external expression of the balance between a wide range of internal and external social, cultural and economic perceptions. Its expression as 'a choice' today is unlikely to be identical to its expression as 'a choice' tomorrow.

Two important points emerge from this. First, expressions of choice at any one moment are inherently unstable, at least in terms of their *precise* specification, and possibly in terms of their essential components. This idea of instability of choice will be explored further below. Second, any desire at a policy level to alter the macroscale patterns of choice preferences requires actions that will change perceptions and understandings both amongst all the influencing factors in choice (young people, parents, teachers and the media, for example) and across the whole time span of choice. Changing choice patterns in relation to university entrance, for example, requires changing attitudes in relation to decision-making as far back as primary school entrance and the attitudes of primary school teachers. This is, in part, because for many years those approaching HE choice will continue to have had their fundamental perceptual frameworks established by implicit and explicit influences since their childhood, and will be making choices in the context of traditional attitude and value systems. In addition, though, those frameworks can only be changed by modifying the messages and images that build them in the minds of key influencing people – and that takes time. Herein lies one of the great paradoxes of 'choice' for policymakers. While choice makes the system more responsive to the wants and needs of individuals within society, it makes the exercising of any form of political control to shape choice much less easy and much less predictable in its outcomes.

The family context of choice

Choice is the product of complex processes taking place within the context of an individual young person's family. Just as the family is a highly diverse phenomenon, so the precise operation of the choice process in this environment will be highly diverse. Roles and influences change over time, and family membership may change over time. The family environment is also a melting pot in which the experiences past and present of every member of that family contribute to a constantly re-emerging model of the world with which individuals interact.

The family environment is, of course, a product of its social situation. We have shown in earlier chapters the contrasts between choice in middle-class and working-class contexts. This may reflect differences in the importance of economic and social factors in lifestyle models, differences in educational and social histories, and differences in the 'cultural capital' of individuals and families. Such differences are clearly not just based in social class, but, as we have seen in relation to further and higher education 'choice', interact in different ways with the cultural values of particular ethnic communities.

Identifying the influence of the family in the choice process of younger children is not difficult. Five year olds do not choose their own school. Their parents do, on the basis of their own values and aspirations for their children (whether long-term or short-term, career-focused or social-context focused). By the time choice of secondary school is required the influence and autonomy of the child have grown such that they contribute, in most cases, to the shaping and making of choice. For all children, though, the choice will be explicitly constrained by the family's 'models' of education and training and their value and importance in relation to social and economic objectives. The relative influence of different family members must be underlined here, for fathers, mothers and siblings do not play identical roles with equal weight in choice. The role of mothers in searching and refining and the role of fathers in confirming choices emerges quite strongly from the research evidence we have presented.

Beyond the age of 11 adolescence moves the young person into the role of decision-taker as the family context encourages, allows, or, in some cases, resists, the growing individuality and self-responsibility of the child. The family context of attitudes and values, though, has huge unconscious persistence in the decision-making of 14–18 year olds, and we must regard the choices that are made during this time as being, for most young people, a synthesis of inherited values and emerging individual values. The choices of young people are never free of the influence of their family, with the implication that replication of choice and values from generation to generation is a significant element in understanding broad patterns of choice in education and training markets.

The social context of choice

The social context of choice has two distinct meanings. In general terms it describes the broad social and cultural environments within which an individual and their family live. It is strongly related to social class, and is defined by the attitudes and values of particular social groups. The expected link between social class, social status and choice has emerged very clearly in relation to each of the choice points we have considered. Broadly speaking, middle-class aspirations relate strongly to notions of economic advancement and social status, while working-class choice is focused more strongly on the young person's own preferences and the desire to preserve social acceptability. Just as choosing is strongly linked to social class, so we have identified a number of strong links between choice patterns and ethnicity.

Social context, though, also has a second meaning, as we are reminded by Maguire *et al.* (2000), for it also relates to the immediate social and leisure life of an individual. It is in this context that the pressures to establish or preserve self-esteem, and to make decisions that support group identity are found. These pressures are important in shaping choice. In relation to school choice, it is the social context of the parents which is important, but by the time choice is being made at 16+ or 18+ this combines, and is probably overshadowed by, the pressures on the young people themselves. The growing significance of lifestyle as a theme in the development of personal image is one we have stressed elsewhere in this book. Lifestyle is intimately involved with social relations, not leisure and social status in relation to peers and other groups. We would suggest, therefore, that the expansion of 'lifestyleism' will see a growing influence on choice of factors relating to this aspect of the social context of young people and their parents.

The institutional context of choice

The second important environment of choice influence is that of the young person's school or college. We have seen in relation to choice at each of the key break points in the education/training system that the role of individuals from within school, and of the overall ethos and value system of the school, are important in shaping perceptions and images. At primary school, headteachers are important gatekeepers to subsequent stages of education, while class teachers implant in children, knowingly or unknowingly, a range of cultural perspectives and values, as well as specific career, education and labour market 'knowledge'. At secondary school these roles continue but are added to by the impact of formal and informal careers education and guidance, and, as the child approaches 16, the promotional messages emanating from post-16 education and training providers. Several aspects of this institutional context appear to be of particular importance in the choice process.

First, the interaction of institutional 'messages' and 'parental' values is important, for they may act as positive reinforcement to each other or, through contradictions and conflicts, provide substantial dissonance in the thinking of young people and their families. In general terms, for example, we can assume that the emphasis on academic pathways and examination achievement in a context of middle-class values in most independent schools will reinforce the parental perspective on choice and pathways through education. This synergy may generate an almost irresistible pressure towards certain FE and HE choices amongst young people in this context. In contrast, the contradictions we have identified earlier between school values and the values and aspirations of some sectors of, particularly working-class, communities, may generate very significant tensions for young people caught between them. This battleground makes choice and decision-making substantially more challenging for such young people, for any choice will compromise the values of one of the key influences in their lives – school or family. Justifying and announcing choices in such a context will be much more problematical and challenging to self-esteem, as we shall consider later.

Second, the knowledge and guidance of teachers other than careers teachers is of importance in shaping perceptions, yet we have shown in Chapter 8 how the accuracy and reliability of that knowledge is questionable. Added to this limited knowledge is the institutional pressure for teachers to push young people towards decisions that are primarily in the school or college's interest because of its own competitive needs. Between them these two dimensions compromise an important part of the information system in choice, and may handicap or at least constrain the choice process for young people.

Third, the role of careers guidance is important as a counter to existing attitudes, knowledge and perception, and is a critical factor where young people from social backgrounds with no family traditions of FE or HE make a choice to pursue such a pathway. Although not without its own organisational needs relating to the aims of careers companies, CEG provides the nearest approximation to 'objective' guidance available to young people in support of their choice processes. CEG, however, is constrained by resources in the extent of its influence, particularly with younger children, and its ability to act as a counter to entrenched perceptions is, therefore, limited.

Fourth, the role of marketing and promotional strategies is important. These have emerged as a very important influence in choice, perhaps more by providing 'just-in-time' information to enable choices to be justified rather than in fundamentally changing the choices that may be made. In relation to primary and secondary school choice the relationship between parents and schools, and its strong community context, means that a relationship marketing approach, with an emphasis on word-of-mouth, is the only effective mechanism for this communication. With FE and HE choice, though, transactional marketing processes become more important, although relationship marketing may still be significant in some market segments, particularly in recruitment into training pathways. Such promotional strategies may not be important for changing choice, but they are a very important element of the psychological processes of choice justification and announcement. The interaction of promotional activities and young people's choice processes is an area of important research for the future.

The primacy of academic pathways

A dominant theme that emerges from the analysis of choice from five to 18 is the importance of academic pathways as the most frequent choice of young people, and the market value that academic choices appear to possess. For active choosers, whether they are parents of three year olds or 10 year olds, or young people themselves considering post-16 pathways, the dominant themes in their choice relate to accessing academic pathways. University entrance seems to represent the kite mark of economic and social success in the wider community, and is perceived as the gateway to economic enhancement, social status and lifestyle benefits by most young people. Access to university is itself seen as only achievable by the pursuit of academic pathways through post-16 education, and active choosers appear to make their choice at any key point so as to optimise the chance of pursuing a successful academic route at later stages of their individual pathway.

At all stages, non-academic pathways are seen as the option of those not able or willing to access academic routes. Vocational choices are perceived as a second choice option, and, therefore, as the refuge of those with a track record of not reaching their initial educational goals and ambitions. Despite the pursuit of equity between academic and vocational programmes by government policy, there is still little belief in the community that vocational pathways can deliver the ultimate goal of university entrance. This is strongly the perception that underpins the value system of middle-class parents, most teachers, and most active choosers amongst working-class communities, and which strongly shapes the choices of young people and their parents about education and training options.

The role of perception and image

Within any decision-making process, whether related to education/ training choice or the purchase of consumer goods, an important element is an individual's belief and understanding of the benefits and disadvantages of choosing each particular option. This is a form of 'cost-benefit analysis', but is based not on vigilant information searches and a rational process of decision-making but on a partly conscious and partly subconscious process bringing together fact and feeling, ideas and image. Central to this process is the role of perception, for to the individual it is their perception of the world that is the objective reality on which this cost-benefit analysis is made. In Chapter 8 three forms of image in career choice were iden-tified – contracted images, that an individual has constructed for themselves from their own experiences; delegated images, which are acquired from other people's perceptions; and derived images, that emerge from the media. These images interact to create the indi-vidual's overall perceptual model of any component of the choice they are engaging in, and this will be true for both the young person and the adults who are involved in advising, formally or informally, that choice.

This creates three interesting issues in understanding choice. First, the perceptual models held by each person will be unique, which will in turn provide a unique input into the choice-making process. Understanding choice at the micro-level, therefore, can only be achieved through seeking to identify an individual's personal constructs. Second, it is important to recognise that any form of guidance, information or input from a third party is itself the product of that individual's own personal perceptions. Since educa-tion and training choices are largely concerned with decisions about an adult world that young people have not directly experienced, almost all their perceptions will have been passed through the filter of other people's perceptual models before reaching them. Under-standing this issue, and seeking to make young people aware of the need to question the delegated images they receive, is an important part of 'careers literacy', and needs to be a high priority in any form of CEG.

Third, we must recognise the great significance of the media in the lives of all sectors of the community, and the importance within media communications of the creation of image linked to the objectives of a consumerist society. 'Lifestyle' has become an important element both in formal marketing by organisations and in the general approach adopted by the media. Our research suggests that derived images from the media are important in creating and amending the perceptual constructs young people have in relation to careers and the labour market. The values these images embody find a fertile site in young people's developing models of society and their place within it. In particular, the importance of images of lifestyle in shaping choice in education and training markets must be recognised. The 'holistic lifestyle view of careers' that we have identified (Chapter 8) as important in choice underlines the central role of media images in developing perceptions as part of such personal decisions. Understanding choice requires us, therefore, to examine closely the images and values the media portray in relation to the labour market and education/training. In addition, though, seeking to modify perceptions rapidly may only be achievable through re-presentation of images and ideas through the media.

The reinforcement of self-image

It is implicit within any discussion of education and training pathways that young people are preparing, and being prepared, to assume a role within adult society. This is not simply a technical process of providing them with knowledge and skills, but is a highly complex psychological process in which the individual seeks to make sense of their own physical, emotional and social maturation. To compound the psychological challenge, at the very time when young people are developing their own social and personal roles and values, society also requires them to make decisions relating to work and education that may have quite a fundamental impact on their whole lives. From this perspective it is perhaps surprising that so few young people find this a quite insuperable demand.

Central to all this is the development of self-image by the individual young person. Identifying who they are, what their relationships with family, friends and the wider community can be, and seeking a role in the adult world, is built around creating, protecting and expressing self-image. At the points in the education/training pathway where a young person plays a central role in their own choices (i.e. choice at 16+, 18+ and in choices of career), it is clear that protecting self-image is a key process. Choices are made that give credibility to the individual in the eyes of those around them of personal importance, particularly their peers. Information searching is based on identifying the best way of justifying choice when it is announced to peers. Understanding choice at such stages requires us to identify the value systems of the peer group within which an individual does, or would like to, live their personal life. In the context of the growing media emphasis on lifestyle images amongst both their peers and older adults, this process may become even more significant in the education/training choice process in the future. At 16 or 18 the lifestyle and values they espouse are unlikely to be those of their parents! However, the peer and friendship groups within which they operate will probably have emerged from the social environment in which their parents placed them as younger children. The hidden hand of parental influence will be clear, if somewhat modified, in the attitudes and values of the peer group, therefore.

Protecting self-image is not a process unique to young people, of course. Our analysis of school choice, where parental influence is very substantial, has shown that adults operate the same psychological processes as their older teenage children will in due course. School choice is in no small measure a statement of the values, beliefs and social status of parents, who are seeking recognition from their own peer groups for the decisions they make. Within broadly defined social groups the common themes in school choice are a reflection of the shared values of the group. Expressing those values in words, actions and decisions is one way in which self-esteem and group identity and membership are reinforced. In the context of independent school choice (Chapter 4) we have explored in detail some of the issues relating to the creation and announcement of choice. This suggests that it is the public declaration of choice to peer groups which is the major psychological challenge to be met. Exploring the mechanisms for defending and justifying school choice in different social groups will be an important arena of future research.

Choice, defaulting and dissonance

A strong theme that has emerged from the analysis within this book has been the high expectations of children, young people and their parents throughout the decision-making process. While some of this is, inevitably, an encouraging measure of the existence of hopes and dreams in human nature, there is, nevertheless, an exaggerated expectation of achievement at each choice point. In school, higher proportions of children expect to enter lottery jobs and high-status jobs than society can support. In relation to formal public examinations at 16 and 18, young people predict they will achieve substantially better GCSE and A-level results than the objective performance data would suggest. At 16 and 18 more young people aspire to enter academic pathways in FE and HE than the system will accept.

The reasons for this over-optimism are complex. In part it reflects the underlying values of society that support the pursuit of high aspirations. This is a message strongly peddled by schools and by government, and also by parents who inevitably wish to see their children be successful both for their own sake and also to enhance their social status as parents. It also reflects the psychological process of promoting self-image, in the context of a society which gives social, economic and market primacy to success in academic pathways and to the lifestyle outcomes of success in the labour market. There is also a strong belief in luck or chance, a belief that things will fall into place, based on a serious over-estimate of the likelihood of such chance events occurring. This is no more than the over-estimation of the likelihood of success that has made the National Lottery in the UK so popular a form of recreation.

The consequence of this over-optimism, though, is that for many young people the reality of their eventual choice is one that emanates from a failure to achieve their original personal goals. Their choices are second (or lower) choices, and they must go through the process of defaulting to lower ambitions in pathway and career choice arenas. This is, of course, not only personally challenging, but also challenging to the protection of self-esteem which is so important in choice making. The resulting dissonance that emerges from the choices they can make *and* operationalise provides a strong personal challenge to be met, and which may be the root of much of the instability of choice amongst those who pursue pathways other than successful academic routes.

Rationality and sub-rationality in choice

The development of enhanced choice in education has been founded on an unquestioning policy view of choice as an economically rational process. Examination of this idea in relation to generic choice processes and the psychology of choice (Chapter 2) has shown that this is an untenable view. The evidence from the analysis of education/training choice elsewhere in this book has confirmed that we must not base any true understanding of decision-making and choice on such models. This is not to say, though, that there is a complete absence of pattern and principle to choice, or that it is a non-rational process. We have shown clearly how, at the micro-scale, we can identify some factors as more important than others (e.g academic achievements are frequently the most important factor in choice), and that it is possible to predict the broad picture that will result from the choice outcomes in particular market environments.

Rationality is also a feature of choice, but the impossibility of a fully rational choice process means that most choices are rational only in part. Individuals appear to have a commitment to rationality, too, in that they will seek to justify decisions based on emotional and perceptual judgements in logical, rational terms, often to defend themselves from accusations of a poor decision or an over-commitment to feelings rather than logic. Rationality can be constructed where none is obvious to outside observers, and on the flimsiest of evidence!

Overall, therefore, we should describe choice in education and training arenas as either sub-rational or, according to Hodkinson and Sparkes (1997), pragmatically rational, i.e. rational within the confines of limited information, the inherent human desire to minimise effort, and the pressure to preserve self-image in the announcement of decisions. Just as individuals may be seen to be satisfied with making a decision that is 'good enough' rather than an optimising choice, so their choice process may be seen as 'rational enough'. A decision to use the local community comprehensive school may have been made, for example, to preserve acceptability within the family's social arena and peer groups, but may be justified as a decision made on grounds of proximity or the child's choice to remain with friends. Where the truth really lies between these ideas is hard to determine, and, in practice, both forms of justification for the choice are rational. What we are seeing is not a non-rational process but a choice of justification strategies.

Stability and instability of choice

The use of the term 'choice' in relation to education and training pathways can be misleading, for the term has an implication of irrevocable commitment to a line of action or behavioural strategy. It suggests that choice is the ultimate culmination of a rational, reasoned process, and once made will not be revisited. This is an invalid and naïve view of choice and the choice process, for we have shown that many 'choices' are unstable, and are subject to change, modification and reversal over short or long periods of time.

Some choices are stable of course, in that they are not changed, although this should not imply that the chooser never considered that they should be changed. In general, the most stable decisions are those relating to accessing academic pathways and entry into high-status careers. This is for two reasons. First, they are the choices with the highest market value, the aspirational high ground for most individuals. Their achievement is likely to have minimised post-choice dissonance and generated most satisfaction amongst both the chooser and their family and social circles. Second, such decisions close few alternative pathways. Academic pathways leave many future choices open, since they are more generic than many of the vocational pathways. In addition, they involve minimal (if any) defaulting, preserving this option for later occasions. For young people this combination of high peer acclaim for the choice and minimum compromise of alternatives seems to be a win–win choice, and is likely to be highly stable and persistent.

Other choices have much less stability, though, for they are more likely to generate dissonance and feelings of sub-optimal achievement. They will generate less self-esteem and less recognition amongst peer groups. They will be constantly subject to review and re-appraisal. The evidence from choice in relation to vocational pathways and employment at 16+ has stressed the mobility of young people between choices, and confirms that we cannot be confident that any specific choice has long-term or even short-term persistence or stability.

Instability does not just apply to choices made at the points of transition within the education/training environment. The choice process is long term. Accessing it at any moment will stimulate the revelation of a choice, which is simply the preferred option at the time. Such perspectives are constantly subject to reappraisal on the basis of new information and perceptions, and are subject to change. They are inherently unstable for, as Foskett and Hesketh (1997) suggest, the choice process

> ... involves many iterations and reiterations in relation to specific educational choices with a continuous matching, re-matching

and filtering of new perceptions and available information within the existing choice structures of both pupils and their parents.

(Foskett and Hesketh, 1997, p. 302)

We must regard instability of choice, therefore, not as a sign of a failure in the process, but as an integral part of choosing. Stability is a much less common state than instability in this environment.

Modelling 'choice' in career, education and training markets

In examining some of the patterns and themes that have emerged from a consideration of young people's choice it is possible to begin to construct a conceptual model of the choice process. A starting point for such a model is provided by two existing conceptualisations of choice, both derived from analysis of choice at 16+. These are the models developed by Hodkinson, Sparkes and Hodkinson (1996), and by Maguire, MacRae and Ball (2000), the latter of which is in itself a development of Hodkinson *et al.*'s model. Hodkinson and Sparkes perceive choice as emerging from the interaction of young people with their *habitus*, key experiences in their personal life histories, stakeholders in the post-16 market place, and a number of horizons of action. An 'horizon for action' is 'the area within which actions can be taken and decisions made' (Hodkinson, 1995, p. 5), and will be defined in part by objective realities of the range of circumstances and options available and in part by subjective narrowing of that range on the basis of each individual's perceptions. As a result such horizons for action may be broad or narrow, complex or simple.

Maguire *et al.* (2000, p. 14) have extended this model in two ways. First, they suggest that there are 'three critical arenas of action and centres of choice making', which interact in the shaping of choice – the arena of family, home and domesticity; the arena of work, education and training; and the arena of leisure and social life. Second, they suggest that the choice model must include both spatial and temporal components. The arenas of choice operate within localities defined by the individual's personal spatial zone of operation, and are dynamic over time, with histories and future expectations and aspirations as well as a continuously changing present.

These models are valuable in demonstrating the broad socio-cultural spheres which interact to shape a young person's decision or choice. However, they provide little by way of an understanding of the processes of choice within the individual's mind, and they need extending to provide a perspective that is more generically applicable than just within the context of choice at 16+. The analysis of choice within this book is the basis of our own model of choice and decision-making in education and training markets (Figure 9.1).

The four components of the model are 'Context', 'Choice Influencers', 'Choosers' and 'Choice'. The chooser operates within a context that is defined by the full range of components of their individual life – their home, their institutional environment (work or school), their social existence, their lived space (i.e. the geographical locations that their lives encompass), and the social, cultural, economic and policy environment within which each of these operates. This context provides the backdrop to choice, the panorama of the individual's life which defines their own existence. Each element within it comprises people, processes, culture and values, each of which will contribute to the whole environment of choice.

This context provides not just a passive, inert background of

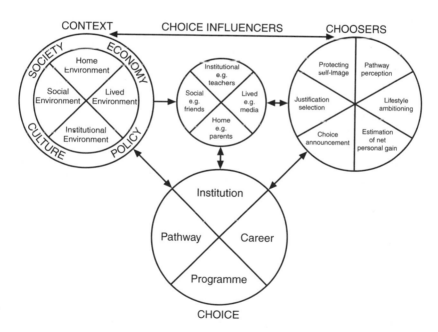

Figure 9.1 Model of choice and decision-making in education and training markets.

implicit influences on choice, but also active explicit influences, and this is represented in the model by the Choice Influencers. These influencers may be people or they may be processes such as media communications. The difference between the passive 'context' and the active 'choice influencer' can be illustrated with reference to the role of a child's school in the choice process. Its passive influence lies in its mere existence as a component of the child's life, albeit imbued with strong value-laden implicit messages about the world of work, education and training. Its active explicit influence, though, emerges when it engages with the choice process directly through the ideas and actions of teachers and careers teachers. Such choice influencers act as an important intervening filter on the perceptions of the environment that an individual chooser may have. Where these influencers are people, whether they are teachers, friends, peers or parents, they will be engaging in a range of psychological processes to generate their own interpretations of the environment and preferences for choice. These are described below in our consideration of 'choosers'.

The notion of 'Chooser' is important within the model. We have recognised that the question of 'who chooses' generates different answers in relation to each young person and to the particular choice point they have reached. The chooser of a child's primary school is not the child, but will be an unequal partnership decision between mother and father. At age 11, the child will contribute to this partnership choice, and by 16 or 18 will be the dominant partner in the choice. By this stage the role of each parent will have been relegated to their contribution through the long-term drip feed of attitudes, values and perceptions into the young person's psyche. We cannot know exactly who the chooser is, therefore, in any individual case. Whoever it is, though, we can identify a range of psychological processes they will be applying to the choice on a continuing basis, whether they are a mature adult, child, adolescent or young adult. These will be:

a   the construction of perceptions of careers, and of FE and HE options, from contracted, delegated and derived images *(pathway perception)*;

b   the construction of lifestyle ambitions from similar sources *(lifestyle ambitioning)*;

c   the comparison of perceptions and lifestyle images in an informal estimate of net long-term and short-term personal gain *(estimation of net personal gain)*;

d   the comparison of perceptions and lifestyle images with the need to protect and enhance self-image in the social and cultural context that the individual operates within *(protecting self-image)*;

e   the selection of *post-hoc* justifications to preserve self-image and group identity *(justification selection)*;

f   the announcement of a choice within the social and cultural environments where the individual operates *(choice announcement)*.

There is no implication in this description of the internalised psychological processes of the choosers that this is a rational, sequential and essentially positive process of choice. Our analysis of the generic principles of choosing futures earlier within this chapter has emphasised how many choices are second-best options, or are simply a default residual after other options have been rejected or have simply not been acted upon. Whether the process is active, passive, positive or negative, the psychological processes described here will operate, although their relative significance, order of occurrence, and interaction may differ from person to person.

From this interaction of context, choice influencer and chooser, will emerge a 'Choice'. That choice is not fixed or irrevocable, however, and itself is subject to interaction with the other components of the model, and hence subject to change. It will be conditional not only on the individual achieving the necessary achievements to allow them to pursue that choice, but also on the choice having sufficient stability to survive the reconsideration that it will be subject to. It has an internal dynamic as well as being part of the dynamic nature of the process shown in the overall model. It is important to recognise, therefore, that choosers may revisit any of the stages many times, as significant changes in context (e.g. policy changes), or new information provided by choice influencers (e.g. CEG input), are drawn to the chooser's attention.

Travelling the pathways of education and training

The model we have described above provides an objective view of the nature of choice in education and training markets. Our interviews with many young people and their parents through our research suggests, however, that to each individual the story of their choosing and the way in which they follow 'their' pathway is more a narrative of a personal history than a systems model can portray. We believe the choice process may be perceived, therefore, like a journey, where decisions and choices made along the way determine, not individually but through the product of their interaction, the final destination to be reached.

The pathway through education and training that begins formally when a child enters primary school becomes increasingly complex in the route that takes young people through to 18 years of age. The path divides repeatedly, offering a wider range of destinations at each junction, while at the same time the quality and effectiveness of the signposting reduces further along the path. There *is* one main pathway which many can choose to follow, which is the academic path through secondary school, A-levels and on into university. University education is the 'emerald city' at the end of this particular yellow brick road.

The path becomes narrower as young people progress along it, though, and cannot accommodate all who might wish to stay on it. Some leave by choice, some fall off the path by accident, some are pushed off in competition with others to stay on. Those who leave are forced to take less well signposted side roads. Some of these side paths suggest in their signposts that they can lead to the emerald city, but the route they follow is more tortuous, more likely to be subject to diversions and obstacles to progress, and is perceived by young people and their parents as, in fact, leading somewhere other than university. Government policy has, of course, sought to help solve congestion and confusion in this particular road network. They have taken steps to widen the main path so more people can follow it, to improve (and widen) the side roads of alternative routes, to ensure that more of the side routes reach university, to provide tourist promotional materials for alternative destinations, and to enhance the signposting, for the side roads are still the routes taken by most people.

To make matters more difficult, those who leave the main pathway are often those who are the least capable at map reading and with a more limited idea of what the destination is that they are aiming for. These young people run the risk of wandering the side roads for a long time without reaching an attractive destination. As a result, the guides have simple advice for those embarking on the route – 'stay on the main path unless you can be sure that the destination of a side road is assuredly where you want to go'. There are guides along the path (CEG professionals), who can explain the destinations of some of the side routes, and can also show how some side roads rejoin the main path further along. Few listen to their guidance, however, for the message about 'staying on the main road' has been strongly inculcated into travellers before they start and in the early parts of their journey. Guidance comes principally from those who have travelled the route before. Teachers, parents and other adults have made the journey themselves, and believe they know the route's twists, turns, shortcuts and destinations. Time plays tricks with the memory, though, and major roadworks mean that the pathway and its side routes have changed much in recent years. Many of the new side roads and loops are not on their older editions of the map, and so, in accordance with the advice to stay on the main road, many travellers are unwilling to explore alternative choices.

The emergence of a 'main pathway' or a 'well-known choice for all' is partly the result of enhanced choice. In a competitive market, where there is a real intention to expand the overall market there tends to be one major 'product' which emerges as the 'standard'. The more unusual choices are generally taken up by enthusiasts and by the most knowledgeable buyers. In the case of educational choice, as the market expands, the route which everyone knows about becomes the 'best choice' for all – but this is problematic in education because that route is one which is highly selective. This means that those who are least well informed are unable to take the 'standard' route, and have to find their way through a less familiar path.

Choosing futures – some policy issues

As we progress towards a better understanding of how and why young people's choices are made we can begin to consider the implications for a range of meta-scale policy issues in relation to education and training. Three specific policy domains will be addressed here – the policy drive towards widening participation and lifelong learning; the implications of choice for school improvement and the raising of achievement for all pupils; and the future development of careers education and guidance in a context of enhanced choice for individuals.

Choice, lifelong learning and widening participation

'Lifelong learning' has become a central tenet in responding to the international imperative to be responsive to an ever more rapidly changing and globalising world economy. 'Widening participation' is an important element of this commitment for it focuses on encouraging more individuals to engage in learning at all stages of education and training. As Blunkett (1998b, p. 1) has indicated:

> To achieve stable and sustainable growth, we will need a well-educated, well-equipped and adaptable labour force. To cope with rapid change and the challenge of the information and communication age, we must ensure that people can return to learning throughout their lives.

However, despite this commitment to education and training, there is still much to be done to promote the notion of a 'learning society' (DfEE, 1998b). Only the embedding of a culture of self-development by and for individuals, which builds on entitlements and responsibilities (CBI, 1989), will achieve this social and economic goal, and rhetoric and policy achieve such fundamental social change only slowly. It is in the choices and decisions of individuals that the key to achieving a 'learning society' is to be found. Choices about learning at all stages through to age 18 are rooted in the earliest decisions made by and for young people, which are themselves based in deeply ingrained perceptions of the nature and value of learning pathways that are available. Amongst young people and their parents learning is seen as the route to economic and social benefits leading to an enhanced lifestyle. Its value is not intrinsic, but extrinsic, and lies in the payoff to the individual later in their life. Furthermore, vocational training and education is seen as a 'just in time' form of learning with a smaller and more immediate payoff than academic learning.

We must assume that this is also true of decisions made throughout the individual's adult life. Expanding participation of adults and organisations in learning, therefore, requires more than simply 'selling' learning to them. First, it requires a fundamental understanding of the psychological processes of choice that those considering renewed participation must engage in, and in particular a recognition that a choice 'to participate in learning' will only be made where individuals can enhance or preserve self-esteem and group identity, and not expose themselves to the risk of failure. Second, if widening participation is based on vocational training or leisure-based learning then it will not possess much perceived value in individuals' subliminal calculations of personal gains and losses from learning – and if the gains to be made are not substantial to the individual, then they will be insufficient to overcome the inertia of non-participation.

Our final comment in relation to widening participation/lifelong learning relates to the imperative of researching adult choice, and choice processes in relation to career change, FE/HE participation decisions amongst adults, and the psychological barriers to choosing to learn (Hemsley-Brown and Humphreys, 1998). Although we can begin to make policy suggestions on the basis of extrapolating our model of young people's choice, we can only be confident of our perspective with evidence from specific research programmes.

Choice and school improvement

Our second policy field for comment relates to the issue of school improvement. We have demonstrated in Chapter 1 that there is increasing evidence that current market models for choosing secondary schools do not lead to enhanced achievements in school in total, but have the negative impact of increasing social polarisation. So if markets and parental choice polarise the raising of standards so that some advantaged schools do well by their pupils and the disadvantaged schools do not, what are the alternatives? Choice appears to now be too embedded into the libertarian value systems of governments and societies in many countries to countenance replacing it with a command system of allocating school places. Indeed, those proponents of markets in school choice would contend that the deficiencies of quasi markets lie in the constraints imposed by government. Free up the markets from much or all of the government intervention, and the system, they suggest, will deliver both quality and equity objectives in the long term (Tooley, 1996, 1997).

Such enthusiasm is not widespread, however, for as Lauder and Hughes (1999) indicate, the baseline inequalities between schools, as a result of differences between their catchment communities, means that such an outcome will not be achieved. They suggest, as an alternative, that the answer must lie in some form of constrained choice, through what they term 'state-mediated choice', which they believe would have the dual advantages of preserving parental choice while preventing the worst excesses of polarisation. Such state-mediated choice would enable parents to express preferences, but would allow local authorities or government to ensure that the final pattern of pupil allocation did not promote inequalities between the schools. The mechanisms of such a process are more challenging to conceptualise than the principle, however, for they will require a challenge to the newly acquired rights of individuals to choose freely the education their children receive. There remains a long social and political battle ahead over the balance between the right to choose and the rights of society and the individual to be protected from the potential negative impacts of choice.

Careers education and guidance

A central consideration in our analysis within this book has been the role of careers education and guidance (CEG). Its role in shaping and informing choice, particularly in relation to post-16 and post-18 options for young people has become clear, and its potential to fulfil the crucial role of 'market maker' within the choice systems of education and training is substantial. Despite government rhetoric and some central funding and policy direction to enhance the role and scope of CEG, however, it remains a service constrained from operating in the arenas where it can be most effective. We have shown how the development of images and perceptions of careers and education/training pathways is well established by the time young people enter adolescence, such that when CEG 'kicks in' in the secondary school much of its potential for influence has been lost. By then, many young people are unwilling or unable to make effective use of CEG, and the service is only of value to those dealing with the cognitive dissonance of recognising their inability to achieve previously chosen target careers or pathways. CEG is of most help to those who become aware of the value of pathways outside the normal arenas of action inhabited by those from similar cultural backgrounds, and hence unable to obtain guidance from within their community contacts; and also those seeking a second tier choice.

We believe that understanding choice is itself an important entitlement for young people. If we are to endow them with the rights and responsibilities of choice, we must equip them with the skills to exercise that choice. This requires an understanding of the process of choice and of the influences on choice, and of mechanisms for dealing with the psychological challenges of choice. There is a need for the extension of careers education, therefore, into two domains where it is currently absent. First, it must be developed within the primary school curriculum, not as careers guidance, but as a process of personal development and as part of the notion of citizenship. Citizenship is built on the idea of recognising the contribution the individual can make to society and their rights and obligations within contemporary political and economic systems. Facilitating choice is a key element of that responsibility. Second, this extension of CEG into the primary arena will require an increasing awareness of choice processes and issues amongst teachers, and programmes to support teacher development in this field would seem to be a high priority. There will need to be careful exploration of the mechanisms for achieving this with the positive support of those with responsibility for the whole primary curriculum.

Choosing futures

Consumerism, individualism and choice are central themes in the society and culture of the new millennium across much of the globe. Just as they drive the operation of the retail and manufacturing sectors of the economy, they have underpinned the expansion and diversification of the service sector and encroached in a substantial way into the provision of what were traditionally public sector services. Young people and adults are encouraged by the media and marketing influence in society to express their individualism through lifestyle choices, and choices of education and training have become as much a part of that self-expression as the purchase of consumer goods. Issues of status, self-esteem, cultural capital, and power are implicated as choices are made and options exercised, and amidst such emotive and politically charged issues there emerge winners and losers in the competition for the benefits of education and training.

But where does this leave young people, their parents and their families operating in the new world of enhanced choice in educational and training arenas? While at the macro-scale such debates have provided rich academic and political discussion, the individuals faced with the choice process in their own lives have found a challenging and often contradictory reality that has often made them the victims rather than the beneficiaries of choice. Losers may be seen in terms of the outcomes of the choice process, but the experiences and emotional challenge of choice may mean that some who are winners in terms of outcomes are losers in terms of the necessity of going through a difficult and dissonant experience. The rhetoric of choosing schools, FE and HE pushes parents and young people to see themselves as consumers, not just because they have a right to freedom of choice but also because they have an obligation to improve the system by playing their role as consumers. The language of consumerism is 'writ large' in an explosion of guidance on choice. Official publications, such as the Parents Charter (DfEE, 1994), direct them to exercise this right, while commercial guidebooks purport to provide insider information to support the choice process. At school level, and in terms of FE and HE choice, the emergence of competitive indicators such as guide books and league tables defines the form of the market and the basis of competition in classical consumerist terms.

Throughout this book we have attempted to show how far young people and their parents have come to terms with, or adopted, the emergence of enhanced choice. In particular we have described and modelled the process by which young people choose their futures up to and beyond the age of 18. Choice is an inevitable component of life in a democracy and a market economy, and is a challenge for all young people to engage with in their personal, social and educa-tional/training lives and their subsequent careers. We have shown, though, that choice can be both an opportunity to exercise free will in the pursuit of personal betterment for some, and a lose–lose end game for others, depending on circumstance and opportunity.

Bibliography

Ausubel, D. P. (1958). *Theory and Problems of Child Development.* New York: Grune and Stratton.

Bain, K. and Howells, P. (1988). *Understanding Markets.* London: Harvester Wheatsheaf.

Baker, K. (1988). Speech to the North of England Education Conference, January 1988.

Baker, M. J. (1992). *Marketing Strategy and Management.* Second Edition. Hong Kong: Macmillan.

Ball, S. J. (1993). 'Market forces in education.' *Education Review,* 7, 1, pp. 8–11.

Ball, S. J., Bowe, R. and Gewirtz, S. (1995). 'Circuits of schooling: a sociological exploration of parental choice of school in social class contexts', *Sociological Review,* 43, 1, pp. 52–78,

Ball, S. J. and Gewirtz, S. (1997a). 'Is research possible? A rejoinder to Tooley's "On school choice and social class"', *British Journal of Sociology of Education,* 18, 4, pp. 575–86.

Ball, S. J., Macrae, S. and Maguire, M. (1999). 'In a Class of their Own: classifying and classified – identity and the science of infinite distinctions.' *Paper presented to the BERA Conference, University of Sussex, September 1999.*

Barber, M. (1996). *The Learning Game – Arguments for an Educational Revolution.* London: Victor Gollancz.

Barrett, L. R. (1996). 'Students as consumers – some warnings from America', *HE Review,* 28, 3, pp. 70–3.

Beardshaw, J., Brewster, D., Cormack, P. and Ross, A. (1998). *Economics: A Student Guide.* Edinburgh: Addison Wesley Longman.

Becker, G. (1975). *Human Capital: A Theoretical and Empirical Analysis, with Special Reference to Education.* New York: Columbia University Press.

Beischer, N. (1995). 'Marketing Through the Grapevine', *Inside Education Marketing,* 1, 2, pp. 8–11.

Bennett, R. J., Glennester, H. and Nevison, D. (1992). *Learning Should Pay.* Poole: B.P. Education Services.

Beven, P. (1995). 'Using Personal Construct Theory in Careers Education and Guidance', University of Northumbria at Newcastle, Department of Employment Studies: Research Paper on the UNN Internet Web Site.

Blunkett, D. (1998a). 'Modern Apprenticeships – the popular choice for school leavers', *DfEE 574/98 Press Release.*

Blunkett, D. (1998b). Foreword to *The Learning Age.* London: DfEE.

Bourdieu, P. (1997). 'The forms of capital', in A. H. Halsey, H. Lauder, P. Brown, A. S. Wells (eds), *Education: Culture, Economy and Society.* Oxford: Oxford University Press.

Bourdieu, P. and Passeron, J. C. (1990). *Reproduction in Education, Society and Culture.* London: Sage.

Bowe, R., Ball, S. J. and Gold, A. (1992). *Reforming Education and Changing Schools: Case Studies in Policy Sociology.* London: Routledge.

Bowe, R., Gewirtz, S. and Ball, S. J. (1994). 'Captured by the discourse? Issues and concerns in researching "parental choice"'. *British Journal of Sociology of Education,* 15, 1, pp. 63–78.

Bredo, O., Foersom, T. and Laursen, P. F. (1993). 'Students choice – a model'. *HE Review,* 26, 1, pp. 64–73.

Brehm, J. (1966). 'Post-decisional changes in the desirability of alternatives', *Journal of Abnormal and Social Psychology,* 52, pp. 384–9.

Brighouse, T. (1992). 'External relations and the future', in N. H. Foskett (ed.), *Managing External Relations in Schools – A Practical Guide.* London: Routledge.

Butterfield, S. and Chitty, C. (1997). *In Search of Key Stage 4.* London: ATL.

Callender, C. and Kempson, E. (1996). *Student Finances.* London: Policy Studies Institute.

Caplen, P. (2000). 'How can HE institutions improve support for full time undergraduates making the transition from sixth form into higher education?' Unpublished MA(Ed) dissertation, University of Southampton.

Carroll, S. and Walford, G. (1997a). 'The child's voice in school choice', *Educational Management and Administration,* 25, 2, pp. 169–80.

Carroll, S. and Walford, G. (1997b). 'Parents' responses to the school quasi-market', *Research Papers in Education,* 12, 1, pp. 3–26.

Chisnall, P. (1985). *Consumer Behaviour – 3rd Edition.* London, New York: McGraw Hill Book Company.

Cockett, M. and Callaghan, J. (1995). 'Caught in the middle – transition at 16+', in R. Halsall and M. Cockett (eds), *Education and Training 14–19: Chaos or Coherence.* London: David Fulton.

Cohen, L. and Manion, L. (1994). *Research Methods in Education.* Fourth Edition. London: Routledge.

Coldron, J. and Boulton, P. (1991). 'Happiness as a criterion of parents' choice of school', *Journal of Education Policy,* 6, 2, pp. 169–78.

Confederation of British Industry (CBI) (1989). *Towards a Skills Revolution.* Report of the Vocational Education and Training Task Force. London: CBI.

Confederation of British Industry (CBI) (1993a). *Routes for Success.* London: CBI.

Confederation of British Industry (CBI) (1993b). *A Credit to Your Career.* London: CBI.

Connor, H., Burton, R., Pearson, R., Pollard, E. and Regan, J. (1999).

Making the Right Choice: How Students Choose Universities and Colleges. London: Institute for Employment Studies for CVCP.

Copley, S. and Sutherland, K. (1995). *Adam Smith's Wealth of Nations. New Interdisciplinary Essays.* Manchester: Manchester University Press.

Cox, K. K. (1968). *Analytical Viewpoints in Marketing Management.* New Jersey: Prentice Hall, Inc.

Crequer, N. (1997). 'Employers welcome Modern Apprentices', *Times Educational Supplement,* 5 September 1997.

David, M., West, A. and Ribbens, J. (1994). *Mother's Intuition? Choosing Secondary Schools.* Lewes: Falmer Press.

Davies, P. (1993). 'Towards parity of esteem? Marketing GNVQs'. Occasional Paper 55, Blagdon: The FE Staff College.

Davies, P. (1994). 'Do it again – with conviction', *College Management Today,* 2, 7, pp. 6–7.

Davies, P. (1999). 'Colleges and customers', in J. Lumby and N. H. Foskett (eds), *Managing External Relations in Schools and Colleges.* London: Sage.

Dearing, R. (1996). *Review of Qualifications for 16–19 Year Olds.* Full Report. Hayes, Middlesex: SCAA Publications.

Dearing, R. (1997). *National Committee of Inquiry into Higher Education.* DfEE Full Report, July 1997 (Leeds.ac.uk internet web site).

Department for Education and Employment (DfEE) (1994). *Our Children's Education: The Updated Parents Charter.* London: DfEE.

Department for Education and Employment (DfEE) (1995). *Participation in Education and Training by 16–18 year olds in England 1984/85 to 1994/95.* DfEE News 284/95, 27 July 1995.

Department for Education and Employment (DfEE)/Local Government National Training Organisation (1998a). *Dare to be Different: Challenging Gender Imbalances in Modern Apprenticeships.* London: TSO.

Department for Education and Employment (DfEE) (1998b). Modern Apprenticeships – The popular choice for school leavers. DfEE 574/98, Press Release.

Department for Education and Employment (DfEE) (1998c). *The Learning Age.* DfEE: TSO.

Department for Education and Employment (DfEE) (1999). *Learning to Succeed: a New Framework for post-16 Learning.* London: DfEE.

Department for Education and Employment (DfEE) (1999). *The National Curriculum for England.* London: DfEE.

Department for Education and Employment (DfEE) (2000). *Connexions – the Best Start in Life for Every Young Person.* London: DfEE.

Department of Education and Science (DES) (1991). *Education for the 21st Century.* London: HMSO.

Devlin, T. and Knight, B. (1992). *Public Relations and Marketing for Schools.* London: Longman School Management Resources.

Downs, A. (1957). *An Economic Theory of Democracy.* New York: Harper Row.

Edwards, W. (1954). 'The theory of decision making', in W. Edwards and A. Tversky (eds), *Decision Making.* London: Penguin Modern Psychology.

Edwards, W. (1961). 'Behavioural decision theory', in W. Edwards and A. Tversky (eds), *Decision Making*. London: Penguin Modern Psychology.

Edwards, T., Fitz, J. and Whitty, G. (1989). *The State and Private Education: an Evaluation of the Assisted Places Scheme*. London: Falmer Press.

Erikson, E. H. (1968). *Identity, Youth and Crisis*. London: Faber and Faber.

Falconer, A. (1997). 'A buyer's market': parents' views on what is wanted in the Independent Sector', *Management in Education*, 11, 1, pp. 21–2.

Fergusson, R. and Unwin, L. (1996). 'Making better sense of post 16 destinations: a case study of English shire county', *Research Papers in Education*, 11, 1.

Festinger, L. (1964). *Conflict, decision and dissonance*. California: Stanford University Press.

Foskett, N. H. (1995). *Marketing, Management and Schools; A Study of a Developing Marketing Culture in Secondary Schools*. Unpublished PhD Thesis, University of Southampton.

Foskett, N. H. (1996). Conceptualising marketing in secondary schools – deconstructing an alien concept, in Proceedings of the 'Markets in Education: Policy, Process and Practice' Symposium, University of Southampton.

Foskett, N. H. (1998). 'Linking marketing to strategy', in D. Middlewood and J. Lumby (eds), *Strategic Management in Schools and Colleges*. London: PCP.

Foskett, N. H. (1999). Strategy, external relations and marketing, in J. Lumby and N. H. Foskett (eds), *Managing External Relations in Schools and Colleges*. London: PCP.

Foskett, N. H. (2000). 'Dancing with the Devil – ethics and research in educational markets', in Usher, R. and Simons, H. (eds), *Situated Ethics in Educational Research*. London: Routledge Falmer.

Foskett, N. H. and Hemsley-Brown, J. V. (1997). *Career Perceptions and Decision Making*. Southampton: CREM/Heist Publications.

Foskett, N. H. and Hemsley-Brown, J. V. (1999). *Teachers and Careers Education – Teachers' Awareness of Careers Outside Teaching*. Southampton: CREM/Hampshire TEC.

Foskett, N. H. and Hemsley-Brown, J. V. (2000). *Changing Parental Attitudes to Independent Education*. Southampton: CREM Publications.

Foskett, N. H. and Hesketh, A. J. (1995). *Higher Education Awareness Amongst Year 10 Pupils in Hampshire Schools*. Southampton: Centre for Research in Education Marketing.

Foskett, N. H. and Hesketh, A. J. (1996a). *Student Decision-Making in the Post-16 Market Place*. Southampton: HEIST.

Foskett, N. H. and Hesketh, A. J. (1996b). *Higher Education Awareness Amongst Year 8 Pupils in Hampshire Schools*. Southampton: Centre for Research in Education Marketing.

Foskett, N. H. and Hesketh, A. J. (1997). 'Constructing choice in contiguous and parallel markets: institutional and school leavers' responses to the new post-16 marketplace', *Oxford Review of Education*, 23, 2, pp. 299–330.

Fox, I. (1985). *Private Schools and Public Issues; the Parents' View.* Basingstoke: Macmillan Press.

Friedman, M. and Friedman R. (1980). *Free to Choose.* London: Secker and Warburg.

Fryer, R. H. (1997). *Learning for the Twenty–First Century.* First Report of the National Advisory Group for Continuing Education and Life Long Learning. London: DfEE.

Fryer, R. H. (2000). *Making a reality of lifelong learning.* Inaugural Lecture, University of Southampton.

Furlong, A. and Biggart, A. (1999). 'Framing choices: a longitudinal study of occupational aspirations among 13- to 16-year olds', *Journal of Education and Work*, 12, 1, pp. 21–35.

Further Education Funding Council (FEFC)/OFSTED (1994). *16–19 Guidance.* Coventry: FEFC.

Further Education Funding Council (FEFC) (1997). *Careers Education and Guidance: Good Practice Report.* Report from the Inspectorate, September 1997. London: FEFC.

Gaffney, E. (1981). *Private Schools and the Public Good.* Indiana: University of Notre Dame.

Gewirtz, S., Ball, S. J. and Bowe, R. (1995). *Markets, Choice and Equity in Education.* Milton Keynes: OUP.

Gibson, A. and Asthana, S. (2000). 'What's in a number? Commentary on Gorard and Fitz's 'Investigating the determinants of segregation between schools', *Research Papers in Education*, 15, 2, pp. 133–53.

Ginzberg, E., Ginzberg, S. W., Axelrad, S. and Herma, J. L. (1951). *Occupational Choice.* New York: Columbia University Press.

Glatter, R., Woods, P. and Bagley, C. (eds) (1997). *Choice and Diversity in Schooling: Perspectives and Prospects.* London: Routledge.

Gleeson, D. (1996). 'Continuity and change in post-compulsory education and training reform', in R. Halsall and M. Cockett (eds), *Education and Training 14–19 – Chaos or Coherence?* London: David Fulton.

Gorard, S. (1997). *School Choice in an Established Market.* Aldershot: Ashgate.

Gorard, S. (1999). 'Well. That about wraps it up for school choice research; a state of the art review', *School Leadership and Management*, 19, 1, pp. 25–47.

Gorard, S. and Fitz, J. (2000). 'Investigating the determinants of segregation between schools', *Research Papers in Education*, 15, 2, pp. 115–32.

Gordon, J. (1995). An innovative approach to the comparison of qualifications in Europe: the regional perspective. *European Journal of Education*, 30, 3, pp. 277–93.

Gray, D. and Morgan, M. (1998). 'Modern Apprenticeships: filling the skills gap?' *Journal of Vocational Education and Training*, 50, 1, pp. 123–33.

Gray, J. and Sime, N. (1989). *Extended Routes and Delays – Transitions Among 16–19 year olds – National Trends and Local Contexts.* London: City University.

Guardian, The (2000). Brown scorns Oxford elitism. *The Guardian*, 26 May 2000.

Hall, V. (1999). 'Partnerships, alliances and competition – defining the field', in Lumby, J. and Foskett, N. H. (eds), *Managing External Relations in Schools and Colleges*. London: Sage.

Halstead, M. (1994). *Parental Choice and Education: Principles, Policy and Practice*. London: Kogan Page.

Hammond, T. and Dennison, W. F. (1995). 'School choice in less populated areas', *Educational Management and Administration*, 23, 2, pp. 104–13.

Hargreaves, D. (1992). *Understanding Teacher Development*. London: Cassell.

Harris, B. and Harvey, J. H. (1975). 'Self attributed choices as a function of the consequence of a decision', *Journal of Personality and Social Psychology*, 31, pp. 1013–19.

Hatcher, R. (1994). 'Market relationships and the management of teachers', *British Journal of Sociology of Education*, 15, 1, pp. 41–61.

Hawthorn, R. (1995a). 'Sifting reality from the images of work', *Times Education Supplement*, 7 April 1995.

Hawthorn, R. (1995b). 'Career choice was just right', *Times Education Supplement*, 8 December 1995.

Hawthorn, R. (1996). 'How television can shape the rest of your life', *Times Education Supplement*, 13 December 1996.

Headington, R. and Howson, J. (1995). 'The school brochure: a marketing tool?' *Educational Management and Administration*, 23, 2, pp. 89–95.

Hemsley-Brown, J. V. (1994). 'Marketing the school's sixth form', *Inside Education Marketing*, 1, 3, pp. 2–3.

Hemsley-Brown, J. V. (1996). 'Marketing Post-16 Colleges: A Quantitative and Qualitative Study of Pupils' Choice of Post Sixteen Institutions.' Unpublished PhD Thesis, University of Southampton.

Hemsley-Brown, J. V. (1999a). 'College choice, perceptions and priorities', *Educational Management and Administration*, 27, 1, pp. 85–98.

Hemsley-Brown, J. V. (1999b). 'The state and colleges', in J. Lumby and N. H. Foskett (eds), *Managing External Relations in Schools and Colleges*. London: Sage.

Hemsley-Brown, J. V. and Foskett, N. H. (1997). *Higher Education Awareness Among Year 6 Pupils in Hampshire Schools*. Southampton: Heist Publications.

Hemsley-Brown, J. V. and Foskett, N. H. (1999). *Perceptions of Modern Apprenticeship in Wiltshire*. Southampton: CREM Publications.

Hemsley-Brown, J. V. and Foskett, N. H. (2000). *Factors Affecting Post-Sixteen Choices*. Southampton: CREM Publications.

Hemsley-Brown, J. V. and Humphreys, J. (1998). 'Opportunity or obligation? Participation in adult vocational training', *Journal of Vocational Education and Training*, 50, 3, pp. 355–73.

Herr, E. L. (1997). 'Career counselling: a process in process', *British Journal of Guidance Counselling*, 25, 1, pp. 81–93.

Hesketh, A. J. and Knight, P. T. (1998). 'Secondary school prospectuses and educational markets', *Cambridge Journal of Education*, 28, 1, pp. 21–35.

Hindess, B. (1988). *Choice, Rationality and Social Theory*. London: Unwin Hyman.

Hirschmann, A. (1970). *Exit, Voice and Loyalty: Responses to Decline in Firms, Organisations, and States.* Cambridge, MA: Harvard University Press.

Hobbs, S., Lindsay, S. and McKechnie, J. (1996). 'The extent of child employment in Britain', *British Journal of Education and Work*, 9, 1, pp. 5–19.

Hodkinson, P. (1995). 'How young people make career decisions', *Education and Training*, 37, 8, pp. 3–8.

Hodkinson, P. and Bloomer, M. (1999). 'Dropping out of FE: the nature and complexity of educational failure.' *Paper presented to the BERA Conference, University of Sussex, September 1999.*

Hodkinson, P. and Sparkes, A. (1993). 'Young people's career choices and careers guidance action planning: a case-study of Training Credits in Action', *Journal of Guidance and Counselling*, 21, 3, pp. 246–61.

Hodkinson, P. and Sparkes, A. (1994). 'The myth of the market: the negotiation of training in a youth credits pilot scheme', *British Journal of Education and Work*, 7, 3, pp. 2–20.

Hodkinson, P. and Sparkes, A. (1997). 'Careership: a sociological theory of career decision making', *British Journal of Sociology of Education*, 10, 1, pp. 23–35.

Hodkinson, P., Sparkes, A. and Hodkinson, P. (1996). *Triumphs and Tears: Young People, Markets and the Transition from School to Work.* London: David Fulton Publishers.

Hogarth, T. *et al.* (1997). *The Participation of Non-traditional Students in Higher Education.* Bristol: HEFCE.

Holland, J. L. (1985). *Making Vocational Choices: A Theory of Vocational Personality and Work Environments.* Englewood Cliffs, New Jersey: Prentice Hall.

Hootkoop, W. and Van Der Kamp, M. (1992). 'Factors influencing participation in continuing education', *International Journal of Educational Research*, 17, 4, pp. 537–48.

Howieson, C. and Croxford, L. (1996). *Using the YCS to Analyse the Outcomes of Careers Education and Guidance*, DfEE. London: HMSO.

Hughes, M. (1997). 'Schools' responsiveness to parents' views at Key Stage One,' in Glatter, R., Woods, P. A. and Bagley, C. (eds), *Choice and Diversity in Schooling: Perspectives and Prospects.* London: Routledge.

Hughes, M., Wikely, F. and Nash, T. (1994). *Parents and their Children's Schools.* Oxford: Basil Blackwell.

Hunter, J. B. (1991). 'Which school? A study of parents' choice of secondary school', *Educational Research*, 33, 1, pp. 31–41.

Janis, I. L. and Mann, L. (1977). *Decision Making: A Psychological Analysis of Conflict, Choice and Commitment.* New York: Macmillan Publishing Co./The Free Press.

Jensen, A. R. (1991). 'Spearman's g and the Problem of Educational Equality', *Oxford Review of Education*, 17, 2, pp. 169–85.

Johnes, G. (1993). *The Economics of Education.* London: Macmillan.

Johnson, D. (1987). *Private Schools and State Schools; Two Systems or One?* Milton Keynes: Open University Press.

Kelly, A. (1989). 'When I grow up I want to be ...: a longitudinal study of the development of career preferences', *British Journal of Guidance and Counselling*, 17, 2, pp. 177–200.

Kelly, G. A. (1955). *The Psychology of Personal Constructs*. New York: Norton.

Kennedy, H. (1997). *Learning Works – How to Widen Participation*. Coventry: FEFC.

Keys, W. and Fernandes, C. (1993). *What do Students Think About School?* Slough: NFER.

Keys, W., Harris, C. and Fernandes, C. (1995). *Attitudes to School of Top Primary and First Year Secondary Pupils*. Slough: NFER.

Kidd, J. M. and Wardman, M. (1999). 'Post-16 course choice: a challenge for guidance', *British Journal of Guidance and Counselling*, 27, 2, pp. 259–74.

Lauder, H. and Hughes, D. (1999). *Trading in Futures – Why Markets in Education Don't Work*. Buckingham: Open University Press.

Le Grand (1990). *Quasi-markets and Social Policy*. Bristol: University of Bristol, School for Advanced Urban Studies.

Levacic, R. (1995). *Local Management of Schools: Analysis and Practice*. Milton Keynes: Open University Press.

Liem, G. (1975). 'Performance and satisfaction as affected by personal control over salient decisions', *Journal of Personality and Social Psychology*, 31, pp. 232–40.

Maguire, M., Ball, S. J. and Macrae, S. (1999). 'Dissenting males: just "ordinary" boys'. *Paper presented to the BERA Conference, University of Sussex*, September 1999.

Maguire, M., Macrae, S. and Ball, S. J. (2000). *Choice, Pathways and Transitions: 16–19 Education, Training and (Un) Employment in One Urban Locale*. London: King's College.

Major, L. E. (1997). 'A foot in the door', *The Guardian*, 10 June 1997.

Martinez, P. and Munday, F. (1998). *9000 Voices: Student Persistence and Dropout in Further Education*. FEDA Report. London: FEDA Publications.

Maslow, A. H. (1943). 'A theory of human motivation', *Psychological Review*, 50, 2, pp. 370–96.

Maychell, K. and Evans, C. (1998). *Leaving at 16: a Study of Factors Affecting Young People's Decision to Leave Full-time Education*. Slough: NFER Publications.

McLean, I. (1987). *Public Choice. An Introduction*. Basil Blackwell: Oxford.

Miller, D. W. and Starr, M. K. (1967). *The Structure of Human Decisions*. Englewood Cliffs, NJ: Prentice Hall.

Minter, K. (1997). 'Marketing in the primary school', Unpublished MA Thesis, University of Southampton.

Modood, T. and Shiner, M. (1994). *Ethnic Minorities and Higher Education*. London: Policy Studies Institute.

Moir, J. (1990). 'Psychological theories and lay accounts of occupational choice, a comparative study of mechanical engineering and nursing undergraduates.' Unpublished PhD Thesis, Dundee Institute of Technology.

MORI (1989). *How and Why Parents Choose an Independent School.* London: MORI.

National Advisory Council For Education And Training Targets (NACETT) (1995). *Review of the National Education and Training Targets.* London: HMSO.

Newscheck (1994). 'Modern Apprenticeships – An introduction by Anne Widdecombe MP', 8 June 1994, 4, 8, p. 4.

Nice, E. (1997). 'Parents, schools and choice: An examination of how parents choose a primary school for their 4 year old children.' Unpublished MA Dissertation, University of Southampton.

Nicholls, A. (1994). *Schools and Colleges: Collaborators or Competitors in Education?* Report for Laser Further Education Council. London: LASER.

OECD (1997). *Parents as Partners in Schooling.* Paris: OECD.

Office for Standards in Education (Ofsted) (1999). *Inspecting Subjects and Aspects 11–18: Work-related Education and Careers Guidance.* London: TSO.

O'Hear, A. (1991). *Education and Democracy against the Educational Establishment.* London: Claridge.

Petherbridge, J. (1997). 'Work experience pre-16: Is the common learning process the solution to its assessment?', *British Journal of Curriculum and Assessment,* 7, 1, pp. 42–6.

Piaget, J. (1953). *The Origin of Intelligence in the Child* (translated by Margaret Cook). London: Routledge and Kegan Paul.

Radford, K. J. (1977). *Complex Decision Problems an Integrated Strategy.* Virginia, United States of America: Reston Publishing Company.

Rajan, A., Van Eupen, P. and Jaspers, A. (1997). *Britain's Flexible Labour Market: What Next?* London: DfEE.

Ranson, S. (1993). 'Markets or democracy for education?' *British Journal of Educational Studies,* 41, 4, pp. 333–52.

Reay, D. (1996). 'Contextualising choice: social power and parental involvement', *British Educational Research Journal,* 22, 5, pp. 581–96.

Reay, D. (1998a). 'Engendering social reproduction: mothers in the educational marketplace', *British Journal of Sociology of Education,* 19, 2, pp. 195–209.

Reay, D. (1998b). '"Always knowing" and "never being sure": familial and institutional habituses and higher education choice', *Journal of Education Policy,* 13, 4, pp. 519–29.

Reay, D. and Ball, S. (1997). 'Spoilt for choice: the working classes and educational markets', *Oxford Review of Education,* 23, 1, pp. 89–101.

Reay, D. and Ball, S. J. (1998). '"Making their minds up": family dynamics of school choice', *British Educational Research Journal,* 24, 4, pp. 431–48.

Reynolds, D. and Cuttance, P. (eds) (1997) *School Effectiveness: Research, Policy and Practice.* London: Cassell.

Roberts, D. and Allen, A. (1997). *Young Applicants' Perceptions of Higher Education.* Leeds: Heist Publications.

Roberts, D. and Higgins, T. (1992). *Higher Education: The Student Experience.* Heist Research Publications.

Roberts, K. (1995). *Youth Employment in Modern Britain.* Oxford: Oxford University Press.

Roberts, K. and Parsell, G. (1988). *Opportunity Structures and Career Trajectories From Age 16–19.* London: City University.

Roberts, K., Parsell, G. and Connolly, M. (1989). *Britain's Economic Recovery – The New Demographic Trends and Young People's Transitions into the Labour Market.* London: City University.

Rogers, E. M. (1983). *Diffusion of Innovations.* New York: The Free Press.

Rule, P. (1992). 'A consumer view of careers education', *Newscheck,* 3, 2, pp. 4–6.

Schein, E. H. (1985). *Organisational Culture and Leadership.* San Francisco, Jossey-Bass.

School Curriculum and Assessment Authority (1996). *Skills for Choice.* London: SCAA Publications.

Schotter, A. (1990). *Free Market Economics.* Oxford: Blackwell.

Scott, P. (1996). 'Markets in post-compulsory education: rhetoric, policy and structure', in N. H. Foskett (ed.), *Markets in Education, Policy, Process and Practice.* Southampton: CREM Publications.

Simon, H. A. (1957). *Models of Man: Social and Rational.* New York: Wiley.

Simon, H. A. (1972). 'Theories of Bounded Rationality', in C. B. McGuire (ed.), *Decision and Organisation: A Volume in Honour of Jacob Marschak.* Amsterdam: North Holland.

Sloman, J. (1999). *Economics.* Third Edition. Englewood Cliffs: Prentice Hall.

Smedley, D. (1995). 'Marketing secondary schools to parents – some lessons from the research on parental choice', *Educational Management and Administration,* 23, 2, pp. 96–103..

Smith, D. N., Scott, P. and Lynch, J. E. (1995). *The Role of Marketing in the University and College Sector: a Study of how Marketing is Defined and Organised in British Universities and Colleges, as Compared with other Service Sectors.* Leeds: Heist.

Stables, A. and Stables, S. (1995). 'Gender differences in students: approaches to "A" level subject choices and perceptions of "A" level subjects, a study of first year students in tertiary education', *Educational Research,* 37, 1, pp. 39–51.

Stillman, A. and Maychell, K. (1986). *Moving to Secondary School. Who Decides? A Questionnaire for Parents.* Slough: NFER/Nelson.

Stokes, D. (1999). 'Small Enterprise Management in the Public Sector: The Marketing of Primary Schools.' Unpublished PhD Thesis, Kingston University.

Super, D. (1953). 'A Theory of Vocational Development', *American Psychologist,* 8, pp. 185–90.

Taylor, M. J. (1992). 'Post-16 options: young people's awareness, attitudes, intentions and influences on their choice, *Research Papers in Education,* 7, 3, pp. 301–33.

Thomas, A. and Dennison, B. (1991). 'Parental or pupil choice – who really decides in urban schools?' *Educational Management and Administration,* 19, 4, pp. 243–9.

Thompson, G. *et al.* (1991). *Markets, Hierarchies and Networks, th* *of Social Life.* London: Sage Publications.

Thrupp, M. (1999). *Schools Making a Difference – Let's Be Realistic.* ham: Open University Press.

Tooley, J. (1996). *Education Without the State.* London: IEA.

Tooley, J. (1997). 'On school choice and social class: a response to Bai. Bowe and Gewirtz', *British Journal of Sociology of Education*, 18, 2, June 1977, pp. 217–30.

Trow, M. (1998). 'American perspectives on British Higher Education under Thatcher and Major', *Oxford Review of Education*, 24, 1, pp. 111–30.

Tuckett, A. (1997). *Life Long Learning in England and Wales. An Overview and Guide to Issues Arising from the European Year of Lifelong Learning.* Leicester: National Organisation for Adult Learning (NIACE).

Unwin, L. (1992). *Young People's Attitudes to Youth Training.* Warrington: NORMID Training and Enterprise Council.

Unwin, L. (1996). 'Employer-led realities, apprenticeship past and present', *Journal of Vocational Education and Training*, 48, 1, pp. 57–68.

Veblen, T. (1899). *Theory of Leisure Class.* New York: Macmillan.

Von Hayek, L. (1976). *Law, Legislation and Liberty – Vol. 2, Rules and Order.* London: Routledge and Kegan Paul.

Vondracek, F. W., Schulenberg, J., Skorikov, V., Gillespie, L. K. and Wahlheim, C. (1995). 'The relationship of identity status to career indecision during adolescence', *Journal of Adolescence*, 18, pp. 17–29.

Vroom, V. (1966). 'Organisational choice: a study of pre- and post-decision processes, *Organisational Behaviour and Human Performance*, 1, pp. 212–25.

Walford, G. (1999). 'Review of Woods, P., Bagley, C. and Glatter, R. (1998). "School Choice and Competition: Markets in the Public Interest?"', *Educational Management and Administration*, 27, 2, pp. 200–1.

Walters, G. (1998). 'The choices made by Year 6 pupils and their parents at secondary transfer.' Unpublished MA(Ed) Dissertation, University of Southampton.

Waslander, S. and Thrupp, M. (1995). 'Choice, competition and segregation: an empirical analysis of a New Zealand secondary school market, 1990–93', *Journal of Education Policy*, 10, 1, pp. 1–26.

Watts, A. G. (1972). *Diversity and Choice in Higher Education.* London: Routledge Kegan Paul.

Watts, A. G. and Young, M. (1997). 'Models of student guidance in a changing 14–19 education and training system', in R. Edwards, R. Harrison and A. Tait (eds), *Telling Tales: Perspectives on Guidance and Counselling in Learning.* London: Routledge.

West, A. (1992). 'Factors affecting choice of school for middle class parents', *Educational Management and Administration*, 20, 3, pp. 212–22.

West, A. and Varlaam, A. (1991a). 'Choice of high schools: pupils' perceptions', *Educational Research*, 33, 3, pp. 205–15.

West, A. and Varlaam, A. (1991b). 'Choosing a secondary school: parents of junior school children', *Educational Research*, 33, 1, pp. 22–9.

West, A., David, M., Hailes, J. and Ribbens, J. (1995). 'Parents and the process of choosing secondary school: implications for schools', *Educational Management and Adminstration*, 23, 1, pp. 28–38.

West, A., Noden, P., Edge, A., David, M. and Davies, J. (1998). 'Choices and expectations at primary and secondary stages in the state and private sectors', *Educational Studies*, 24, 1, pp. 45–60.

Whitehead, G. (1981). *Economics Made Simple*. London: Heinemann.

Whitty, G., Power, S., Edwards, T. and Wigfall, V. (1998). *Destined for Success? Educational Biographies of Academically Able Pupils*. Swindon: ESRC Project Report.

Whitty, G., Power, S. and Halpin, D. (1998). *Devolution and Choice in Education: The School, the State and the Market*. Buckingham: Open University Press.

Willms, J. and Echols, F. (1992). 'Alert and inert clients; the Scottish experience of parental choice of schools', *Economics of Education Review*, 11, 4, pp. 339–50.

Wilson, J. (1991). 'Education and equality: some conceptual questions', *Oxford Review of Education*, 17, 2, pp. 223–30.

Winn, S. and Stevenson, R. (1997). 'Student loans: are the policy objectives being achieved?' *Higher Education Quarterly*, 51, 2, pp. 144–63.

Woodrow, M. (1998). *From Elitism to Inclusion: A Guide to Good Practice in Widening Access to Higher Education*. London: CVCP.

Woods, P., Bagley, C. and Glatter, R. (1998). *School Choice and Competition: Markets in the Public Interest?* London: Routledge.

Worchel, S. (1971). 'The effect of simple frustration, violated expectancy, and reactance on the instigation to aggression.' Unpublished doctoral dissertation, Duke University.

Wyn, J. and Dwyer, P. (1999). 'New directions in research on youth in transition', *Journal of Youth Studies*, 2, 1, pp. 5–21.

Appendix A

Centre for Research in Education Marketing – major research projects

1994–96   **'Post-16 Markets' Project**

A national study of young people's decision-making at 15/16 in relation to post-16 education and training pathways. Funded by Heist.

Principal publication:

Foskett, N. H. and Hesketh, A. J. (1996). *Student Decision-Making in the Post-16 Market Place*. Leeds: Heist Publications.

1995–97   **'Pupils' Knowledge and Awareness of Higher Education' Project**

A study in southern England, examining what children aged 10, 14 and 17 know and understand about higher education, how those perceptions are formed, and how this feeds into HE aspiration. Funded by Hampshire TEC.

Principal publications:

Foskett, N. H. and Hesketh, A. J. (1996). *Higher Education Awareness Amongst Year 10 Pupils in Hampshire Schools*. Southampton: CREM.

Foskett, N. H. and Hesketh, A. J. (1996). *Higher Education Awareness Amongst Year 8 Pupils in Hampshire Schools*. Southampton: CREM.

Hemsley-Brown, J. V. and Foskett, N. H. (1997). *Higher Education Awareness Amongst Year 6 Pupils in Hampshire Schools*. Southampton: CREM.

1996–97   'Career Perceptions and Decision-Making (CAPDEM)' Project

A national scale study of how young people develop images and perceptions of particular careers, and how this shapes their career decision-making. The study focused particularly on careers in nursing and engineering. Funded by Heist.

Principal publication:

Foskett, N. H. and Hemsley-Brown, J. V. (1997). *Career Perceptions and Decision Making Amongst Young People*. Leeds: Heist Publications.

1997–98   'Perceptions of Nursing as a Career' Project

A national scale study of how nursing is perceived by young people and how this influences career choice in relation to nursing and other medical careers. Funded by the Department of Health.

Principal publication:

Foskett, N. H. and Hemsley-Brown, J. V. (1998). *Perceptions of Nursing as a Career Amongst Young People*. London: Department of Health.

1997–98   The 'Marketisation of the Careers Service' Project

A case study of two privatised careers services, exploring the implications of privatisation for the nature of careers education and guidance available to young people. Funded by Heist.

Principal publication:

Hemsley-Brown, J. V. and Foskett, N. H.(1998). *The Marketisation of the Careers Service*. Leeds: Heist Publications.

1998–99   'Teachers' Awareness of Careers Outside Teaching (TASCOT)' Project

A study of how the images that teachers other than careers advisers have of specific careers, and how this contributes to the images and models of the labour market conveyed by teachers to their children, both implicitly and explicitly. Funded by Hampshire TEC.

Principal publication:

Foskett, N. H. and Hemsley-Brown, J. V. (1999). *Teachers and Careers Education – Teachers' Awareness of Careers Outside Teaching.* Southampton: CREM.

1998–99   **'Perceptions of Modern Apprenticeships – the Wiltshire Study'**

A detailed analysis of the market for modern apprenticeships in contrasting localities within a southern English county. The study examined the perceptions of young people, parents, schools, teachers, careers advisers, training organisations and employers, and considered how these perceptions 'make the market' for modern apprenticeships. Funded by Wiltshire and Swindon TEC.

Publications forthcoming.

1999–2000   **'Parental Attitudes to Independent Education' Project**

A study of choice, satisfaction and decision-making by parents and young people in a number of independent schools in southern England. The project focused, *inter alia*, on the nature of financial planning for independent education, the impact of the demise of the Assisted Places Scheme, and the role of a range of choice justification strategies by parents. Funded by a consortium of independent schools.

Publications forthcoming.

1999–2000   **'Choice at 16+ in Inner London' Project**

A large-scale quantitative and qualitative analysis of the choice process at 16+, with a particular focus on attitudes to training, especially the modern apprenticeship. The nature of the sample in the study enabled some important patterns to emerge in relation to ethnicity and gender. Funded by FOCUS TEC.

Publications forthcoming.

Index